Future Tense

Future Tense

THE CULTURE OF ANTICIPATION IN FRANCE BETWEEN THE WARS

Roxanne Panchasi

Cornell University Press
Ithaca and London

First published 2009 by Cornell University Press
Printed in the United States of America

Library of Congress Cataloging-in-Publication Data

Panchasi, Roxanne.
 Future tense : the culture of anticipation in France between the wars / Roxanne Panchasi.
    p. cm.
 Includes bibliographical references and index.
 ISBN 978-0-8014-4670-2 (cloth : alk. paper)
 1. France—Intellectual life—20th century. 2. France—Social life and customs—20th century. 3. France—History—1914–1940. I. Title.

 DC389.P36 2009
 944.081'5—dc22

                        2008055481

Cloth printing   10 9 8 7 6 5 4 3 2 1

Contents

Illustrations

Acknowledgments

I could never have conceived of, let alone completed, this project without the help of a number of people and institutions. I would like to thank the Social Sciences and Humanities Research Council of Canada, Rutgers University, the Institute for Advanced Study, and Simon Fraser University for the funding that made possible more than a decade of research travel and writing. I am also grateful to the staff at the Bibliothèque nationale de France, the Bibliothèque de documentation internationale contemporaine, the Bibliothèque de l'Arsenal, the Bibliothèque historique de la ville de Paris, the Service historique de l'Armée de Terre, the Bibliothèque du Film, and the Fondation Le Corbusier in France. Alexandre Ragois at the Institut français d'architecture, John Frederick at the University of Victoria's McPherson Library, and the Interlibrary Loan staff at Simon Fraser University's Bennett Library all provided invaluable assistance during the final stages of editing and image preparation.

The Department of History at Rutgers University was and remains an extraordinary scholarly community. During my years of graduate study there, I was fortunate enough to work with a group of outstanding professors. I am honored to have studied under the supervision of Bonnie G. Smith, a scholar who remains for me a model of intellectual daring backed by careful research and good, clear writing. I learned so much from her about how to be a historian and I cannot thank her enough for her guidance and patience over the years. Jennifer Jones was a wonderfully smart and kind teacher from my first visit to the Rutgers campus in 1993 to my last one as a student in 2001. I am grateful to Omer Bartov for his encouragement of this project from its early stages. Matt Matsuda continues to dazzle me with his intellectual creativity and good humor. I thank him for his enthusiastic support and for his insightful reading of an early version of the manuscript. Norma Basch, Belinda Davis, and Alice Kessler-Harris taught me to think more critically and more broadly in ways that shaped the questions that I explore in this book.

Other scholars and readers have offered their time and advice over years of research and writing. Mary Louise Roberts generously agreed to meet with me and to look at chapter drafts before most outside readers do, and her comments on the dissertation were extremely helpful. Joy Dixon, Sophie McCall, Paige Raibmon, and Sylvia Schafer all read versions of the entire manuscript at different stages, and I am grateful for their very useful comments and suggestions for revision. Tamara Chaplin, Richard Jobs, Richard Keller, Todd Shepard, and John Stubbs all offered valuable advice on various chapters, and on the project as a whole. The guidance and suggestions I received from John Ackerman and the readers at Cornell University Press have greatly improved the clarity and overall quality of this book. I also thank Susan Barnett, Teresa Jesionowski, and Jack Rummel, the copy editor, for their hard work and patience. Dale McCartney also provided me with editorial assistance during this process. I am also grateful to the editors of *differences* and *Historical Reflections/Réflexions historiques* for publishing articles that were earlier versions of the first and third chapters of the book.

The best thing about graduate school was the community of friends I was lucky enough to find there. To this day, I can sit with Miriam Bartha in any kitchen, in any city, and feel at home. Kimberly Brodkin, Tamara Chaplin, Richard Jobs, Patrick McDevitt, Carla MacDougall, and Daniel Wherley were truly the best friends a historian-in-training could have asked for. I only wish there were fewer kilometers between us all now. A supportive (but tough!) writing coach and an extraordinarily caring friend, Jennifer Brier has, quite literally, been the encouraging voice in my ear throughout the process of writing this book. Our regular phone conversations have sustained me through this and many other challenges. "Send it to me!" she said. And I did, over and over again.

In Paris, wonderful friends have helped see me through periods of research, writing, writer's block, and more writing, all the while teaching me more about France than I could ever learn from any book. Yahn Jeannot was and remains a *guide de France* unlike any other and I am indebted to him for the French lessons, the driving lessons, and much more. Abhaya Kaufman has made so much space for me—in her life and in her apartment—since we first met over a decade ago, and I thank her for every m². I am also grateful to Sophie Alexinsky, Olivier Delcourt, and Ségolène Robin for their generosity and friendship.

In Vancouver, a community of colleagues and friends has helped me to settle into the city and into professional life in so many ways over the past eight years. Hilary Mason and Joy Dixon were my first friends in this new place, and their continued love and support mean the world to me. Full of good humor and sound advice, the faculty and staff in the Department of History at Simon Fraser University have made writing this book while teaching so much easier than it would have otherwise been. I would especially like to thank Elise Chenier, John Craig, the late Ian Dyck, Jacob Eyferth, Karen Ferguson, Mark Leier, Sheilagh MacDonald, Derryl MacLean, Janice Matsumura, Heather Skibeneckyj, Mary Lynn Stewart, John Stubbs, and Tessa Wright. Other friends, within and outside the academy, have been incredibly important to me over the past several years. I am particularly indebted to Courtney Booker, Susan Brook, David Chariandy, Susan Cho, Anna Dow, Tim Fuller, Kat Hindmand, Paola Iovene, Eugene Katsov, Sophie McCall, Robert McMillan, Michael Prokopow, Paige Raibmon, Peg Rettino, and Tiffany Werth.

I would also like to express my gratitude to my mother Firdaus, my sister Gazelle, my brother-in-law Johan, my niece Sophia, and my nephew Max. The first three housed me, fed me, and encouraged me to keep going so many times throughout this process. The last two are the most adorable people I know. I continue to miss my late father Mak Panchasi.

Christopher Pollard entered my life (again) just as I was finishing this book. I will never be able to thank him enough for his love and patience during its final stages. He is my closest reader and my favorite accomplice. Now that this adventure is over, I cannot wait to see what sort of trouble we will stir up next.

There is one last person whose contributions to this book I must acknowledge. Joan W. Scott has supported this project, and my career as a whole, in ways that I could not begin to enumerate here. She has read everything I have published, from the roughest of first drafts through many, so many, revisions. Her scholarly example, integrity, kindness, and encouragement have helped make possible every page of this book and so I dedicate them to her.

ROXANNE PANCHASI

Vancouver, British Columbia

Future Tense

"The Future": A Useful Category of Historical Analysis

This book is an experiment in the history of "the future." Drawing on French sources from the years between the world wars, its chapters explore representations of the body, the city, and military security, as well as definitions of culture and civilization across domestic and international spaces. In the pages that follow, labor, design, and home efficiency experts propose "modern," elegant appliances as supplements to wounded and tired bodies; architects and urban planners discuss whether skyscrapers should be banned from the city of Paris; military strategists and representatives in the French Chamber of Deputies consider the defense of the nation's territory and the construction of a "Great Wall" on its borders; a series of French authors travel to "America," publishing accounts of their journeys across an ocean of space and time; and a number of French delegates declare their opposition to Esperanto in the early assemblies of the League of Nations. Moving from the local to the international, while remaining attentive to connections between them, this is a book about temporality and culture that takes up "the future" as a category of historical analysis.[1]

o   o   o

In France, as elsewhere in Europe, many felt that the First World War had effected a deep change in them. Among them was the phenomenological psychiatrist Eugène Minkowski, who in 1918 began to outline an essay entitled "Comment nous vivons l'avenir (et non pas ce que nous en savons)," or

"How We Live the Future (and Not What We Know of It)." Minkowski later described this never published work as a "systematic study of those phenomena directed toward the future, of the relationships among these phenomena, and the way in which they participate as a whole in the contexture of the lived future."[2] In his formulation the experience of the war—"the duration"—was a temporal phenomenon that had made anticipation a salient feature of everyday life. "During the war," Minkowski observed, "we were waiting for peace hoping to take up again the life that we had abandoned." But life could not continue in the same way after four years of battle, the loss of so many lives, and an unprecedented scale of material devastation in France. According to Minkowski, when the war was over "a new period began, a period of difficulties and deceptions, of setbacks and painful, often fruitless efforts to adapt oneself to new problems of existence." For years after the conflict, the psychiatrist's ruminations on time "lay dormant."[3]

Minkowski's focus on temporality, the human experience of time, built on the ideas of Henri Bergson, a philosopher whose work emphasized the distinction between a public, quantifiable time and a more authentic and private, *lived* time. For Bergson, time was subjective, and he used the term "duration" to understand the variable human sense of temporality, an experience that could not be measured scientifically.[4] Taking up this notion of *lived* time in his study of human psychological disorders, Minkowski developed his thoughts on temporality in *Lived Time (Le Temps vécu)*, published in 1933. Throughout this work Minkowski privileged the future as the true temporal orientation of human life, a temporality lived in a more direct and immediate fashion than any fleeting sense of the present, or any recollection of the past remembered or reconstructed. Particularly interested in notions of progress and human perfectibility, Minkowski emphasized the "intimate connection…between the lived future, on the one hand, and the ideal or…ethical tendency toward the good…on the other."[5] According to Minkowski, the lived future could be understood through the analysis of various phenomena, including two modes: (1) *activity*, or the actions that human beings engage in that are oriented toward some future goal or objective, and (2) *expectation*, a form of anticipation with more of a sense of the inevitable about it. The future "expected" seems to come of its own accord, regardless of any human attempts to shape or control it. It is a future of determined outcomes, of fates and destinies. Minkowski argued that individuals need a balance between these two modes of *living* the future. He further suggested that a range of psychopathological problems might be explained in terms of a patient's disrupted sense of temporality and of a faulty sense of the future in particular. Without a healthy consciousness of the movement from past, through present, to future, human beings might suffer from an overwhelming sense of regret—an excess of memory—and an inability to imagine or project themselves imaginatively forward in time. Minkowski understood this problem with the temporal continuum as a fundamental cause of psychological suffering.[6]

Future Tense takes up Minkowski's emphasis on anticipation as a crucial dimension of human experience. I began this project as a student of European history interested in twentieth-century French culture. It seemed to me that the scholarly literature on modern France had become caught up in the pursuit of the "past tense," the politics and history of historical consciousness itself. For many years now, "memory" has functioned as a central conceptual paradigm that historians have worked to define and deploy in their readings of French culture and national identity in the modern period. Beyond the French case in particular, the range of scholarly work on memory has been tremendously important in methodological terms, constituting a complex field of debate across the disciplines—from psychology, anthropology, and literary studies to political and cultural history.[7] Within the discipline of history, the literature on the "Great War" of 1914–18 in particular has emphasized memory in its consideration of the war's legacies and in debates over whether or not the conflict constituted a watershed moment for the emergence of a distinctive European modernity.[8]

It has now been more than two decades since the appearance of the first volume of Pierre Nora's monumental edited collection _Les Lieux de mémoire_ (_Realms of Memory_).[9] In a series of seven volumes published between 1984 and 1992, Nora and his collaborators explore a range of symbolic sites, or _lieux_, of French national memory, including the Château de Versailles, the tricolor flag, and the national anthem, "La Marseillaise." While there has been much interrogation of Nora's project, the collection has nevertheless influenced the work of a number of scholars who have emphasized memory (and forgetting) in their examination of the French, European, and more global past.[10] "Commemoration," "mourning," "amnesia"...these have become keywords in the study of French society, politics, and culture from the Revolution of 1789 to World War I, from Vichy to the histories and aftermaths of empire. Numerous analyses have highlighted the ways in which the experience and remembrance of the past work continually to define and challenge the idea of France as a nation, all of them starting out from the basic assumption that "even memory has a history."[11] This rich body of work on "sites," "realms," "crises," and "vectors" of memory, the nation's celebrated symbols and historic events as well as its enduring traumas, has placed the question of temporality at the center of historical inquiry. Perhaps most important, this literature has demonstrated that the objects and strategies of national cultural memory at a given moment tell us just as much, if not more, about the *present doing the remembering* as they do about the *past being remembered.*

Deeply indebted to the historical scholarship on memory, *Future Tense* rests on the premise that the future anticipated at a particular historical moment can tell us a great deal about the cultural preoccupations and political perspectives of the *present doing the anticipating,* in this case the interwar years in France. The point here is not to evaluate the truth or falsity of the futures imagined and expected between 1918 and 1939. Rather, I seek to explore "the future" *as history,* as a set of ideas and representations of the nation in time that takes particular forms at different historical moments. While not all interwar visions of the future achieved the "success" of concrete realization, the cultural and political imaginaries they forged and illustrated render these future-oriented sources vital sites of historical inquiry. Thus, for example, a playful magazine spread from 1933 offering images and descriptions of "Paris in the 21st century" is valuable to the present work as a representation with real effects, a primary source that reveals the concerns of the historical moment and actors that produced it. It is, in short, a historical document, linked by its cultural vocabulary to the archives of urban planning, military strategy, international diplomacy, interior design, science fiction, and travel literature.

In each of the chapters in this book, I examine how a range of interwar French observers tried to render "the future" visible in different ways, giving meaning and content to its mysteries and unknowns. The representations of the future illustrated in these five case studies depend on two inextricably linked ways of figuring "the future" that were also ways of thinking about, remembering, and commemorating "the past": (1) as trace and (2) as disappearance. In the interwar years, certain encounters in the present—meetings between the human and the machine, the organic and the artificial, the civilized and the "less" civilized, the national and the international—appeared as premonitions of the future. Just as some ideas and objects served as traces of the past in the present, so too did others—skyscrapers and airplanes, for example—appear as traces in the present of a *future* world, its technologies, and possible transformations. The future was also a rhetorical device, a way of framing potential changes to French society and ways of life (already underway in some cases) as out of step with the nation's history and cultural traditions. These were transformations that could both fascinate and alarm contemporary French observers in the interwar years: mechanization and automation; architectural modernism and urban planning; new possibilities for war and military invasion; the expansion of American cultural, economic, and political power; the international dreams of a common language and the peaceful settlement of disputes between world nations.

If certain objects appeared as traces of the future, artifacts whose presence seemed to provide evidence of a world to come, they also often suggested the disappearance of other cultural phenomena. A skyscraper could signal the erasure of one or more historic monuments, for example. Many visions and predictions focused explicitly on the absences in an imagined future. In the chapters that follow, then, I am also concerned with the contours of what I will call an anticipatory "discourse of disappearance." Each chapter examines the future by looking at perceptions of and predictions about the possible, likely, or even inevitable disappearance of an object invested with deep cultural meaning. Five such objects are the focus of the book: the whole, healthy, and organic human body; Paris, the nation's capital; the French border (particularly the border with Germany); French *civilisation;* and the French language itself. Representations of a future without these phenomena expressed contemporary uneasiness about perceived threats to "Frenchness," the erosion of a "True France."[12] In the interwar period, these threats included the technological transformation of everyday life; the increasing power and cultural influence of the United States; the possibility of German military invasion; and the forces of "internationalism," from aesthetic modernism to communism.

This is not to say that all observers in France during this period regarded the future with foreboding. In the chapters that follow, readers will encounter many who "looked forward" optimistically, understanding temporality and change in terms of technological "progress," national growth, and human evolution. At the same time, whether utopian or dystopian, the range of images of the future I explore contributed to a cultural remembrance of things not yet past. In particular, the anticipatory mourning or celebration of a "traditional" French culture *in advance* of its demise was, in its own way, an example of what historian Svetlana Boym has described as the nostalgic "hypochondria of the heart."[13] In Boym's formulation, nostalgia operates as "hypochondria" in its frequent expression of longing for things, places, and ideas that never really existed in the first place.[14] While Boym's focus is the representation of the past, on memory, exile, and diaspora, her framework has crucial implications for my analysis. The representation of "the future" framed as progress and/or loss included the anticipation of the memories of the present. The futures I explore here were all visions that expressed a kind of cultural "premourning," a nostalgic longing for French values and cultural phenomena that *had not yet disappeared.* Rather than seeking to restore a loss already suffered, this anticipatory nostalgia was meant to preclude the disappearance of a national culture that many thought to be imperiled.

The "culture of anticipation" that I explore in these pages is thus necessarily tied to the culture of memory and mourning so prominent in historical work on the period after the First World War. The experiences of the past helped to shape the nature of anticipation, just as they contributed to the cultural and political preoccupations of the present in the interwar years. Drawing on the insights of "collective memory" studies, this is a work that seeks out and explores the nature of "collective anticipation" during the years between 1918 and 1939.[15] By identifying and linking cultural evidence and images that might otherwise appear to be disconnected, the book demonstrates how anxieties and hopes for "the future" shaped the concerns of the present. At the same time, it suggests that images of the future took different forms in response to contemporary political, cultural, and social developments. At both the individual and collective levels, the cultural imaginary of "the future" was linked to past experience and to the traces of that experience in the present. This relationship between past, present, and future did not flow in only one direction, however. In this book, I argue that many of the images and objects of anticipation—the cultural phenomena identified with "the future"—contributed to the shaping of national cultural memory in this period. One of the broader aims of this study, then, is to reveal the ways in which representations of "the future" and a collective "culture of anticipation" may have contributed to eventual forms of remembrance and commemoration.

o   o   o

The chapters of this book follow a set of themes and resonances rather than a chronological sequence or narrative of the years from 1918 to 1939. I have organized them in terms of five concentric circles, moving outward from local to more international sites of cultural anticipation.[16] The first three chapters focus on the domestic, urban, and national spaces of France. Moving from the body, to the city, to the border, these chapters are "national" in their objects while referring conceptually to broader ideas and ideals with international implications. Considerations of the body at work and at rest were tied to broader questions about a "universal" human nature; planners interested in the future of Paris engaged repeatedly with the models (and specters) offered by international aesthetic movements and agglomerations such as New York and Chicago; strategies for the defense of the border could not be conceived or implemented without a deep sense of panic about the threats to the nation from beyond its boundaries, by land, sea and air.

The fourth and fifth chapters consider in more explicit terms the "nationality" of the future, including the representation of "America" and France as cultural opposites. The publication of Georges Duhamel's *Scènes de la vie future* in 1930 was a defining moment in the rhetorical and imaginative identification of the French "future" with the American "present." French contemporaries of Duhamel also identified the future with "America," drawing on the dichotomies of nature and technology, organic and artificial, civilization and barbarism. In this set of cultural binaries, the future could signify the disappearance of civilization altogether as it threatened the demise of French *civilisation* in particular.

The final chapter takes another step beyond the borders of the nation to consider the role of France in international diplomacy and politics. Here I analyze the arguments of French promoters and detractors of "Esperanto," an international, auxiliary language, the use of which the League of Nations considered seriously in the early 1920s. The debate over Esperanto held particular significance for France given the historic role of French as the lingua franca of international communication. Threats to the predominance of French suggested the diminishment of the nation's influence and power in world affairs while raising the specter of the disappearance of national sovereignty and culture.

o   o   o

The themes and issues I explore in this book are temporally fluid, held together by the somewhat leaky historical container of the *entre-deux-guerres*, or interwar period. The First World War and the defeat of 1940 were important watershed moments in French history and the years "in between" bore both the memorial and anticipatory *traces* of these major events.[17] I recognize the dilemma of defining attributes or characteristics as exclusive to these twenty years. Some of the questions raised in this period—some of its most vital sites of cultural and political debate—certainly seeped into the years on either side of 1918 and 1939. At the same time, "enclosed" as they have been in histories of twentieth-century France, these years constitute a crucial moment for exploring the relationship between representations of past and future, between what the philosopher of history Reinhart Koselleck has termed the "space of experience" and the "horizon of expectation."[18] Koselleck's frame, which offers a means to exploring the relationship between experience and expectation, between perspectives on the past and anticipation of the future, is useful for thinking about temporality in the interwar period. During these two decades, the future, as well as the past, expectation and experience, figured in debates about "Frenchness," competing ideas about the definition, preservation, and protection of a sense of national identity and culture.[19]

The "culture of anticipation" that I examine here was not exclusive to these two decades in French history, nor was it unique to France itself. A study of the futuristic imagination might easily engage with other, perhaps more obvious, sites and cases: Soviet Russia, Fascist Italy, or Nazi Germany, for example. These societies all engaged in radical social and political experiments. They drew on national histories while planning revolutionary national futures. In addition to political ideologies and transformations elsewhere in Europe, a range of aesthetic and literary movements—modernism, futurism, constructivism, cubism, and surrealism—reimagined time and space, memory and anticipation during the interwar years. In the French context, however, these different political and aesthetic models exercised a distinct influence on representations of past and future in relationship to existing political and social policies, definitions, and practices of national culture.

"Modernity," that hotly contested notion, appears often in these pages as voices from different political and cultural milieux refer to themselves and others as "modern," "modernist," or marking a break with the "traditional." I do not seek here to define "modernity," a term that remains the subject of intense scholarly debate within and beyond the field of French history. Nor do I seek to judge French culture and society in relation to a normative timeline of "modernization." Instead of asking, let alone answering, whether France is or has ever been "modern," I examine the history of the markedly temporal vocabulary used to imagine and organize change, one which often relies on the strictest opposition between past and future, backward and forward. Throughout, the idea of cultural *prosthesis* is critical to my analysis of representations of the future at once memorial and anticipatory, a field of imagination in which "modernity" and "tradition" figured as mutually constitutive rather than mutually exclusive cultural constructions.[20]

Finally, while this is not a work of science fiction, its sites of historical analysis do draw some of their inspiration from the themes and interrogations of that fantastic literary genre: What will the cities of the future look like? What are the possibilities of technology, the potential threats it poses, and the solutions it offers? What will become of human civilization and culture in the decades and centuries ahead? Will there be an end to national and international conflict, or an intensification of human strife, even global destruction? The grammar of a "future tense" essential to these questions shaped my research methodology for this study. First, I examined science fiction novels, short stories, and even films from the period, linking their preoccupations to the so-called nonfictional (but no less imaginary) worlds of urban and military planning, diplomacy, technological design, and cultural commentary. Certain themes and images appeared again and again: the possibilities and threats of technology; cities and architectures "of the future"; the fear of military and territorial invasion; the trope of "Old World" versus "New World" cast in terms of an opposition between a Europe represented by France, and the United States of America; and the ideal of universal cooperation and peace. Consulting a range of published and unpublished sources (including newspapers, magazines, novels, and monographs), I sought out evidence and images of cultural anticipation in interwar France, sources whose titles began with "The future of" and "Will we...in the year 2—?" *Future Tense* is, therefore, a history of "science fiction" in the broadest possible sense of the term. The traditional sources of future-oriented fiction are only one route to this exploration of a much larger cultural desire, the yearning to make the as-yet-unknown known, projecting what has been and is into glimpses and shadows of what might become.

CHAPTER 1

Machines for Being

In December 1933, *Le Miroir du monde,* a popular illustrated weekly in France, called on its writers to report on the world in the year 2933. In their opening remarks, the editors announced: "The Christmas issues of most magazines are filled with an abundance of memories drawn from a picturesque past. This year, *Le Miroir du monde* breaks with tradition: to amuse our readers, we invite them to turn their thoughts to a distant future."[1] The magazine's experiment was not the only one of its kind to appear in France during the interwar years. Other popular publications engaged in similar attempts to inform and entertain, devoting columns, articles, and entire issues to the consideration of the world to come in fifty, one hundred, even a thousand years. Weeklies like *Illustration, Lecture pour tous, VU,* and *Sciences et voyages* published their own accounts of anticipated developments in transportation, medicine, and communication, imagining the future transformation of human cities and ways of life.[2] *Lecture pour tous,* for example, devoted an entire segment of their Christmas 1932 issue to representations of life in 2002.[3] Launched in 1919, *Sciences et voyages* published numerous articles focused on science and technology in France and throughout the world, predicting futures both near and distant.[4] Alongside coverage of established and emerging scientific knowledge, including the projection of the future, *Sciences et voyages* also published science-fiction stories in serial form.

On its cover, *Le Miroir du monde*'s "XXXth century" issue featured an illustration of a cityscape, its towering buildings reaching into the clouds and overshadowing the people in the streets below. Inside the issue, article titles considered various aspects of everyday life in the future: "Will We Live without Money in the Year 2933?" "Robots, Our Slaves," "Travel 2933: Interplanetary Voyages," "Ten Centuries of Medical Progress," "The Sterilization of Sentiments," and "One's Entire Life Spent in a Chair!" The authors of these reports wrote from the imaginative perspective of 2933, adopting pseudonyms like "Mademoiselle Coco" and "Professeur Nietzsche-Bergson Rognonas," fanciful names that referred to historical and contemporary personalities (Coco Chanel, Friedrich Nietzsche, and Henri Bergson) who would have been well known to many readers in France in 1933. According to the editors, authors had been given free rein, having been asked only to remain "within a generally optimistic frame" and to depart from the assumption of "ten centuries of technological progress." While acknowledging the possibility of negative events and changes over the next one thousand years, the editors believed this emphasis on progress would make for more engaging reading than descriptions of "populations reverting to primitive ways after some sort of global upheaval."[5]

Among the articles featured in the issue was "Un millénaire de gastronomie," a report tracing one thousand years of human culinary history from the perspective of 2933. Its author identified himself as "Cur XLVII," the "head of the archives" of the Académie des gastronomes. Adopting the name "Cur," this anonymous writer referred to the real-life interwar French culinary expert "Curnonsky." This "Curnonsky" of the thirtieth century claimed to have researched the evolution of human eating habits, delving back as far as the "appalling" menus and appetites of the "early twentieth century." He cited with disdain the indulgence of a meal served in Lyon in 1933 with its courses of duck with foie gras, lobster, creamed artichokes, and soufflé, all specialties of French cuisine. "It would take five hundred years," he asserted, "for a more rational cuisine to evolve." Thanks to advances in the field of "chemical synthesis," "the ancient superstition attached to wine had disappeared long ago." As early as the twenty-second century, "the best wines of France, Spain and Italy" had been "standardized" and transformed into an "American-style drink." Linking developments in food to those in travel, "Cur" also noted, "After the definitive conquest of aviation and the ever-increasing rapidity of modes of transportation, the pace of life no longer permitted humans to linger with such primitive pleasures."[6]

Other contemporary accounts also focused on the food and drink of a future world. The introduction to *Lecture pour tous*'s special issue in 1932 described a celebration of the publication's one hundredth anniversary in 2002, praising a meal prepared "in the 1900 style" accompanied by wines

"from the reserves of the Bordelais, Burgundy and Champagne." The magazine noted these wines to be "less appreciated than the synthetic wines
discovered around 1990." Expressing a comical nostalgia for traditional
French wine, the magazine emphasized the "synthetic" as an obvious sign of
everyday life in the future. Elsewhere in the issue, another writer described
the challenge of designing clothes for "women who move at 500 kilometers
per hour." She recalled with amazement the slower-paced life of "the 1930s
when people ate two meals a day, sat down, went to restaurants and...didn't
take nutritional pills."[7]

In these descriptions (of 2002 and 2933), authors looked "backward"
to the present (1932 and 1933 respectively). Considering how their own
worlds might appear from the tomorrows they conjured, they constructed
distant memories of the present by imagining the future. This type of retro-
spective gaze revealed something about what these authors understood as
the markers of progress and change. The trope of a historical perspective
from the future also allowed these commentators to reimagine their own
time, historicizing their own epoch *in advance*.

Looking back to the twentieth century as he looked forward to the thirtieth, *Le Miroir du monde*'s "Cur" claimed "the problem of food" had been
"simplified" for centuries. The evolution of "rational eating" habits had
led to the eventual elimination of "the tedious chore of food preparation"
with all foods coming from a centralized factory. A typical menu by the
beginning of the thirtieth century might include the following items: "pow-
dered herb soup, compressed turbot tablets, two pills of refrigerated beef."
Finally, human beings turned to the development of alternative nutritional
techniques including "hypodermic injections" and the eventual perfection
of a "super-surgery suppress[ing] all of the digestive organs." This surgical
method "reconstructed the whole anatomy of the human body according to
the principles of reason." By 2933, "Two daily injections and one monthly
injection of reconstituting serum" had become "sufficient to maintain the
normal and regular functioning of the human machine." Calling on readers
to remember "the names of those vanished organs which likened Man...to
the basest species of animals: the stomach, the liver, the pancreas, the
intestines...[and] the belly," the author of *Le Miroir du monde*'s fictional
culinary genealogy hailed the rational overhaul of the most basic human
functions: "Human science had, little by little discovered ways of eliminating all needs...surpass[ing] all forms of pain, of appetite and desire."[8]

Like the other articles in *Le Miroir du monde*'s special issue, "Un millénaire de gastronomie" took a humorous approach to the future while poking
fun at the present. The idea of a "foodless utopia" expressed the lighthearted

and optimistic tone of the magazine as a whole. The use of comic illustrations, along with hyperbolic descriptions of a future dominated by rational
processes and mechanical devices, all contributed to the tongue-in-cheek
quality of the magazine's meditation on 2933. But "Un millénaire" concluded somewhat wistfully. According to this narrative of "progress," the
thirtieth-century human beings who had been "liberated" from their organic functions and emotions eventually felt perhaps the most fundamental human need: the need for need itself. "Cur" went on to describe how
the human inhabitants of Mars, Saturn, and Venus (planets fully colonized
by the year 2933) realized that "nothing was so monotonous as a world
without desire." They resorted eventually to the use of "psychocerebral
wave" technology, a neurological intervention that allowed them to channel
and live vicariously through the emotional and appetitive thoughts of less-
evolved civilizations. Linking the technological enhancement and so-called
improvement of the body to a deep sense of physical and psychological
loss, the article ended on a rather somber note: "The signals transmitted to
us...allow us to relive all of the sensations of distant eras, a little bit like
the way in which, long ago, amputees continued to suffer the pain of their
absent limbs."[9] Technology might enable, supplement, and even eliminate
body parts and functions. Taken to extremes, however, the body's *prosthetic*
enhancement would, in the future, feed a profound nostalgia for a more
primitive, organic humanness. The image of an amputee longing for whole-
ness could express this desire in powerful, visceral terms.

The analogy between a highly evolved humanity in the year 2933 and
amputees haunted by "phantom limbs" was more than incidental. However exaggerated, even absurd, the images, tropes, and associations at work
in "Un millénaire" pointed to a set of cultural preoccupations that figure
centrally throughout this chapter and resonate through the rest of this
book. Focusing on human appetites and needs, this *prosthetic* representation of the future reflected a much broader and profound fascination with
the changing relationship between technology and the human body in the
wake of the First World War. The images of popular science and culture
in this period fixated on an artificial and synthetic future, making reference to a number of contemporary projects to transform human bodies
and everyday lives through the use of a range of machines and devices. The
future imagined in the pages of *Le Miroir du monde* extrapolated from an
increasingly mechanized, standardized, and rationalized present in 1933,
depicting a variety of hybrid forms that might lead to the eventual triumph of
the artificial over the organic in all aspects of life. The article on French
eating habits and cuisine also mobilized a persistent dichotomy between

essentialized understandings of "New" and "Old" world civilizations and ways of life, opposing a "traditional" culture (represented here by French food and wine) and a synthetic culture of the future (typified in this instance by "American-style" beverages, nutritional powders, and pills). This is a theme I will return to at a number of other points in this book and especially in chapter 4, "The Future is a Foreign Country."

In this chapter, I focus on three discursive sites that served as contemporary traces of the kind of future outlined in "Un millénaire": the prosthetic rehabilitation of soldiers returning from the First World War; the rationalization of domestic space and housework; and the design of modernist furnishings and interiors. As part of a larger project of national recovery that began even before 1918, scientists and labor experts in France developed strategies for the reintegration of soldiers to the workforce as they strove for the revival of the nation as a whole. While all adult males were important for these efforts, none could better represent reconstruction than the wounded soldier in need of physical and social reeducation and rehabilitation. Engineering the recovery of disabled men through the scientific rationalization and prosthetic extension of their bodies, experts like the French scientist Jules Amar proposed a smooth transition back to work and civilian life.

Proponents of the movement to "modernize" housework in France in the 1920s and 1930s applied a similar framework of rationalization to the home. Domestic experts like Paulette Bernège promoted the "automatic kitchen," looking to the use of labor-saving devices and strategies in the home as a means to liberate housewives from the burden of domestic chores. Combining the latest home appliances and methods with a sexual division of labor that had preceded the war, Bernège's was, in its own way, a *prosthetic* vision in which wives and mothers would be aided in their supportive and nurturing roles by time-saving strategies and technological supplements.

During this same period, the modernist architect Le Corbusier and his design collaborator Charlotte Perriand outlined theories and furnishings for the home that also relied on the strategies of rationalization and mechanization, as well as the vocabularies of prosthesis and rehabilitation. Defining furniture as a system of "tools" completing human lives and bodies, a set of machines intended to revolutionize the spirit and intellect, Le Corbusier and Perriand anticipated a more rational, human subject enabled by an "orthopedic" interior design. Proposing "machines for living" as solutions to the problems of human fatigue and weakness in the modern world, Le Corbusier and Perriand imagined a "new man of the future" enabled by restful and ordered spaces furnished with sturdy "equipment."

Promising the liberation of humanity via the elimination of various needs, these projects drew on the methods of industrial production and scientific management articulated by Americans like Frederick Winslow Taylor and Henry Ford.[10] During the period, these models increasingly exerted their influence in a European context where fascination with the science of human labor had been apparent since the end of the nineteenth century.[11] The application of these methods and strategies certainly raised significant fears about human "progress," particularly in the wake of a war that had employed advanced technological means toward terrible and destructive ends. Even those who remained optimistic after four years of industrial slaughter were divided in terms of which strategies they deemed most effective for the advancement and improvement of human lives. Still, the human engineers I discuss here generally viewed technology as an enabling force, a means to the true realization of human potential. These different French voices called on the machine as the model for a human subject whose time, space, and behavior might be structured and modified more ideally in the future. Within this framework, a variety of tools and objects served as *traces* of the future. According to their advocates and designers, these *prosthetic* limbs, appliances, and furnishings could allow human beings to achieve their most noble goals, their time and energy freed up by the substitution of mechanical devices and strengths for human labor and weaknesses. Interrogating the definition, capacities, and limits of the body, this range of interwar projects—of extension, improvement, and relief—pushed and blurred the boundaries between the organic and the artificial, the animate and the inanimate, human and machine. In doing so, they anticipated the disappearance of the vulnerable beings that were the focus of their efforts.

The Mechanical Arm

The French experience of the First World War left individual and national wounds that cut across bodies, families, and entire landscapes. An estimated 8.4 million French men had been mobilized between 1914 and 1918 and more than 1.4 million, or 16.8 percent, of those men died. Historians of the war have pointed out that French losses were higher than those experienced by any of the other "Great Powers" and more significant when considered in proportion to population.[12] The number of French soldiers either killed, wounded, missing, or taken prisoner during the war amounted to more than 75 percent of the men mobilized while German victims totaled 50 percent. While Germany ultimately lost more individual soldiers during the war than any other nation (more than 2 million men), France's lower birth rate and higher rate of mortality relative to Germany in the decade before the war meant that the demographic effects of these losses were, in the end, greater in the French context.[13] Beyond actual deaths, many of the men who returned from the front suffered from physical and psychological damage that would never be completely undone.[14] Approximately 40 percent of the men mobilized had been wounded on at least one occasion, and half of their numbers were wounded a second time. One hundred thousand men were wounded more than twice and at least 300,000 men were categorized as war disabled, or *mutilés de guerre,* by the end of the conflict.[15] For the soldiers who had literally lost parts of their bodies in the brutal years between 1914 and 1918, the *cicatrix* separating battle front from home front seemed to have been permanently drawn.

Well before the war's end, the French government looked to strategies for the management of returning soldiers, including the prosthetic reconstruction of the bodies of those men who had lost limbs or been otherwise mutilated in battle. Introducing the fatigue and labor expert Jules Amar to an audience assembled in Paris in 1916, Paul Painlevé, the French minister of public instruction, expressed his conviction that "human science could, in a number of cases, repair what seemed irreparable."[16] Painlevé's remarks reflected a larger wartime and postwar commitment to the rational management of the destructive and disordering effects of the war experience. As director of the French Laboratoire de prothèse militaire et du travail professionel during and after the war, it was Amar's duty to address the trauma experienced by men severely wounded in battle. His contribution to the project of normalization focused on the physical reconstruction of the disabled soldier's body and his reintegration to work and society.

Amar's approach was one that he and a number of other European experts had been working on for some time. He was part of an established group of scientists in France and Germany who had, since the last decades of the nineteenth century, studied the working body as one governed by the laws of thermodynamics. These scientists regarded the human body as a vital system of energy that could be measured and manipulated to improve its productive capacity. As historian Anson Rabinbach has pointed out, the science of labor that emerged in late-nineteenth-century Europe applied a "productivist calculus" to studies of the body, developing a notion of the "human motor" tied to a rational, "social ethic of energy conservation."[17]

Shortly before World War I, these European scientists reconsidered their work in light of Taylorism, an American system for the rationalization of production. This system of "scientific management" proposed a revolution in the organization of production that included the breakup of work into a series of basic steps, an emphasis on maximum efficiency in the performance of these tasks, and the standardization of models for the design of tools and machines. Taylorism also established a relationship between wages and output, rationalizing managerial and administrative functions. At first, scientists like Amar expressed suspicion of Taylorism as a nonlaboratory system intended to serve the interests of management alone. Like many of his colleagues, however, Amar came to believe that it could be productive to apply the principles of the science of labor, including the rationalization of the body, to the very real conditions of the shop floor while addressing the issues of operation and administration.[18]

Beginning his work with the French Ministry of War in 1907, Amar brought this mix of scientific analysis and production strategies to his work with the military.[19] Scientific management of the body and production worked particularly well in the consideration of battle, informing studies of the soldier's physical capabilities and the organization of labor in preparation for and during combat. This framework also helped structure Amar's ideas about demobilization and the soldier's transition to the civilian labor force. In his discussion of the rehabilitation of wounded soldiers returning from the front, Amar highlighted the importance of "organiz[ing] the work of the wounded, in such a manner that each shall fill his true place in the social machine, contribute as best he can to its operation, and thereby advance towards prosperity." The postwar revival of French industry, agriculture, and commerce depended on the efficient and full redeployment of labor power in all sectors. According to Amar, 80 percent of those wounded in battle could be reeducated. "The wounded soldier, or the victim of amputation," Amar insisted, "possesses a capacity for work that is perfectly capable of complete utilisation; he represents a *value* which is sometimes *integral*." Amar also emphasized the willingness of most war-wounded to return to work. He noted that among the wounded, soldiers were particularly eager to adapt to their new circumstances, approaching their rehabilitation with "an admirable spirit of courage, coolness, and resolution." Amar insisted on how important it was "*to utilize human capacities rationally*, even when they are diminished," noting that this was critical not only to the "material and moral future of many thousands of French families," but to the recovery of the French nation as a whole.[20]

The rhetoric of "the social machine," a family and nation dependent on the able and willing male body, mobilized disabled men otherwise reliant on forms of social assistance. In addition to its possible implications for national economic recovery, the disabled male body troubled the definition of men in terms of their labor power and a gender ideology that historically placed the male provider at the center of the family, the economy, and the nation. Amar devoted special attention to the challenge of putting amputees back to work in order to prevent their decline into "inaction, hours of idleness made gloomy by anxiety."[21] Reintegrated to the workforce, these men contributed their labor and avoided acting as a drain on national economic resources, including dependence on government pensions and assistance.[22] Putting the male body to work in peacetime relied, as it had in wartime, on the identification of productivity with masculinity and the interests of the nation. When Amar identified the rehabilitation of the disabled soldier with the fate of the nation as a whole, he gestured toward the equation of individual male productivity with masculinity and prewar gender roles. His program for the rehabilitation of amputees made explicit the challenge of the return to work and family involved for all soldiers, both in terms of the collective capacity to forget the horrors of the wartime experience and the reestablishment of the prewar gender roles that came to symbolize a return to normalcy after the war.[23] The scarred and mutilated body of the war amputee thus became a privileged site of national recuperation.

Beyond addressing economic and social vulnerabilities, work also held the potential to heal the psychological trauma experienced by individual men. Amar's explanation of the phenomenon of "phantom" limbs felt by amputees was typical of his rational approach. According to Amar, it was the "memory of industrial or professional life" that brought on the "illusion" of a "phantom" limb. The true cause of an amputee's pain and suffering was both "mental" and "physiological." Amar believed firmly that this problem could be resolved "in a few months" through rehabilitation and "the resumption of daily work" that could physically soothe the amputee while "lessen[ing] the danger of [his] nervous degeneration." Apart from the physical relief this could have, Amar noted "the moral advantage of bestowing upon the war-cripple a certain sense of energy, and a feeling of hope as regards the future." There was nothing that science could not explain or undo; even the seemingly irrational "haunting" of "phantom" limbs could be addressed by his method. While other physicians who had studied the phenomenon tended to prescribe rest as a route to healing, Amar's philosophy of rehabilitation viewed idleness as the source of an amputee's physical and psychological pain. His program could thus be understood as a form of "work cure."[24]

Rationalization was crucial to the reintegration of soldiers who required physical rehabilitation and reeducation on their return from the front, and the body of the disabled soldier fit easily within the scientific study of labor. In the case of the amputee in particular, the absence of parts of the arms or legs, or of entire limbs, did not affect the procedures involved in the analysis of their productive capacity and strength. This framework already imagined the body as a series of interdependent parts, assuming the fragmentation of corporeal systems of energy and force. Therefore, the very real fragmentation of the amputee's body presented little difficulty for the quantification of that body by the science of work. As a scientist of labor, Amar did not discriminate between so-called "whole" bodies and those from which certain parts were missing. In his rationalized model, every body represented a set of productive *values* that could be measured and manipulated in the same way. In order to determine the strength and "functional value of stumps," Amar employed devices such as the "ergometer," a combination bicycle and respirator, and the "ergograph," a weighted system for measuring the strength of fingers and hands. These devices were adapted only slightly in order to measure the force and energy of the disabled body. Differences among disabled men, and between the disabled man and the "able-bodied" man, merely produced different data: different lengths of stumps, different measurements of strength and energy output.[25]

After assessment and measurement, the second stage of an amputee's rehabilitation was the fitting of an appropriate prosthesis. The amputee equipped with the right prosthesis could be trained to operate the appliance, returning to his former employment in some cases. When this was not possible, he could be reeducated to perform some other, more suitable work. As early as 1916, Amar had developed his designs for a "working arm," a device that would make him famous on both sides of the Atlantic (figure 1.1). The working arm consisted of a steel rod articulated at the elbow to which a series of basic tools could be attached, the most common being a pair of universal pliers. Amar attempted to distinguish the need to "make up for a function lost or greatly reduced" from any attempt to "replace the limb or missing segment." He maintained that the prosthesis, while "by definition...anatomical," was "in truth...physiological and utilitarian." "The principle of design was efficiency, not aesthetics," Amar insisted. "There was no point in trying to copy the human arm; it was the arm's use-value that had to be reproduced." Amar went on to note that, "while [the prosthesis] copies Nature, it is not a slave to it." The aim was not to deprive certain workers of more realistic and lifelike prostheses. Many forms of industrial work had become so specialized that it was more practical and efficient to replace fingers with hooks, hands with pliers or magnets, than to attempt to recreate an organic human hand.[26]

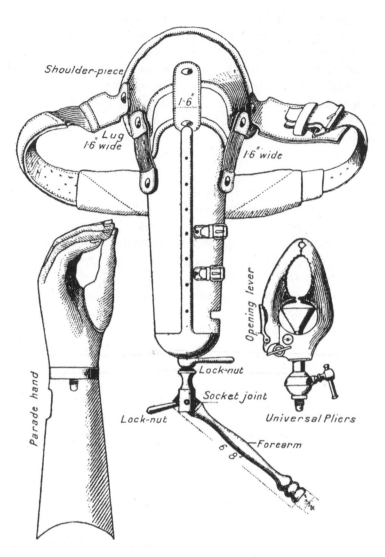

Shoulder-piece

Lug
1·6" wide

1·6"

1·6" wide

Opening lever

Parade hand

Lock-nut

Socket joint

Lock-nut

Universal Pliers

Forearm

1.1. The "Working Arm." Jules Amar, *The Physiology of Industrial Organisation and the Re-employment of the Disabled*, 1918.

Rehabilitation had an intimate, as well as an industrial side, however. The practice of private life still required the human hand (or at least its appearance) as its most appropriate "tool." Amar seemed to understand that the reintegration of the disabled body extended beyond the restoration of its function at work. His "worker's arm" also came equipped with a *main*

de parade (parade hand) attached to a leather sheath formed to the forearm.
According to Amar, this prosthetic hand "responded to a well-accepted aesthetic." In the fabrication of a "show" hand, Amar acknowledged that the
purely functional tool would not do outside of the work/shop context. If
only the arm's "use-value" mattered in the workplace, the aesthetics of the
natural body would resume their importance during a working man's hours
of leisure.[27]

If he criticized the complicated "luxury" appliances of German and American design, Amar nonetheless predicted that in France, "in the near future," prosthetic designs might reveal a "progress that takes into account
both elegance and utility."[28] When Amar designed the more sophisticated
"mechanical arm" that included an articulated hand, it was its "natural"
appearance that made the design successful. This new mechanical arm, complete with fingers that opened and closed, simulated more accurately than
the "working arm" the movements of an organic human hand. Controlled
by a cable attached to a band fitting around the chest, the mechanical hand
could be made to open or close in direct relationship to the wearer's deep
inhalation and exhalation, movements that would expand and contract his
chest. Amar designed this feature to eliminate sudden movements, making
the hand seem more natural in its operation. Not all workers would require
a mechanical arm, according to Amar. But in what he termed the "liberal
professions," the line between utility and elegance could not be drawn as
easily as in a more industrial context. While a factory worker's hand might
be replaced effectively with a set of pliers, a man working in a professional
setting would require not only the functional value, but also the appearance
of a real arm. Different types of work called for different degrees of mobility
and different levels of approximation of natural, human hands. The simula-
tion of the organic body was, in certain situations, part of the function and
use-value of the appliance.

Amar's project of prosthetic reconstruction employed a practical "science
fiction" of the body in which the reintegration of the disabled man seemed
rationally and technologically manageable. Carefully designed appliances
could enable certain types of work, as well as the relatively inconspicuous
execution of leisurely activities in public. Amar expressed his excitement
about the degree to which his new mechanical arm permitted the amputee
to "go about all of the normal practices of life in public... drinking out of a
glass, removing his hat, playing the violin, as well as performing certain forms
of vocational work: drilling wood, planing, etc."[29] The photograph of a soldier in the image below (figure 1.2) is an example the aesthetic normalization that was part of the design for Amar's mechanical arm and articulated

1.2. "Accountant, seated at a café table." Jules Amar, *The Physiology of Industrial Organisation and the Re-employment of the Disabled,* 1918.

hand. In the photograph, a man, seated in a café, lights a cigarette. What could be more "natural," more "French"? A patron seated at another table might recognize him as a soldier because of the medals he wears. If not for these signs of valor in battle, an onlooker might not think about the horrific war in which this soldier lost the limbs now replaced by feats of technological design. The fingers were mechanical, but functional. Despite the stiffness of the cold, shining metal, these hands seemed to do everything that human hands might. The body could be reconstructed. Normal life could be resumed. Everything could be returned to the way it once was. The use of photographs like this one testified to Amar's faith that prosthetic technology could be used to restore more than just the productive capacity of the disabled man. Amar's publications included images whose central aim seemed to be to show that the "elegant" prosthesis held the promise of a man's complete rehabilitation in all aspects of public and private life.[30] In spite of initial disclaimers about the purely utilitarian aims of prosthetic design, Amar was careful to emphasize just how close to nature the well-designed prosthetic appliance could come.

The case of a hand completed, not with universal pliers, but with metal "fingers" suggested a new relationship between hands and tools. If industrial labor had reduced human body parts to tools, prosthetic technology increasingly imagined certain tools as if they were human, capable of replacing organic body parts. An artificial limb may have been artificial like any other tool, but it was differently valued in symbolic terms *as a limb*. Close approximations of human limbs could help to efface the terrible memory of the wartime experience that the disabled soldier seemed to permanently embody. In addition, the "elegant" prosthesis could alleviate possible anxieties about the melding of men and machines, the dehumanization of labor in a rationalized system of production, and the animation of wood, metal, and leather that prosthetic technology involved.

The mechanical approximation and replacement of human body parts also raised another set of issues about the body's erosion in the face of technological advances. The amputee's body reconstructed represented more explicitly than any other the fantasy of the man-machine hybrid that was, at one and the same time, the dream and the nightmare of industrial production, its rationalization, increasing mechanization, and automation.[31] Fixating on the limb as the principal site of a man's productive value and reconstructing that limb with nonhuman, nonorganic materials, Amar normalized the body's partial replacement with a mechanical device. While the animation of the inanimate prosthesis was linked to an organic body, Amar's use of prosthetic substitutes for human body parts pointed to an uncertainty about the status of the whole, natural, male body whose functional value and elegance he was working to restore. How could the replacement of organic limbs with nonhuman, mechanical devices work to assuage fears about an eroding masculinity tied to productivity if contained in that replacement was the suggestion that the human body might not be entirely necessary? The male body completed by technology could function as the best example of the possibilities of individual and national reconstruction. From another perspective, however, this hybrid of man and machine made the threat of that body's eventual disappearance apparent.

As a project of restoration, Amar's work on the body was, in many ways, oriented toward the past, the return of the soldier to work and family. In its emphasis on productive capacity, the rehabilitation of the amputee also underlined a shift in thinking about the body that had begun before the war. The amputee's body made explicit a problem that was already evident in factories and industrialized agricultural sites throughout the nation: the increasing dehumanization of human labor. The nonnecessity of the entire, articulated human body for certain forms of work and production opened up a space for the body without certain limbs or parts; it also made room for a functional body enabled with prostheses that only partially simulated the functions and the appearance of human limbs. While Amar never explicitly addressed the broader or longer-term implications of his work, his designs provided a very literal embodiment of where the relationship between all human beings and machines might be headed: a future without organic bodies or needs.

Toward an Automatic Kitchen

The soldier's was not the only body whose management served as an emblem of national reconstruction and revival in the interwar years. The First World War had wrought a massive transformation of French society as whole. The traumatic impact of battlefront violence and death, coupled with shifts in the sexual division of labor at home, brought about a fundamental interrogation of the traditional family as the foundation on which a stable and peaceful society might be imagined and reconstructed. Of the men who survived the war, many returned from the front unable to take up their prewar positions as breadwinners and heads of households. Many French women had entered the workforce for the first time during the war, often in industries previously reserved for male labor. This revolution on the home front enacted a set of changes to domestic economies and roles, the effects of which outlasted the years of military conflict. The tremendous loss of life further exacerbated an already low French birthrate. It was in this atmosphere of instability that pronatalists and conservatives expressed increased concern regarding women's bodies after 1918. Their anxieties focused on abortion, contraception, and images of the "new woman," that social and cultural emblem of a traditional femininity undone.[32]

In this context, it was therefore not surprising to hear the question: "What will domestic life in the future be like?"[33] Emphasizing technological invention as the engine of social transformation, one interwar observer imagined a future private life filled with labor-saving and recreational devices, telephones and home appliances, including "machines for food preparation, washers, various vegetable peelers, choppers, salting devices, fat-removers for meat." Once again, food took center stage in the imaginative description of everyday life in the future. In this version of the future, homes would become communal dwellings equipped with a range of helpful machines and devices, their "modern kitchens... filled with small, quiet, clean, tidy appliances without flames or smoke." Electricity would be "the soul animating" these machines, releasing human beings entirely from the "onerous tasks" and "cares of everyday life."[34]

Amar deployed strategies of rationalization and mechanization to the rehabilitation of soldiers and workers. In the 1920s and 1930s in France, Paulette Bernège championed these techniques as answers to the domestic challenges of French housewives. A member of the Comité national de l'organisation française (CNOF), Bernège was also the founder of the Ligue de l'organisation ménagère in 1925. She published a number of books on the subject, including *Si les femmes faisaient les maisons* (1928), *De la méthode ménagère* (1928), and *Les Rapports financiers entre époux* (1929). Drawing extensively on the work of the American household and consumer expert Christine Frederick, Bernège also published numerous articles in the magazines *Mon chez moi* and *L'Art ménager*.[35] In these publications, Bernège waxed enthusiastically about increased efficiency and organization in the performance of household chores and tasks, extolling the value of machines and appliances that might enable the woman at home to accomplish her domestic duties while saving time and energy.[36]

A number of historians have discussed and debated the "new woman" as the embodiment of the challenge to "traditional" gender roles in the first part of the twentieth century, the female incarnation of the problem of "modernity."[37] The image of this independent woman, unfettered by the bonds of marriage, liberated in her sexuality and dress, certainly did capture the imagination of many contemporary observers in the interwar years. The movement for scientific management in the home was a striking example of an attempt to "liberate" the *femme au foyer* (housewife) while maintaining her role as the keeper of the hearth. Encouraging women to take advantage of technological conveniences *within* the boundaries of an idealized domestic sphere, advocates of rationalization like Bernège saw themselves as improving the lives of wives and mothers, transforming drudgery into efficient techniques, housewives into skilled workers, empowered consumers, and prudent administrators. In doing so, however, these domestic reformers continued to rely on the notion that women were somehow uniquely suited to house work, to serving the best interests of men and society as a whole.

Bernège called on French women to take up domestic rationalization as a social obligation, a duty to French families and to the nation. She identified the efficient organization of their households as women's contribution to the order and stability of French society declaring:

> No more words, no more complaints, no more indifference. To work! More than ever, men need the level-headedness, in a practical sense, of the productive, patient and ordered work of women. Against the disorganization that surrounds us, let us oppose the unshakable barrier of the organization of our homes and of women's work.[38]

Bernège promoted the *arts ménagers,* or household arts, as a means to enable economic recovery and national strength. While she insisted on the uniqueness of her version of domestic scientific management as one catered to the specific needs and values of the French household, the idea of "America" loomed large in Bernège's prescriptions for the French housewife. Bernège gathered some of her inspiration from American models. She also mobilized "evidence" of American superiority to prod French women to action. Throughout the articles in *Mon chez moi,* Bernège and her collaborators made reference to a national economy whose strength began at home, reminding women: "It is imperative...that you realize how far behind our country is, how much we waste our precious resources." She likened the gap between France and the United States to the difference between urban and rural households within France, claiming "if the modern American housewife had to prepare a single meal in a French woman's kitchen, you would hear her moan and sigh just as you would if you found yourself in the discomfort of the countryside. The same abyss separates the two."[39] French economic weaknesses had been greatly exacerbated by the experience of the war.

In 1926, Bernège devoted an entire issue of the magazine *Mon chez moi* to the household economy, asserting that it was the woman in the home who could serve as the key to revitalizing the nation.[40] In 1933, Bernège suggested the mechanization and rationalization of the domestic sphere could "serve as an example for the entire derailed world economy." In the domestic sphere, these strategies were to be valued for their orientation toward the prosperity and comfort of families and, by extension, the nation as a whole. Bernège argued that the mechanization of "the masculine world of industry, commerce, and finance" took instead as its "dominant and often exclusive aim the maximization of profit and material wealth, without a humane counterbalance of happiness and leisure." The "feminine" rationalization of the home and housework, on the other hand, had the nobler goal of "improved quality of life" rather than profit.[41]

Bernège based her program on the assumption that the housewife performed meaningful and productive work, that certain laws governed her labor, like the labor of any worker. In her discussion of time management, budgeting, and the organization of household space, Bernège often insisted that "the household enterprise is comparable to an industrial enterprise."[42] In her framework, the home became a site for the negotiation of female labor and the rendering of maximum output from machines that could aid women just as they aided workers. The home was a workshop, a business to be managed and administered. At the same time, the division of labor characteristic of rationalized factory work was not quite the same in the context of the home. As another contributor to *Mon chez moi* pointed out in 1923, the rationalization of domestic work was unique in that the terms of household labor demanded that women perform multiple tasks, operate a range of different machines, and employ a variety of skills. In the home, women functioned as workers and supervisors at the same time, managing the enterprise as a whole while executing the individual tasks required across a range of skill levels. "Modern" housewives were uniquely powerful as workers in that they were simultaneously the owners and the operators of machines. Unlike many husbands, these women were their own bosses in a workplace they managed themselves.[43]

Believing that home appliances and rational techniques could enable the most noble human goals and achievements, Bernège insisted that French women "Modernize!"[44] Bernège offered a solution to the "crisis of the home" weighing heavily "on female shoulders," noticing that this burden had become even greater "at the very moment when intellectual and social life calls out to women." It was understandable for women to cry out, "Where is the financial reward?... How does one find the time to accomplish the material tasks and 'live' intellectually, cultivate one's interest in the arts, go out, see the world, etcetera?"[45] By using labor-saving devices and appliances, women could free up time, thereby improving the quality of their individual and personal lives while contributing to the nation as a whole.

Bernège encouraged women to use the appropriate equipment for cooking, cleaning, and washing as a way of protecting their own physical and intellectual health and expanding their horizons in life. Reminding women that "health is very precious," Bernège urged them to learn how to use "tools that simplify, mechanize and liberate," and "entrust their work to machines that will do it as well...and much more quickly."[46] She instructed women: "Before each object in your kitchen, you should now ask the following questions: Is this the one that will save the most fuel, the most effort, the most work, the most time? And you should only be satisfied when you finally have the tool with the best output."[47] Bernège further suggested that women model their own performance after the machines intended to serve them. Monitoring their own expenditures of time and energy, women should be careful to maintain maximum output and production. "It is necessary to turn all women into household athletes," Bernège declared.[48]

Characterizing housewives as workers and athletes, Bernège argued that women needed to subject themselves to the "minute observation of [their] time and work." This "chronometric" evaluation of women's efforts could hold a "highly educational value" because it "reveals surprising wastes" of time. Bernège offered the example of "unmaking and making a single bed," a task that "without methodical reflection," would take "12 minutes." Following a close examination of "the movements involved," Bernège declared the task a "3-minute" endeavor. In another illustration, Bernège focused on food preparation, comparing the time required to perform simple functions without training to a more efficient, rationalized approach: "Peeling a half-kilo of potatoes, with an ordinary knife, without method or training: 9 minutes; with a peeling knife, a good position for working, excellent lighting and a little bit of practice: 5 minutes."[49]

These strategies not only suggested women use machines; they suggested that women emulate machines, that they consider their own bodies and behavior in the same terms used to evaluate their appliances. Employing the strategies of time management and the careful organization of domestic tasks—applying the same standards and criteria to their own movements and performance that they should use to evaluate their appliances—women could live fuller, more humane lives. Bernège invested labor-saving techniques and devices in the home with the promise of an improved life for families in general and a more evolved life for women in particular. By rendering their labor more efficient, women might develop a more cultivated, pleasurable existence, using their increased leisure time to explore more fulfilling activities. Regardless of the possibilities she promised women, however, Bernège maintained a vision of the domestic sphere as a uniquely female domain.[50] She never directly questioned the "fact" of women's responsibility for household management in her program for domestic rationalization. Nowhere in her writings did she explicitly challenge the notion that a woman's primary role was that of homemaker, however "modernized." Furthermore, neither emotion nor affect appeared in the discussion of this rationalized home; Bernège emphasized a woman's relationship to machines rather than her relationship to other human beings such as a husband or children. Traces of a more conventional femininity lurked in the details of Bernège's plans for a highly productive and efficient domestic life for women, however. Admiring Frederick's "modern" kitchen in 1933, Bernège noted that it included "a little nook in the wall for a powder box with a mirror placed above it, allowing the cook, leaving her stove, to powder her nose and make herself beautiful before going to the table."[51]

The project to restore disabled men to their productive capacities through the use of prosthetic appliances was troubled because the increasing obsolescence of their laboring bodies was implied in the structures and strategies used to repair them. Reimagining the housewife in "prosthetic" terms, advocates of domestic rationalization and home appliances in the interwar years unwittingly called her very future into question. In a 1925 article entitled "A La recherche du 'home scientifique,'" Jean Labadie, a contributor to the magazine *Science et la vie,* pointed to the increasing rationalization of domestic life and activity. Extolling the benefits of labor-saving devices such as the washing machine, the dishwasher, and the vacuum cleaner, particularly in the fight against germs and bacteria, Labadie also acknowledged limits to the use of these appliances. "As soon as we speak of the 'scientific home,'" Labadie noted, "we think of automatic spaces in which tasks are entirely performed by ingenious electrical appliances." According to Labadie, this sort of "mechanical intrusion upon our daily lives, which we must distinguish from our 'work' would be frankly intolerable." Asking, "Must our existence be literally plugged into an electric current, put at the mercy of cogs in a machine, all in the name of achieving automation at its fullest?" Labadie responded with a clear and resounding "no."[52] But the figure of the automated household that featured importantly in the discourse of domestic rationalization in the interwar years could raise significant questions. If there were already machines capable of performing household duties just as well—and sometimes even more effectively—than women, could those tasks continue to be regarded as essentially "feminine?" If the future of domestic life lay in its automation, how could the home be guaranteed as the sphere and domain of women? The increasing replacement of the housewife's body with a range of mechanical devices threatened the future of another crucial pillar of the family on which the nation itself seemed to depend. What could possibly guarantee femininity, masculinity, and a gendered division of labor if new methods transformed the roles and definitions of wives and workers, imagining both in mechanized terms while substituting their bodies and body effects with a range of machines and appliances? The engineers and authors of the culture of mechanization of the interwar years extrapolated a more efficient future from the traces they detected in electrical appliances and efficient designs. Their prescriptions and premonitions thus contributed to a culture of anticipation that suggested the disappearance of household work and the demise of long-standing domestic arrangements and roles.

Machines for Living

> Events are unfolding, the notion of furniture has disappeared.
> It is replaced by a new term: "household equipment."
>
> —LE CORBUSIER, *Precisions on the Present State of Architecture and City Planning* (1930)

Proponents of domestic management like Bernège were not alone in their program to rationalize the home in the interwar years. In 1929, the interior designer Charlotte Perriand published a rather unique manifesto, a two-page statement on the subject of furniture. The editors of *The Studio,* the magazine where Perriand's "Wood or Metal?" appeared, hailed the designer as a "champion of new ideas," praising her "original style."[53] Perriand's manifesto referred to a series of furnishings that she had designed while working in the Paris atelier of the modernist architect Le Corbusier. In it, she claimed metal had enacted a "revolution" in furniture "as cement ha[d] done in architecture." Perriand championed metal over wood, identifying the former as a material enabling more efficient mass production than the latter. She argued that metal was more durable, practical, and aesthetically appealing than wood, a "vegetable substance, in its very nature bound to decay." Perriand predicted a future in which metal and other truly contemporary materials might better meet the needs and "solve the problem of the new man." This "new man" was "the type of individual who keeps pace with scientific thought, who understands his age and lives in it: The Aeroplane, the Ocean Liner and the Motor are at his service." This "man of the XXth century" required a new home, a "resting place" furnished with strong, functional, and hygienic "equipment." Only the "new interior" revolutionized by metal furniture could keep the "new man" from feeling like "an intruder," a feeling he could not avoid "when surrounded by antique furniture." Perriand celebrated this new design imperative as evidence of a "modern mentality," "a healthy life in a mechanical age" in which it was essential to "keep morally and physically fit."[54]

Reflecting on a decade of collaboration with Le Corbusier and his cousin Pierre Jeanneret from 1927 to 1937, Perriand identified herself in her 1998 autobiography, *Une vie de création* (*A Life of Creation*), as part of a team whose business was "building, or rather conceiving the future."[55] Perriand executed her designs in keeping with a theoretical framework that Le Corbusier had laid out in his writings on the home and its furnishings. As early as 1921, Le Corbusier had called for a revolution of domestic architecture and space in which the new home should be understood as a "machine for living in."[56] Later on, in the fourth of a series of ten lectures that Le Corbusier gave in Buenos Aires in 1929, the architect recalled his first use of the term *machine for living*. He noted that the term was a "phrase that caught on fast" and bemoaned the fact that he was "beaten" with it "on both sides of the barricade." "If the expression has infuriated," he explained, "it is because it contains the word 'machine,' representing in all minds the idea of functioning, of efficiency, of work, of production."[57] In his writings and presentations, the architect repeatedly defended the machine as "an event of...capital importance in the history of mankind," arguing "that it is legitimate to credit it with the role of conditioning the human spirit." He viewed the machine positively as the force behind "a reformation of the spirit across the world."[58]

Le Corbusier articulated a design program for the contemporary interior that he linked to a highly rationalized plan to renovate and modernize cities like Paris.[59] Le Corbusier saw his revolution in architecture as one that should affect all facets of life, from the organization of the city, to the specific design of chairs, beds, cabinets, and other everyday objects. In his scheme, the rational human being residing in the ideal home, furnished with the right "equipment" constituted the foundation of the "Radiant City" of the future, the urban center of a more evolved human society. Le Corbusier imagined a future human life based architecturally on the standardization of highly functional living units. Within these units, the vital issue of furniture required serious attention. According to the architect, "the renewal of the plan of the modern house cannot be undertaken efficiently without laying bare the question of furniture."[60]

Decrying "the purgatory of the daily life of modern men imprisoned in the houses of the preindustrial age," Le Corbusier argued that the home should be subjected to the same rational management and organization as any workplace.[61] He challenged any notion that these rules of efficiency and productivity be suspended in the domestic sphere. Relaxation required management and efficiency as well. Like Bernège, Le Corbusier believed the domestic sphere required a change no less revolutionary than the transformation of industry and the world of business. Using the example of the banker who organizes his work environment, Le Corbusier praised his attention to functionality and productivity in the interest of profit. But while the architect applauded the progress of design in the workplace, he lamented the fact that the same "banker..."

> proud of his office furniture.... [W]hen he gets home, he is welcomed by a load of curios capable of exploding the manometer of reason if one could fix a manometer of thoughts on our skulls. Here at home, he no longer works, he doesn't produce; he can lose, waste his time, trouble his spirit, wear it out, lie to it. It is of no importance; he is resting, he has no competitors.[62]

Like the rationalization of housework, Le Corbusier's program for interior design reflected intense concern with the economies of space and of time. When the architect proudly surveyed his plans for "modern" living spaces, he noted "one can move around easily; gestures are rapid and exact, storage automatic." Efficiency was key, enabling *minutes gained, every day; precious minutes.*"[63] Calling for the application of the same strategies to the interior and intimate spaces of human life as those being applied in the industrial sphere, Le Corbusier imagined a design revolution in which "the dwelling, the office, the workshop, the factory...will use new forms of standardization, of industrialization, of efficiency."[64] Furniture should be designed and intimate space managed to enable productivity not unlike that of the shop floor or the factory. "Furniture is [*sic*] tools," Le Corbusier maintained. He insisted domestic objects be understood in strictly functional terms as "equipment" rather than decoration. He praised the standardization of office furniture from the "form and dimension of letter paper" to the "precision, efficiency, purity of forms and lines" of desks, tables, and file cabinets.[65]

Le Corbusier claimed his designs were based on an understanding of human needs. He argued that these needs were universal, "not very numerous," and "very similar for all mankind, since man has been made out of the same mould from the earliest times known to us."[66] While intellectually, human beings might vary, Le Corbusier insisted that the physical characteristic of the human body remained constant: "If our spirits vary, our skeletons are alike, our muscles are in the same places and perform the same functions."[67] Interior design and architecture should reflect and inspire this purity and rationality. If standardization could apply to the home and its furnishings, it was because human beings and their lives could also be understood in terms of standards:

> Our needs are daily, regular, always the same; yes, always the same. Our furniture corresponds to *constant, daily, regular functions*. All men have the same needs, at the same hours, every day, all their lives. The tools corresponding to these functions are easy to define. And progress, bringing us new techniques...gives us the means to carry them out infinitely more perfectly and efficiently than in the past.[68]

Le Corbusier's sense of human needs corresponded to a model of the body as a "machine" composed of "the structure, the nervous system, the arterial system."[69] As such, human bodies and behavior could, like any other machines, be engineered, rationalized, and optimized for maximum efficiency.

If Le Corbusier's emphasis on efficiency in the home linked his designs to the work of domestic experts like Bernège, his discussion of the human body also shared a great deal with Amar's discourse of physical rehabilitation. This was particularly evident in his focus on the human limb: "We all have the same limbs," he noted, "in number, form and size; if on this last point there are differences, an average dimension is easy to find."[70] Just as Amar evaluated the functional value of limbs and stumps, Le Corbusier also understood the human body as a system of energy and force comprised of basic component parts and measurable elements. The objects that Le Corbusier identified as essential to domestic and intimate functions were intended "in proportion to our limbs...adapted to our gestures."[71] In *L'Art décoratif d'aujourd'hui* (*The Decorative Art of Today*), published in 1925, Le Corbusier redefined interior furnishings as "human-limb objects" intended to adequately maintain a "technico-cerebral-emotional" equilibrium fundamental to human comfort and well-being.[72] The way to ensure the maintenance of this equilibrium, according to Le Corbusier, was to return to the "compass" of human beings themselves, to design objects on a human scale based on standard human functions. He argued that "nature is indifferent" and that it was the purpose of human invention to compensate for the inadequacies of the natural human body, the fact that "we are born naked and without armor." Rather than a traditional conception of decorative art as "decorative," Le Corbusier called for an understanding of furniture not just as "tools," but as *artificial limbs*. Amar himself had made the identification of the two one of the defining features of the prosthesis. Le Corbusier suggested furniture be understood as prosthetic, life-enhancing substitutes for human effort, "machines" compensating for human physical weakness. According to the architect, this prosthetic model explained the history of human invention and construction:

> For our comfort, to facilitate work, to avoid exhaustion, to refresh ourselves, in one word to *free our spirit* and distance us from the clutter that encumbers our life and threatens to *kill it,* we have equipped ourselves through our ingenuity with *human limb-objects,* extensions of our limbs.

Following this logic, Le Corbusier claimed, "decorative art becomes orthopaedic [*sic*]."[73] In this instance, the fantasy of a body completed by technology took the form of a design strategy that imagined home furnishings as prosthetic appliances enabling an improved future life.

Developed in collaboration with Le Corbusier, Perriand's *chaise longue* exemplified this orthopedic and prosthetic approach to furniture design and was the basic model of what eventually became known as the "LC chair" or the "machine for sitting."[74] Perriand identified the chaise longue as one in a series of "resting machines for ease and pleasant repose."[75] In a number of photographs taken to illustrate the design (figure 1.3) Perriand appeared in a reclined pose with her legs raised, her skirt draping over the side of the chair, and her head turned away. She seemed to be asleep. Plans for the display of Perriand's furnishings at the 1929 Salon d'Automne in Paris, included a sketch of a woman resembling Perriand in this same pose.[76] The image of a body at rest illustrated the effectiveness of an interior design based on the detailed study of human motion and anatomy. Years later, Perriand noted that the "chair designs were directly related to the position of the human body."[77] Her sketches included the study of several physical poses that informed the furnishings she produced. Just as Amar grounded his project of rehabilitation in a science of fatigue, Perriand designed "machines for resting" based on analysis of the human body as a system of energy and force prone to exhaustion. While Amar's was, ultimately, a "technology of work," Perriand, departing from similar principles, developed a "technology of rest."

In his writings about furniture, Le Corbusier underlined the vision of the chaise as a therapeutic "machine for resting." In his formulation, chairs performed different functions. As a general rule, he argued, "*seats are for resting.*" Of course, not all chairs were designed strictly for this purpose. Le Corbusier acknowledged a variety of seating functions, observing, "Depending on the time of day, depending on one's activities, depending on the position one takes in a living room (and which we can change four or

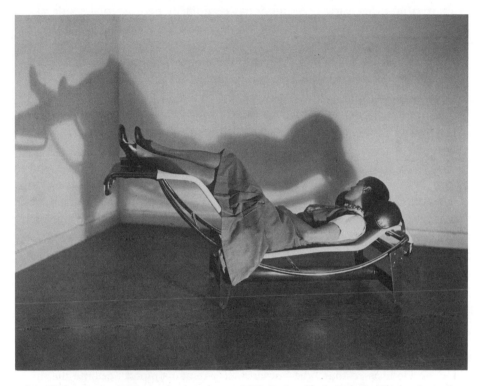

1.3. Charlotte Perriand resting on the chaise longue, 1928. Designed by Le Corbusier, Charlotte Perriand, and Pierre Jeanneret. Photograph. DR-Archives Charlotte Perriand. Photo Credit: Banque d'Images, ADAGP/Art Resource, New York. © 2008 Artists Rights Society (ARS), New York/ADAGP, Paris.

five times in an evening), there are many ways to be seated." Pointing out that "chairs are an instrument of torture that keep you awake admirably," Le Corbusier admitted that "for work...one sits 'actively.'" There were other seating possibilities as well:

> I sit down to talk: a certain armchair gives me a decent, polite manner. I sit down "actively" to hold forth, to prove a hypothesis, to propose a way of seeing: how this high stool is suitable to my attitude! I sit optimistic, relaxed; this Turkish stool of Istanbul, 35 centimeters high and 30 centimeters in diameter is a marvel; I could stay there for hours without tiring, *sitting on my behind*.[78]

While all of these human-limb objects served particular purposes, Le Corbusier pointed to the chaise longue as the ultimate orthopedic device, set apart from other forms of functional equipment because of its sole and noble aim—to facilitate rest:

> But here is the machine for resting. We built it with bicycle tubes and covered it with a magnificent pony skin; it is light enough to be pushed by foot, can be manipulated by a child; I thought of the Western cowboy smoking his pipe, his feet up above his head, leaning against a fireplace: complete restfulness.... It is the true machine for resting.[79]

Not unlike Bernège, Le Corbusier argued that human happiness and liberation lay in the possibilities machines opened up for "one's internal life, one's true life."[80] In order to be truly fulfilled, Le Corbusier maintained, human beings must relinquish the distraction and irrationality of decoration for the efficiency of functionality. With the "precious minutes" gained through the use of the right "equipment," a spiritual revolution might be enabled through design: "And perhaps we shall have the pleasure of thinking about something, during that hour of rest, that hour of relaxation, at home? That is the root of the matter; to think something."[81] Creating a restful physical environment, equipment for the home could enable the true self-realization of individuals from within.

Le Corbusier's goal was not, however, to turn human beings into machines. He insisted that "the human factor remains intact" despite the machine revolution "since the machine was invented by man to serve human needs."[82] At the same time, there was little mention of any affective ties or attachments that intimate spaces and objects might reflect or embody in these treatises on the replacement of decorative art and furniture with "machines for living," "equipment," and "human-limb objects." While the "machine for living" aimed to facilitate increased human happiness and enjoyment, there was minimal representation of either of these things in its depictions. Despite the human and spiritual rhetoric of the theory behind this rationalization of domestic space, plans and photographs remained relatively silent about the place of human bodies and emotions in the machine for living. Few of the photos of these furnishings and spaces included actual human beings. According to architectural historian Alice Friedman, this was because Le Corbusier "preferred to show the rooms completely empty or as settings for evocative, dreamlike tableaux suggesting absence rather than the presence of real-life occupants with their own tastes and preferences."[83] When bodies such as Perriand's did appear, they were often depicted as passive, even melancholy. The mood of Perriand's dramatic poses was somber rather than joyful or energized.

The orthopedic model of interior design took fatigue to be an inevitable and almost natural state of human existence. Just as the rehabilitation of the disabled male body highlighted technology's promises and threats to transform the working man, the weary and weak body in need of rest underlined the contradictions of a technology of leisure and comfort. Identifying human intellectual and spiritual liberation with the elimination of physical effort, designs for "the machine for living" took the incapacitated, even infirm body as a kind of model for humanity. While both Le Corbusier's and Perriand's writings emphasized sport, health, and vitality in the contexts of homes and cities reconceptualized on a human scale, the body at rest in these machines for living always seemed so tired. Le Corbusier worried about the frail state of human bodies when he pointed out that "modern life—office and factory—by its sedentary regime, its reduction of physical effort, weakens organisms and makes the nervous system anemic."[84] A problem thus lurked in the design of the chaise: how could this "sedentary regime" be disrupted or altered if the purpose of the machine for resting was, ultimately, the facilitation of human incapacity and the elimination of physical effort? There was something fundamentally *unwell* about this imagination of the home and its furnishings. The conceptualization of furniture as "artificial limbs" took the human body to be incomplete, in need of reinforcement and enhancement. Like the wood of antique furniture, the human body could also be described as an organic "substance, in its very nature, bound to decay" and this vulnerability stood at the heart of the orthopedic model for modernist furniture.[85] Indeed, there was a connection between the "machine for sitting" and the more overtly orthopedic designs of the period. Advertisements for chairs with aims similar to the LC chaise peppered popular magazines of the period such as *Illustration*. Aesthetically and functionally the LC chaise resembled the "Surrepos" chair designed by the French Dr. Pascaud (figure 1.4). Having met with Pascaud himself, Le Corbusier was familiar with the Surrepos. The architect's sketches made reference to this particular model and the images of Perriand seated in the LC chair clearly took some inspiration from advertisements such as this one.[86]

Drawing on the form and function of the orthopedic, the LC chaise was also part of a broader culture of anticipation preoccupied with the possibilities of rest and ease in the future. The machine for sitting in the form of a mechanical chair eliminating the need for human effort appeared as a compelling emblem of a less physically strenuous future. A fully automated chair appeared as an icon of the future in *Le Miroir du monde*'s visions of life in the year 2933 cited at the beginning of this chapter; one contributor imagined a world in which one's "entire life" might be spent in a chair

1.4. The "Surrepos" chair. *Illustration*, 1929. Courtesy of the McPherson Library, University of Victoria.

equipped for reading, listening to music or the news, and resting.[87] When "Zig and Puce," popular cartoon characters of the 1930s, traveled in time to the twenty-first century, they discovered a completely mechanical chair in one of the "strange dwellings" of the future.[88]

Neither Amar, nor Bernège, nor Le Corbusier and Perriand reflected directly on the problems or contradictions inherent in their designs for human bodies, homes, and lives. The projects of physical rehabilitation, domestic scientific management, and rational interior design focused on providing solutions to human physical and psychological limits and obstacles. Regardless of the claims to human enhancement and liberation, however, these systems of design could not help but highlight human weaknesses and inadequacies. While they championed the progress of humanity through the development of technology, their frameworks for understanding the human body depended on the translation of human functions and behaviors into mechanical parts, functions, and systems. Beyond this conceptual dehumanization of the body, these systems also suggested in various ways that human beings might be considerably more vulnerable and ultimately less efficient than the technological devices intended to liberate them. And if a kind of universalism regarding bodies and minds ran throughout the conversations above, the human subjects at stake in these French representations included soldiers, workers, wives, and mothers, social types essential to the agenda of national recovery from the past, as well as hopes for increased national strength and prosperity in the future. Designing and anticipating worlds without work and effort, these models and approaches to the organic body pointed to the latter's very disappearance. Traces of an eventual "inanimation" of human life could be found in pliers, vegetable peelers, even chairs.

Civilization without Feelings

> Modern life has placed everything under the sign of outrageous speed: everything goes at 500 kilometers per hour: science, travel, feelings.
>
> —JACQUELINE IV (pseudonym, actual author unknown), "Chez le grand couturier: Les dernières super-élégances," in "Féeries de l'avenir," special issue of *Lecture pour tous,* December 1932

The notion that technological advancement would bring about an inevitable inanimation of human bodies and lives appeared again and again in representations of the future in the interwar years. In 1926, *Sciences et voyages* solicited the input of a number of important experts, asking the question: "What discovery would benefit mankind the most?"[89] The magazine also asked these experts to identify what they found most problematic for human survival and happiness in the present and into the future. In his response to the survey, Professor Charles Richet, a member of the Institute of the Academy of Medicine stated "without hesitation" that a vaccine against tuberculosis would be the most beneficial invention in the decades to come. In "second place," he offered the capacity to use solar energy and power "to replace carbon and petrol," resources he predicted would be exhausted within one hundred years.[90] Professor Gustav Barrier, a former president of the Academy of Medicine, suggested "the defense against aerial warfare, toxic gases, the expansion of wireless technology, the use of hydroelectric power...cures for syphilis, tuberculosis, [and] cancer."[91] His colleague Professor Jules Renault, also of the academy, was certain that central heating would top all other future inventions, transforming domestic comfort and aiding in the prevention of illness and disease.[92] Departing from the themes of disease, energy, and comfort, Professor Auguste Rateau suggested "it is not the scientific questions that are of primary importance, but the social ones that threaten...to bring catastrophe."[93] He was neither specific about the nature of these social threats, nor did he suggest possible solutions. Marcel Boulenger, a member of the Academy of Science claimed the real problem was aural. Boulenger was convinced "that the infernal noise of modern cities stuns men." "I do not believe in progress," he complained, "when it brings such commotion, certainly not!" What human beings most needed was "a silent discovery!...[one] that might muzzle the horrible din of the streets and avenues."[94]

Each respondent to the magazine's survey found his own way to lament some current malaise or to express hope for the progress of some human comfort. But it was Professor Maurice Hanriot of the Academy of Medicine who seemed to sum up the problem of the human condition and its solution in the most metaphysical terms. Hanriot looked forward to a future "when we will be masters over life, avoiding disease, maybe even old-age,...when we will be masters of our thoughts, avoiding faulty reasoning, discord and politics." He went on to describe a "golden age" when "we will know...how to live well and think clearly." "The discovery that will be the most likely to do mankind the most good?" he asked. "A machine to destroy the passions." Without emotions, human beings "would have pure hearts, knowing nothing of hate or envy." "It would be perfect," Hanriot added, "if they could be unaware of love." Having articulated the solution to humanity's dilemma, Hanriot expressed his doubt that any such utopia might achieve fruition in the future. "I fear that the invention of this machine does not depend on engineers or experts," he wrote. "Once invented, such a machine would be sabotaged by our merciless instincts."[95]

Professor Hanriot identified the source of human suffering with human emotion, the ability to feel intensely, from the depths of loathing and despair, to the heights of joy and love. Hanriot's utopia would be a world rationally transcendent of the emotions that lead human beings to love or hate, or to engage in politics. If human beings could be freed from their baser instincts, the passions that destroy their ability to think clearly and live in harmony, they might be capable of overcoming their physical limitations and vulnerabilities as well as the spiritual impediments to happiness and peace. Hanriot dreamed of a machine that might function in this doubled way. Although the "machine to destroy the passions" would function like any other enabling tool or device, the specific purpose of this machine would be to transform human beings into a living species devoid of feeling or emotion, to enact the mechanization and rationalization of human subjectivity itself.

Hanriot was not alone in fantasizing about human progress as the evolution away from emotion and sentiment. Another contributor to the *Le Miroir du monde* panorama of life in the year 2933 with which I began this chapter looked back from the future to the world of "sentimental relations in 1933," describing it as follows:

And what do we see? A general and permanent exasperation of sensibilities to the detriment of reason; contempt for all thought and analysis, the triumph of improvisation; the cult of the gratuitous gesture. We love? We use a revolver. We have some ambition? We immolate our rival in the furor of public opinion. . . . Politics is sentimental.

Using the trope of the future to express his disdain for the conflicts and problems of the present, the author imagined a world freed of these problems and conflicts, declaring: "We can say that the year of grace 2933 marks, on the contrary, a memorable date. We have suppressed everything." He went on to mock love, in particular, as an ancient phenomenon, long abandoned by a more evolved humanity:

Love? Who would indulge himself today to give meaning to this word . . . so barbaric? Love has not been felt for a long time. By forbidding the carrying of weapons . . . we have, little by little, exhausted the expression of jealousy . . . Men have learned to see in women nothing but companions and no longer mates. No more pernicious novels . . . We read nothing but economic manuals now. No more films that climax with a kiss! . . . No more strolls under the moonlight, no more love letters! Our vocabulary on this front has, happily, been transformed.[96]

Echoing Professor Hanriot's expert response, this entertaining characterization of the future also emphasized the potential of machines to liberate human beings from their most powerful enemy: human nature itself.
Despite its absurdity, however, there was something serious about this
play with the idea of a future without love. "Do machines fight amongst
themselves?" the contributor to *Le Miroir du monde* asked. Imagining a
"day...when we will no longer be anything but numbers" this picture of
the future appeared ambivalent.[97] On the one hand, it seemed to regard the
present with disdain as an irrational time of human conflict and destruction. On the other, it seemed to mock the very notion that such a project to
eliminate the passions could result in anything but a world ridiculous in its
rationality and passionlessness.

This idea of a future humanity devoid of emotion pushed to humorous
extremes a French preoccupation with the artificial, the mechanical, and
the rational that had been intensified by the experience of the First World
War. In different ways, Amar, Bernège, Le Corbusier and Perriand, Hanriot,
and others linked human liberation to the suppression of human need and
desire. All of these figures viewed a kind of inanimation as the path to better qualities of human physical and intellectual life in the future. Taking
the prosthesis as the model for the relationship between the human and the
machine, they also suggested the eventual disappearance of the very humanity they purported to reinforce and improve. Beyond the employment of
technology as an aid and a supplement, they imagined the application of
mechanical models and rational techniques to the human body and behavior. As such, their strategies of technological reconstruction, enhancement,
and substitution implicitly and explicitly interrogated the very substance of
human "nature." In their attempts to secure a more humane world through
the progress of technology, these contributors to an interwar culture of
anticipation inadvertently pointed to an uncertain future of "the human"
itself.

CHAPTER 2

The City of the Future

Just before the end of the First World War, military strategists in France undertook the construction of an entire city, a city of lights. They decided to call it "Paris." Responding to the threat of aerial attack, the army developed an elaborate plan to build this second Paris, a trompe l'oeil that could pass for the city from above, just northwest of the real Paris, near the suburb of Maisons-Lafitte (figure 2.1). Situated at a place on the Seine where the river bends in much the same way as it curves through the capital, *Faux* Paris was part of a larger scheme that included two other false target locations. One at l'Orme de Morlu, northeast of Saint-Denis, replicated the train stations and tracks of the Gare du Nord and the Gare de l'Est. The other, located directly east of the city, simulated an industrial park. Together, the three decoys held the potential to mislead enemy pilots, diverting possible strikes away from the capital. An expert electrician named Fernand Jacopozzi had proposed the idea to the French Ministry of War early in 1918. Given that aerial attacks on Paris were most likely to occur after dark, Jacopozzi's plans included illuminating structural mock-ups of the city's key landmarks and monuments. Observers hailed the designs as remarkably convincing visual deceptions that simulated very well the nighttime appearance of the capital and its environs. In 1920, one author noted that Jacopozzi's "Gare de l'Est, with its lighting effects of trains running, [would] remain a *chef-d'oeuvre* of the genre."[1]

The stakes involved in developing this counterfeit of the nation's principal urban center included the safety of millions of citizens and the protection of

2.1. "Faux Paris." Lt. Col. Arsène Vauthier, *Le Danger aérien et l'avenir du pays*, 1930.

the seat of the French government. During the First World War, the introduction of new military weapons and means of attack had rendered civilians as well as soldiers vulnerable in unprecedented ways. Having explored
the morale, mobilization, and militarization of those on the "home front,"
historians have recently begun to focus their attention on how the violence
and destruction of the war itself more directly affected the lives and landscapes of civilians.[2] Indeed, capital cities such as Paris were "special cases."[3]
Furthermore, closest to the front lines, the French capital was a target unlike London or Berlin.[4] Germany had attacked the city from the skies most
intensely in the first and final years of the conflict. A total of twenty-four
air raids and three zeppelin attacks against the city from 1914 to 1918 resulted in the death of more than 250 Parisians and several hundred more
wounded. The German military had also employed long-range guns stationed on the ground to bombard the city. By the end of the conflict, the
combined attacks on Paris resulted in almost 600 deaths and between 1,200
and 1,500 wounded.[5]

The military halted construction of false target sites like *Faux* Paris with the armistice in November 1918. Yet the generation of phantasmatic versions of the capital did not end, just as it had not begun, with the war. Historically, Paris had been as much a set of ideas as a physical terrain inhabited by people, buildings, and vehicles. By the interwar years, the urban landscape was already the focus of a range of investments in both the past and future of the French nation. If *Faux* Paris had emerged as a response to the realities of wartime, the "real" Paris that the project imitated was also, in its own ways, a space of imagination, memory, and anticipation in the wake of the conflict.

The first chapter of this book showed how the body functioned as a crucial site for the negotiation of both experience and expectation in the interwar years. In this chapter, I explore a series of representations of Paris as a "city of the future" that expressed the complex relationship between memory and anticipation after 1918. Rich in its historic significance, the city was also a place of futuristic fantasy. Even before the war, the French capital had had a number of incarnations as a "city of the future" in literary and artistic representations, and urban and architectural designs. By 1900, Paris had acquired a reputation as a "modern" city in the national and international imagination. A point of intersection for high art, bourgeois culture, and mass spectacle, Paris could symbolize fashion, luxury, and refinement. The city also seemed to embody the decadence and degeneration that cultural and political conservatives feared epidemic in fin-de-siècle France.[6] In the past, Paris had served as both a center of state power and a breeding ground for ideas and movements that threatened political instability and disorder. The legacies of 1789, as well as the subsequent upheavals of the nineteenth century (in 1830, 1848, and 1871), shaped the discursive and political territory on which debates about the city took place into the twentieth century. Since at least the end of the eighteenth century, Paris had been a city of revolution, the capital of a long history of social conflict and class struggle within France.[7]

In the second half of the nineteenth century, Jules Verne was perhaps the most famous French author to consider the capital of "tomorrow." Verne completed *Paris au XXe siècle* (*Paris in the Twentieth Century*) in 1863.[8] Set in an imaginary Paris of 1961, Verne's panorama of urban life focused on Michel, an impoverished young poet whose literary sensibilities and creativity would be undervalued in the twentieth-century society Verne envisioned. *Paris au XXe siècle* included scenes from a fast-paced urban life saturated with machines. In Verne's century to come, electricity would power "the one hundred thousand streetlamps of Paris" that lit up "at one and the same moment," "countless carriages" would speed along Parisian boulevards, and the city's inhabitants would communicate using telegraphs and a precursor of the fax machine. In the world of the novel, however, the celebration of this technological advancement is tempered by Michel's discomfort in this city of (too many) lights.[9] Through Michel's melancholic response to this so-called human advancement, Verne anticipated a twentieth-century sense of loss and nostalgia for the capital as it appeared during his own era.

Other French authors and illustrators in the nineteenth century imagined Paris as "city of the future." Albert Robida's nineteenth-century depictions of the next century were also dominated by electricity, movement, and advanced forms of communication. Published in the late 1880s and early 1890s, Robida's *Le Vingtième siècle* (1883), *La Guerre au vingtième siècle* (1892) and *Le Vingtième siècle: La vie électronique* (1897), included scenes of a future Parisian life as Robida imagined it.[10] In these illustrated texts, Robida focused on changes in transportation (including the metro and air travel), the transformation of warfare, and gender relations. At the turn of the century, Armand Gervais, a French toy manufacturer, commissioned the commercial artist Jean-Marc Côté to produce a set of illustrated "cigarette cards" to commemorate the fin-de-siècle celebrations in France in 1900. Conjuring an imagined future to mark this historic moment, the cards depicted a variety of scenes from "the year 2000." These included a series of humorous images of a technologized and mechanized Parisian life. Côté's illustrations were, like Robida's, parodies that used the trope of "the future" to comment on the political and cultural ideas and fashions of contemporary society.[11] While these authors' depictions of Paris as a "city of the future" were ultimately less gloomy than Verne's, all three writers privileged the French capital as the altered landscape of a world to come.

Representing the "city of the future" was not just the domain of science fiction in the decades before World War I, however. In France, architects and administrators at the local, regional, and national level also began to consider more seriously the importance of city planning and design, of anticipating the future in concrete terms. One of the best-known, prewar visions of a "city of the future," complete with towering buildings, was socialist architect Tony Garnier's "Cité industrielle." Garnier developed his plans for an industrial city between 1899 and 1904, eventually publishing his work in 1917. His designs reflected both an aesthetic and a social mission for architecture, an imperative to respond to the changes of an advanced, industrialized society in terms both technologically progressive and humane. Garnier's city became a model for many of the urban and architectural visions that followed in France. He was one of the earliest advocates of the use of metal and reinforced concrete in construction, materials that became critical to the plans of architects like Auguste Perret and Le Corbusier. Le Corbusier, whose ideas about the body and domestic design appeared in the first chapter of this study, looked to Garnier as an originator of a *contemporary* rather than a classical approach to architecture and the study of cities and their planning known as *urbanisme*.[12]

In France, the physical violence and material damage of the years between 1914 and 1918 radically altered perceptions and discussions of urban space in general and the French capital in particular. After the German invasions of Belgium and France, it became virtually impossible to discuss the nation's urban centers without reference to those areas devastated during the conflict. While Paris survived the war relatively intact, the legacy of the towns and villages left in ruins by the war continued to shape ideas about the capital in the years ahead. Paris could serve as a living monument to the war dead, a tribute to the nation's suffering, and a testament to its past and present glory. The memorialization of the war experience was one of a number of imperatives that pushed the transformation of cities throughout France. Paris, the nation's largest urban center, exhibited like no other French city the challenges of industrial society. The renovation of the capital after 1918 included strategies for coping with the problems of population density and traffic circulation. Furthermore, an acute sense of anxiety about possible political unrest in the capital heightened awareness of deteriorating conditions, particularly for the city's poorer residents. Existing social and economic problems exacerbated by the First World War underlined long-standing concern about the possibility of yet another large-scale upheaval, particularly in the wake of the Russian Revolution of 1917. The influenza epidemic of 1918 also raised concerns about health, hygiene, access to housing, and overcrowding in the city.[13] While none of these concerns originated entirely with the war, the recent conflict created a sense of urgency on all fronts.

In debates over solutions to these challenges confronting Paris, a multiplicity of plans and visions expressed different versions and definitions of "the future" itself. While "the future" could signify the protection and preservation of the past in the years ahead, it could also mean the erasure of history and tradition, the substitution of national "patrimony" with novelty for the sake of improvement. Some French planners and architects envisioned the capital of the future in terms of a "Greater Paris" extended *horizontally* beyond the city's historic boundaries. They offered expansion outward as a solution to problems of growth and density. Others, like Le Corbusier, anticipated the transformation of Paris in *vertical* terms, including the construction of taller and taller structures to free up space on the ground. Height was virtually synonymous with the "city of the future" in architectural terms. Although Le Corbusier was not alone in his emphasis on verticality, his visions of Paris as a "contemporary," "radiant" city became a principle point of reference for the "city of the future" in France during the interwar years. The skyscraper, the architectural feature at the heart of plans outlined by Le Corbusier and others, became a kind of fetish, the contemporary trace of the future in terms of urban space and development. For those conservative observers who sought to protect national culture through the preservation of historic monuments and architecture, the skyscraper threatened to radically alter the landscape of the capital, endangering the city's historic core, by replacing the structures of the past with new and, more menacing still, *international* forms.

While "Greater Paris" and the "Radiant City" focused on changes to the aesthetic features and physical dimensions of the capital, military security remained an important concern for urban planners long after the armistice. As *Faux* Paris illustrated, civilian population centers had become increasingly likely targets in an age of "total" war. "Greater Paris" relied on the removal of the nineteenth-century fortifications that surrounded the capital, defenses that had been obsolete perhaps from the moment of their construction. New strategies and weapons had called into question existing definitions of territory, as well as methods of defense, a set of transformations I will explore further in chapter 3. In the context of Paris, the experience and expectation of attack and invasion on both local and national levels shaped anxieties about the capital's vulnerability into the future.

French authors of science fiction drew on these themes and experiences, featuring the city of lights as a center of multiple future worlds after 1918. These writers represented Paris time and again—in alternate presents (parallel universes), near and distant futures—as a metropolis destroyed, burned, devastated, frozen, exploded, and swarmed with outside enemies. In Octave Joncquel's 1921 novel, *Les Titans du Ciel* (The Titans of the Skies), for example, an eyewitness described "the spectacle of Paris destroyed by Martian gases" in the year 1975.[14] Joncquel imagined the 1970s from the perspective of the 1920s, outlining a fictional trajectory of events beginning with the end of the "Great War" in 1918. In André Maurois' 1928 novel, *Deux fragments d'une histoire universelle 1992* (Two Fragments of a Universal History 1992), an outer space diplomatic crisis provoked a lunar attack intended to destroy the Earth and its inhabitants. Maurois' account included details of an assault on Paris. The idea of a public health crisis also played an important role in some of these narratives. In Léon Daudet's 1927 novel,

Le Napus, fléau de l'an 2227 (Napus, Scourge of the Year 2227), for example, a strange virus wiped out human life in the capital, while in Jacques Spitz's 1935 novel, *La Guerre des mouches* (The War of the Flies), swarms of intelligent flies suffocated the city and its inhabitants.[15] In plans for Paris that crossed the domains of architectural design, urban and military planning, the authors of municipal policy and projects in the interwar period also had difficulty representing the capital as a "city of the future" without highlighting its susceptibility to attack and worrying about its disappearance. Like the dystopian visionaries writing much of the science fiction from 1919 to 1939, these French planners often depicted Paris as the fragile center of a nation under threat. Interwar authors of the "city of the future" anticipated the destruction of the capital at the hands of multiple enemies, more or less imaginary: Germans, Martians, meteors, skyscrapers, insects, and architects.

Reconstruction and the "Cities of the Future"

The battles and trenches of World War I left in their wake unprecedented scenes of rural and urban devastation in France. In some cases, entire villages and towns had been decimated, leaving former communities in ruins.[16] Well before 1918, the idea of the "city of the future" acquired new resonance as a kind of antidote to the wreckage of the war.[17] The project of reconstruction in France created both the need and the opportunity to consider the planning of cities and towns with renewed vigor. The idea of reviving the nation one town at a time included war-torn sites, as well as those agglomerations, like Paris, left relatively intact after four years of battle. In the case of cities, national spaces destroyed or ruined in wartime became key points of reference for the discussion of all urban spaces in France. The memory of their destruction played an important role in an urban culture of anticipation throughout the interwar years.

In 1915, the French Chamber of Deputies discussed one of a number of initial proposals for what would eventually become the "Cornudet law" of 1919. After years of debate, the eventual law outlined a program for the planning, extension, and beautification of all cities and towns in France. Named for Joseph Cornudet, the deputy of Seine-et-Oise, the law stipulated: "Every city of 10,000 inhabitants or more is required to have a project of development, improvement and expansion." While a special article in the proposed law dealt with the particular case of cities "totally or partially destroyed, in the course of a war, fire, earthquakes or some other catastrophe," the law prescribed the application of the planning imperative to all "agglom-erations, regardless of their size," including those of "a picturesque, historic or artistic nature." It further insisted on establishing plans for "squares, public gardens, playing fields, parks...as well as those areas reserved for monuments, public buildings and services." Pointing out the need to employ more effective strategies for "the distribution of potable water, the network of sewer water, the evacuation and final destination of waste," the law also charged each French department with the task of assembling commissions to oversee town and city planning, as well as committees dealing specifically with hygiene, monuments, construction, and other projects. Without these provisions, there could be no guarantee of decent levels of efficiency and sanitation in the nation's population centers.[18]

The 1915 discussion of planning legislation focused on the need to orga-nize and anticipate the future of French cities at a moment when a number of the nation's communities confronted severe damage and the threat of further devastation. When France's political representatives began their de-liberations over these ideas, the nation had been at war for several months. Cornudet himself highlighted this coincidence, arguing that the war pro-vided an opportunity for positive change on the urban front. He suggested that it was "following crises and great transformations that the greatest progress had always been made," noting that "for a nation, there is no crisis more grave than the one we are experiencing right now." Cornudet claimed that his proposal of law was the ideal civilian counterpart to military service when he stated:

> We on the home front must honor those who fight in the trenches and begin preparing the cities of the future starting now; let us make them more convenient [and] more comfortable, so that we may find in them improved hygiene, well-being and beauty![19]

The material destruction of the war gave new relevance to the idea of "cities of the future" in the French context. During this period, the "city of the future" could symbolize the future of the entire nation. Just as the sol-dier's body rehabilitated could stand for the recovery of France as a whole, each French village, town, and city could also represent metonymically the projects of national healing and restoration in the aftermath of the conflict. Like wounded parts of the national body, these regions could be repaired and replaced. Legislators like Cornudet envisioned a rational, well-thought-out urban planning that could be applied to the revival of damaged popula-tion centers, the creation of new towns and cities on old city ruins or in new areas, and the extension and improvement of existing villages and cities in France. City and town planning suggested a better future for France, one in which the nation might triumph over the impact of the war without losing sight of the legacies and traditions of the past.

Linking the proposed legislation to both the war effort and the grandeur of the French national past, Cornudet and his supporters privileged the city as a site of material and cultural reconstruction in the wake of war. When Paul Jacquier, the French undersecretary of state for the Interior and deputy for the Haute Savoie, expressed support for Cornudet's proposal in 1915, he underlined urban planning as a key to recovery declaring:

> At the hour when the heroic efforts of our soldiers brings us closer to the liberation of territory, Parliament will honor itself in preparing the restoration, not only of the splendor of the past, but with new splendor, those unfortunate regions of...France where the invader has accumulated so many ruins and so much suffering.[20]

Like Cornudet, Jacquier suggested that the commemoration of the nation's past was not the only means to honor the bravery and sacrifice of soldiers and civilians who suffered losses in the war. Jacquier emphasized the need to "modernize" all French cities in need of improvement "while respecting...the treasures and vestiges of the past."[21] The nation's cities and towns could showcase the glories of French history and tradition, the values soldiers fought to protect. They could also announce and facilitate, by virtue of their beauty, efficiency, and hygiene, the prospective triumphs of the nation in the years to come. In this instance, the cause of national memory might be served through appropriate forms of municipal, regional, and national anticipation.

Strategies for building and urban development articulated during and after the war placed a special emphasis on rebuilding those areas damaged or destroyed in the conflict. As early as 1915, the French government created the Service national des habitations et locaux privés dans les départements dévastés par la guerre to deal with the large-scale destruction of individual homes in entire regions of France. A number of publications on the subject of reconstruction appeared in France long before the armistice as government bodies and professional organizations sought to address the situation as soon as possible. The Société des Ingénieurs Civils held a conference on the subject in November 1915 and the French Société des Architectes diplomés formed the Commission d'étude pour les réconstructions rurales dans les régions devastées par la guerre in 1916.[22]

These French groups confronted massive devastation that was without parallel among combatant nations. An official government report in 1916 included statistics on damage to those areas of France that had been invaded since 1914. According to the report: "Out of 753 communes, 74 saw the destruction of more than three-quarters of the houses; 148 were more than half destroyed." The report claimed that "in total, 16,669 houses had been destroyed; 25,594 had been seriously damaged, [while] 221 town halls, 379 schools, 331 churches had been totally or partially hit." Even though "the majority of these public buildings were quite modest...56 of them were classified as historic monuments." These included the Arras city hall and the Cathedral of Reims. In addition to homes and buildings, "330 factories had been destroyed where over 55,000 people lived in the surrounding areas." By 1917, the Germans ceded 331 additional communes to France. On July 28, 1917, Léon Bourgeois, the French minister of labor, addressed the National Assembly on the subject of damage in these areas. According to his report, 143 of these communes were still "inaccessible." Citing effects on the remaining 168, Bourgeois listed the damage: "10,852 homes... intact, 10,876 partially destroyed, 36,393 completely destroyed."[23]

In the discussion of Cornudet's proposal in 1915, Socialist deputy André Lebey suggested that it was time for legislators to "take advantage of our current circumstances and build a new France, a France worthy of herself."[24] Antoine Borrel, deputy for the Savoie, highlighted the war-torn regions of France while applauding the program to improve all of the nation's cities, towns, and villages. Borrel anticipated the success of the Cornudet law as a set of guidelines "permitting the realization of a maximum of comfort and well-being in the new cities and villages built up from ruins." Borrel looked forward to the changes through which French "cities and villages will emerge more healthy from the ordeal [of the war] and become the cradle of stronger generations." André Paisant, deputy for the Oise department, agreed with Borrel, declaring:

> I think the time could not be better chosen to draw up the plans of our future cities than one at which a barbarous enemy has just gratuitously destroyed all of those old stones, and those old walls on which our history was no doubt written, but which could only have been maintained out of a taste for tradition or a familial piety that at times have run counter to our current notions of aesthetics and hygiene.

The war had inflicted terrible losses, but it also offered new hope and possibility by granting the nation a clean slate on which to implement positive changes. Paisant claimed that it was his "dream...that on the ruins of the same France that others sought to crush, of that old France that we loved so much...will emerge a new and rejuvenated France, its grace attesting to its vitality and eternal strength." While Paisant cautioned those responsible for planning to pay sufficient attention to "the evolution of modern life," he saw this consideration of the "modern" needs of urban existence as consistent with the preservation of a distinctively French tradition. According to Paisant, the "air and light" prescribed to France's cities by the Cornudet law were part of "the nation's patrimony."[25] Indeed, Cornudet had insisted earlier that the whole idea of urban planning was one that had "been called for in France for a very long time," that it was a "French idea like so many others."[26]

In their 1917 study, *La Cité de demain dans les régions devastées* (The City of Tomorrow in the Devastated Regions), architects Jean-Marcel Auburtin and Henri Blanchard also linked the idea of the "city of the future" to wartime destruction and ruins. According to these experts, it was the devastation of the years since 1914 that created the opportunity to consider cities and towns anew. They insisted that "whatever the task of urbanism undertaken might be," it was vital that those responsible establish "a plan that clearly lays out and coordinates all aspects of the problem, taking inspiration (whenever possible) from the lessons of the past, the needs of the present and anticipation of the future."[27] Blanchard and Auburtin saw experience and expectation as equally important. They further argued that urban planning could do more for France than the building of more conventional memorials and monuments to battles or to the war dead. In their words:

> Rather than isolated commemorative monuments, of which there are so many, utilitarian projects conceived beautifully—squares, groups of buildings, etc.—will be constructed; over time, they will become a part of the everyday life of the city, responding to both practical and aesthetic needs, all the while perpetuating the memory of a glorious past.[28]

Pursued correctly, the planning of French cities "of tomorrow" could work to honor and perpetuate the nation into the future rather than focusing exclusively on the memorialization of its past.

The significance of this reference to memorials and monuments to the war dead cannot be overstated. As historian Daniel Sherman has shown, the conception and construction of a range of commemorative sites was a complex process with deep political, cultural, and personal meanings in interwar

France.[29] Linking their ideas for cities to the commemoration of the war, planners of town and city development during and after the conflict tied their concerns and projects to an intricate field of individual and collective memory and mourning. There was no way to conceive of the future in terms of urban development without considering its relationship to ideas about national "tradition" and "heritage." Old landscapes could give way to new ones while remaining mindful of past triumphs and customs. Beyond this, however, the new villages, cities, and towns built on the nation's ruins could also be considered monuments to the war dead. So too could the improvement of cities in need of better housing, hygiene, and circulation. While the varieties of expectation referred to the varieties of experience, the culture of anticipation also included plans for the future of national memory.

When Professor Léon Rosenthal of the Ecole Normale published his *Villes et villages français après la guerre* (French Cities and Villages After the War) in 1918, "more than two thousand communes [were] still occupied by the enemy, in the richest areas of France." Added to these were the regions in "Alsace-Lorraine against which the Kaiser had uttered the most horrible threats." Rosenthal claimed the "regions in the North and the East, ravaged by the enemy" had "instigated [his] study" of the problems facing France's cities in general. The "martyrdom" of these cities was paramount to authors such as Rosenthal who regarded these sites as "first and foremost" in the application of their strategies.[30]

Rosenthal's study addressed the issue of postwar reconstruction as one of the most important features of an overall project of urban revival and renovation in France. Referring to the damage of the war in corporeal terms, Rosenthal wrote that "a huge effort would be required in order to heal these wounds." He added that "this effort would already be enormous if it were only a question of restoring cities and villages to the state they had been in before the war, if it were enough to rebuild the houses, reconstruct the roads, if restitution, in a word, could be accomplished without any new plans." As Rosenthal pointed out, however, "These cities and villages suffered from the same ills...as the rest." He went on to enumerate the problems of hygiene, housing, population, transportation, and organization affecting all French cities and towns, above and beyond the war's impact.

Rosenthal insisted that the postwar reconstruction of French cities must incorporate new strategies to improve the quality of life in all areas when he demanded:

> Will we restore...the hovels where people were exposed to physical and moral disease, to alcoholism and tuberculosis? Will we repair the

unhealthy and inconvenient streets where traffic was constantly para-
lyzed, those poorly outfitted ports, those inadequate stations that were
so difficult to access? Will we restore those infected wells, those foun-
tains supplied with suspect water?

In addition to devastated regions, the war had created new problems of urban
development and growth "throughout the country." Rosenthal highlighted
the "new agglomerations [that] had been formed haphazardly around new
factories" for the production of munitions and other supplies. He noted the
fact that "veritable cities had emerged" during the war while "old cities had
seen their activities and populations transformed." These effects would not
"disappear completely after the war," but would "demand organization."[31]

French planning officials and architects, following earlier voices like Cornudet's, invoked the idea of the "city of the future" as they attempted to
lay the groundwork for national reconstruction and revival in the decades
ahead. The *urbanisme* that emerged out of the double imperative to rebuild
and to plan suggested a future for the French nation founded on organized,
healthy, efficient, and beautiful cities. Taking an approach to the city that
historian Rosemary Wakeman has termed "nostalgic modernism," French
architects and legislators sought to establish order and revive the nation
while respecting the past.[32] Effective planning could efface the destruction
of the war, incorporating the best of "modernity" (new materials and methods) into urban landscapes that would also reflect French tradition, national
historic and cultural achievements.

Greater Paris

During the assembly's discussion of the Cornudet proposal in 1915, Arthur
Rozier, the vice president of the Commission générale de l'administration
and deputy for Paris, recognized the need to draw up specific plans for
the development of individual French cities. Rozier highlighted Paris as a
very "special case" in terms of urban planning.[33] While all cities mattered
as sites of potential national regeneration in the wake of war, Paris, the
demographic and political focal point of the nation, held primacy of place
in discussions that linked the future vitality of France to the vitality of its
urban centers. Paris could serve as a living national museum, displaying
historical monuments and the grandeur of the French past. It could also
function as a canvas on which visionaries and leaders, from the local to
the national level, might imagine and undertake aesthetic and political

projects of various kinds. Planning the future of Paris in the aftermath of war, different voices debated the future of France as a whole. Emphasis on Paris exhibited a sense of national competition with other European cities such as London and Berlin, as well as American cities like New York and Chicago. Some versions of the Paris "of tomorrow" also expressed the hope that the city might become a world center of peaceful international relations after the war, the capital of an eventual "United States of Europe."

The idea of the French capital as a "city of the future" depended on the assumption that Paris was (and would continue to be) a changing metropolis. In 1915, Barthélmy Mayéras, deputy for Haute Vienne described the capital of France as a "monster city."[34] An increase in the numbers of bodies and machines residing in and moving about the city, the appearance and disappearance of architectural landmarks over centuries, and the morphing of city limits in the past, all challenged any rigid understanding of Paris as timeless or immutable in its demographic makeup, its dimensions, or its aesthetic features. A city of slightly more than 1 million inhabitants at the middle of the nineteenth century, Paris had reached a population peak of 2.9 million inhabitants by 1921. Automobiles in particular posed an increasing challenge to streets and passageways that had not been designed with their use in mind. The number of automobiles in Paris doubled between 1922 and 1930, increasing from 150,000 to 300,000. By 1939, this figure would jump to half a million.[35] The physical size and boundaries of the city needed to be reconsidered in light of this growing population density and circulation. Congestion, housing, sanitation, the possibilities of social unrest, and military attack were the most pressing concerns for those who considered the city's future in the interwar decades.[36]

The state of flux of the immediate postwar period was unprecedented. As the journalist Maurice Talmeyr, a contributor to the *Revue des deux mondes,* commented in "Les Bouleversements de Paris: La capitale de demain" (The Upheavals of Paris: The Capital of Tomorrow) published in 1923, "Never before has Paris been so disrupted...so many streets...turned upside down...so many houses designated for the pickaxe, and the fortifications, notably, are in the midst of demolition."[37] Observing the changes in Paris, Talmeyr expressed excitement and some hesitation. Imagining a "colossal future capital," "a monstrous Paris next to which the capital of today will be nothing but a kernel," Talmeyr also inquired: "Following what plans and along what conceptual lines" would this future Paris be constructed?[38] Consideration of this vital question had begun years earlier, and even then, not for the first time.

In his report in 1915, Cornudet had referred to a long history of planning and renovation of the capital, asking his fellow deputies:

> Need I remind you of Haussmann's great undertakings? True, we might regret the straight lines, too straight, lined with houses designed in a banal architectural style; but I ask you, what would Paris be without the sewers, the markets, the great avenues that allow for the passage of tramways, buses and all of our mechanical traffic?[39]

Cornudet invoked here what the architectural historian Anthony Sutcliffe has termed "the biggest commonplace of urban history after the Great Fire of London," the complete overhaul of the capital during the Second Empire under the supervision of the French civic planner Baron Georges Haussmann.[40] Indeed, the regulations and codes established by Haussmann set the aesthetic terms for construction in Paris for decades to come.[41] As Cornudet addressed his colleagues in 1915, the execution of Haussmann's plans remained incomplete and the city continued to carry out extension of the wide boulevards intended to improve the circulation of people, traffic, and goods and to facilitate state control of movement in the capital.[42]

Maurice Talmeyr's declarations in 1923 suggested that the interwar upheaval in the city went beyond even the massive transformation of Paris under Haussmann. While some projects remained incomplete, a number of the changes wrought by Haussmannization had been assimilated into the Paris under consideration in the interwar years. One key factor that set the interwar period apart from the nineteenth century was the introduction of a new set of aesthetic debates. Haussmannization had certainly raised scandal in its restructuring and renovation of the capital, but there was something decidedly historical about its reigning aesthetic. Haussmann's guidelines were neoclassical, striving for compatibility with existing structures and forms while setting new architectural standards. Architectural modernism, in its further break with historical forms and materials, distinguished the interwar period from earlier moments of debate over the future of the capital.[43]

In 1915, Arthur Rozier had noted that the appropriate experts in France would soon undertake the study of "what has been called *le plus grand Paris*."[44] Extending Paris beyond its existing parameters was one way to improve the city and the lives of its inhabitants while addressing concerns about the preservation of the capital's historic center. The expansion of the city into a *plus grand Paris* required two things: (1) a detailed and well-thought-out plan, and (2) the elimination of the fortifications that surrounded the city and defined its limits. The development of "Greater Paris" followed the terms of the Cornudet law and was linked to another, very important piece of legislation the government also passed in 1919. Concurrent with the Paris Peace Conference at which the terms of the Treaty of Versailles were being negotiated, the deputies assembled in the French Chamber debated the decommissioning of the fortified wall of Paris, most of which had been built in the middle of the nineteenth century. Their deliberations lasted several days and the Direction de l'extension de Paris met for the first time shortly afterward in order to coordinate municipal efforts with regional and national plans.[45]

The center of Paris was the most congested area of the city and therefore its biggest problem in terms of density, circulation, and sanitation. By extending *horizontally*, a "Greater Paris" could reduce the pressure on the city's population while respecting the historic and monumental core of the capital. The call for a change to the city's boundaries did not just reflect the imperative to "modernize," however. The end of the First World War loaded the removal of the fortifications surrounding the capital with a deeper cultural and political significance. Their proposed replacement with housing, green spaces, and industrial and administrative installations seemed like a concrete application of the spirit of the newly formed League of Nations. The demolition of the fortifications could also signal an accord between the Parisian middle and upper classes that dominated the city center and the working classes who had, particularly since the era of Haussmannization, moved increasingly into the suburbs *extra-muros*.[46] At the same time, contests over what would replace the fortifications included a class struggle that took the form of opposition between a *"ceinture rouge"* (red belt) of working-class housing and municipal installations feared by those on the political right, and a *"ceinture verte"* (green belt) of parks and gardens. The tearing down of the city's walls could have multiple practical and symbolic effects and resonance.

When political representatives debated the fate of the defensive wall around Paris, they engaged with the military and social histories of the nation as they attempted to anticipate a better future for its most important city. Bordering the city, the fortifications served as a crucial site for the negotiation of experience and expectation. Their proposed removal provided an opportunity for the expression of different perspectives on the past and the future of the city and the nation. Beginning on March 13, 1919, Rozier presented his report and proposal for a law outlining the military decommissioning of the fortifications, the expropriation and sale of the surrounding lands, and plans for the development of the region in general. Rozier noted the French military's longstanding resistance to abandoning the installations, despite attempts by the city of Paris to demolish these as early as the 1880s. Outlining a complicated story of negotiations between the city of Paris and the French government over the sale of the lands taken up by the fortifications, the nature of expropriations, and other issues, Rozier detailed the series of agreements and conventions which had, since the early twentieth century, gradually made removal feasible.

In the discussion that followed, a number of French deputies referred to the fortifications as outmoded. Deputy Claude Nectoux from Aubervilliers, a suburb of Paris, highlighted the fact that, since the construction of the fortifications in the nineteenth century, "pyrotechnics and ballistics [had] made so much progress that everyone knows that they are of no use at all from a military point of view."[47] Jean-Baptiste Abel, the deputy for Toulon suggested that fortifications had become obsolete in Paris and elsewhere when he claimed, "Today, the dogma of the inviolability of fortification has fallen in the face of the all-too-painful lessons of the last war."[48] Louis Nail, the minister of justice and deputy for the Morbihan, underlined these comments, acknowledging that demolition would surely take place "in many French cities." Nail admitted no other choice when "faced with cities trapped within these old walls condemned from all perspectives, that of military experience as well as hygiene."[49] Deputy Paul Mistral, from Grenoble, pointed out that his city was also "suffocating in its corset of fortifications."[50] The Socialist deputy from Levallois, Jean Bon, stated, "The fortifications [in Paris] never served any purpose and will never serve any purpose."[51] Rozier had noted earlier that when the fortifications were built in 1841, republicans "accused the...bourgeoisie...of constructing a wall to strangle and dominate Paris, to facilitate crushing the city in the event that new revolutions, insurrections or uprisings should ignite."[52] Bon underlined the issue of class conflict, pointing out that the only time the defenses had ever been employed successfully, it was not "against the enemy," but in "civil conflicts." Bon was referring to the historic moment when government forces had violently suppressed the Paris Commune of 1871.[53]

Addressing this history, Rozier suggested that demolition could be "doubly symbolic." He hoped the "demolition of the fortified wall" might symbolize "a kind of reciprocal disarmament of parties and a rapprochement of men in the common national project."[54] Rozier's colleagues greeted this statement with great applause. Praising the move on the part of the state and the city to replace the "military" with the "sanitary," Rozier also regarded declassification as a liberation of the French capital from a form of military defensiveness when he declared, "At the hour in which victorious France discusses the conditions of a future peace with its allies, Paris, in removing its stone defense, attests to its trust that the league of nations better shelters it from wars than the outmoded fortifications that were intended to defend it."[55]

The construction of the Cité Internationale Universitaire de Paris (CIUP) along part of the "outmoded" fortified belt that had surrounded the city was perhaps the most tangible example of what demilitarization could mean: the anticipation of Paris as a center for international peace in the future. The idea of using part of the land made available as a result of decommissioning for the construction of an international collection of houses and facilities for students from around the world began to take form immediately after the war. In June 1921, the French Conseil des Ministres approved plans to build the CIUP on bastions of the old fortified wall. Late in 1922, the University Council of the Sorbonne set up a commission to follow the progress of the CIUP and established a committee to promote the project. After demolition of the fortifications in the area, the first house, named after Emile Deutsch de la Meurthe (one of the CIUP's founders) opened in July 1925.[56]

Supporters of the CIUP hoped that this project of "antifortification" would transcend boundaries between nations and work to heal the wounds of the First World War. Bringing together young people from around the world, the generation of the *future,* "the Cité Universitaire would be a privileged site of experimentation in international relations."[57] Looking forward in 1923 to the inauguration of the CIUP, writer Henry Spont claimed, "It is not out of line to think that...affective ties [between young people] established at an optimistic age, will...infuse international relations with more kindness and equity."[58] Spont imagined "three thousand students from all nations provided with books, sun and fresh air...work[ing] in concert toward the harmonious perfection of their minds and bodies, toward the progress of science and the cooperation of their respective nations."[59] In 1930, Henri-Paul Nénot, an architect and a member of the French Académie des Beaux Arts commented that while "in the abstract, Paris should become the capital of a modern Europe...concretely, a program is required." He went on to assert that "a project of this nature (the Cité Universitaire) has already been realized."[60] Over and over again, supporters of the CIUP referred to the institution as a new "wall of the College of Nations,"[61] a project reflecting "both national and international interests," revealing "all of France" as a nation "devoted to the service of peace."[62] The founders and administrators of the project reiterated this objective at subsequent stages of the CIUP's development. In 1936, when the CIUP's president, André Honnorat, inaugurated the "International House," he underlined his conviction that the young people residing there were "the hope of tomorrow."[63] As historian Bertrand Lemoine has pointed out: "The mystique of peace could not, in the spirit of the times, be better served but by the rapprochement of the elite...the Cité would be, down to its physiognomy, a microcosmic representation of the universal ideal that it was intended to propagate."[64]

Despite the project of demilitarization, the military security of Paris continued to play an important role in discussions of the city's future. The new possibilities of war posed different problems for military planners who sought to protect the city. Urban and military strategists alike articulated important connections between the city's improvement and the question of its military vulnerability to attack in the future. When Deputy Rozier presented his report on the subject of Paris' fortifications in 1919, Joseph Cornudet interjected with his own concerns. Cornudet posed a series of questions concerning the exact nature of the plans according to which expansion of the capital might proceed. Emphasizing the importance of ensuring that any development or expansion of the city respect the law he had been so instrumental in instituting, Cornudet also expressed concern about the military question. Addressing the prime minister and minister of war, Georges Clemenceau, Cornudet asked, "What do you plan to do to protect Paris?"[65]

A few years after the 1919 decommissioning of the installations fortifying the capital, Maurice Talmeyr argued that the fortifications surrounding cities like Paris offered little in the way of defense against the possibilities of another war with Germany or any other enemy. Talmeyr underlined their anachronism while anticipating the next war by drawing on a painful example from French military history. In his words, the fortifications "seemed to have become even more illusory against the diabolical wars of the future than the towers of Philippe Auguste or...Charles V would have been against the Prussian canons of fifty years ago."[66] Using the distance between two historical moments separated by centuries to predict the gap between the effectiveness of the city's defenses and the threats of the future, Talmeyr's analogy employed a kind of "retroactive" projection. The future he anticipated relied inevitably on the memory and the rhetoric of history.

In *Le Danger aérien et l'avenir du pays* (The Aerial Threat and the Future of the Country), published in 1930, Lieutenant Colonel Arsène Vauthier explored the implications of the new, aerial warfare for France's cities. Indeed, Vauthier devoted the entire third part of his treatise on the military defense of France against aerial attack to the problem of protecting cities. This section of his book focused largely on debates about urban planning, architecture, and the transformation of Paris. The second chapter of this section was subtitled "An Essay on the Organization of the City of the Future."[67]

In it, Vauthier explored the different aspects of the discussions about the renovation of Paris from the perspective of military defense. He outlined a history of the legislation and measures taken since the war to transform the city. In maps, charts, and extensive calculations, Vauthier outlined the time it would take for attacks from various points outside France to reach the capital, as well as estimates of the kinds of damage different strikes from above might bring about.

An air strike against Paris would likely kill more civilians than one on London or New York. As Edmond Blanc, a frequent contributor to the magazine *Sciences et voyages* on the subject of aviation, pointed out a few years later, Paris was "an ideal target." "If New York and London contain 63 or 148 inhabitants per hectare," he observed, "Paris holds 368, and this is very serious." Underlining the need for concern, Blanc cited the French aviator and politician Charles Delesalle's conclusion that "'at the present time, no system c[ould] defend Paris.'"[68] Authors like Vauthier and Blanc warned their readers that military threats to the city had not gone out of fashion because previous strategies of defense had become outmoded. Responses to the problem included the adoption of precautionary measures of passive defense against military attack within the boundaries of the nation. Alongside the debates about the vulnerable terrain and population of the city, military strategists in France also spent the better part of the 1920s considering the fortification of the nation as a whole as a strategy of defense against the threats of the "next war." I explore this transfer of defense from the *inside* of the nation to the fortification of its *borders* in the next chapter of this book. The practical and symbolic displacement of the walled defense of the capital to the construction of the Maginot Line and the imagined impregnability of a "Great Wall of France" enabled a narrative of the future that was reassuring, if illusory, to some observers. In this more optimistic picture of the future, the enemy would not pass and Paris would not become the site of yet another confrontation between French and German forces.

The "Radiant City of the Future"

In 1920, an unnamed journalist who interviewed the French architect Auguste Perret suggested that what he "had learned about the cities of tomorrow" was that these cities "should be built in new countries." Sharing his thoughts with readers of the French newspaper *l'Instransigeant*, Perret described his plans for a series of *maisons-tour*, or residential high rises, to counter the effects of wild development in the city. Perret proposed wide

avenues enabling the free flow of traffic, skyscrapers equipped with eleva-
tors and walkways to allow for travel between buildings, and metro lines
running into the suburbs. Perret's interviewer described Paris as "a fungus
that spreads haphazardly, independent of the will of men," but expressed
relief that the architect did seem to "adore" the historic capital and the "old
France he knows...better than anyone." According to the interviewer, Perret "did not wish to cause even the slightest harm to either contemporary
tourists or the pilgrims of centuries to come."[69] Perret's vision combined two
different spatial strategies for the growth of cities in the interwar years:
the vertical and the horizontal. Paris could be expanded on the ground,
or toward the sky. While these two approaches were not necessarily mutually exclusive, the architects and planners who debated the development of
the city in this period often used these directional designations to figure a
binary opposition between the historic capital of the nation and the "city
of the future."

The architect whose proposed designs for the city ignited some of the
most heated debates in the interwar years was Le Corbusier. No other architect in France during this period devoted as much energy to theorizing
the *plan*, the mapping of space in anticipation of its development and transformation. In *Vers une architecture* (*Toward an Architecture*), published in
1923, the architect identified three keys to his theory and practice: surface,
volume, and the plan. In his opening, Le Corbusier wrote:

The plan is the generator.
Without a plan, there is disorder, arbitrariness.
The great problems of tomorrow, dictated by collective needs, pose
    the question of the plan anew.
Modern life demands, awaits a new plan for the house and for the
    city.[70]

For Le Corbusier, the plan was at the center of a transformative vision that
could revolutionize and improve the city and the lives of its inhabitants.

Though he had been born in Switzerland and did not officially become
a French citizen until 1930, Le Corbusier knew the French capital well.
Having studied and traveled throughout Europe as a young adult, the architect had come to Paris to work with Auguste Perret in 1907. After several years spent exploring cities like Berlin (where he met Mies van der
Rohe), Athens, and Istanbul, he settled in Paris after the war, starting his
own practice in collaboration with his cousin Pierre Jeanneret in the early
1920s.[71] Throughout his career, Le Corbusier designed a series of private

and public buildings in the city. These included the Villa la Roche (1923) in the wealthy Sixteenth arrondissement, the Salvation Army's Cité de refuge (1929), and the Swiss pavilion at the Cité Universitaire (1930). In numerous articles and book-length treatises on architecture and urban design, Le Corbusier used Paris as a case study and point of reference as he outlined his basic principles and commitment to simplicity, clarity, space, and height.

In much of his writing, Le Corbusier described the need to transform Paris, protecting the city from itself. According to the architect, the phenomenon of the "Great City" in general lacked clarity, "geometry," and had become a "menacing disaster." Paris, a "dangerous magma of human beings" required "a reorganization...necessary to her vitality, health and permanence."[72]

Beginning with the "Ville contemporaine de trois millions d'habitants" (Contemporary city of three million inhabitants) that he exhibited at the Salon d'Automne in 1922, Le Corbusier proposed plans for the transformation of Paris into an ideal, "contemporary" city. Like other projections and representations of the capital, Le Corbusier's vision emphasized and traded on the idea of the capital as a "city of lights" while imagining its future. His designs for a "radiant" Paris included the widening of boulevards to improve traffic circulation, the building of towers to free up the ground of the city at its core, and the expansion of green spaces throughout the urban landscape.[73] Le Corbusier's plans for Paris resembled those he outlined for a number of other cities around the world. It was therefore not entirely surprising that those devoted to a French capital expressive of national culture would have a difficult time seeing what these templates had to do with the specificity of French tradition or Parisian historicity. Paris could be opened up and made a site for international cooperation, but the city should remain undoubtedly "French."

In the proposals for the transformation of Paris that Le Corbusier generated between 1922 and 1935, skyscrapers eclipsed and sometimes replaced the monuments and historic architecture of the capital (figure 2.2). Even the Eiffel Tower would not remain unchallenged by the changes Le Corbusier proposed. In *Urbanisme (The City of Tomorrow and Its Planning)*, his treatise on cities and planning published in 1925, the architect suggested, almost taunted: "When our city is built on the same grand scale, then we shall be in a position to go into the question of the permanence of the Eiffel Tower."[74] No more menacing gauntlet could be thrown down in the midst of discussions about the preservation of the capital and its architecture. Less than forty years old when Le Corbusier displayed his "Ville contemporaine" in 1922, the Eiffel Tower had, despite its youth, come to represent an "essential" Paris, quickly becoming a crucial piece of the nation's *patrimoine*.

2.2. Le Corbusier's "Plan Voisin," 1925. © 2008 Artists Rights Society (ARS), New York/ADAGP, Paris.

Older monuments such as Notre Dame and the Louvre also represented the city's history, but in the French imagination no architectural structure came to symbolize Paris more than the Eiffel Tower.[75]

In a review of the 1922 Salon d'Automne for the newspaper *Le Temps*, the architectural critic Léandre Vaillat described the "Ville contemporaine" as a "city of the future."[76] Vaillat was not alone in his characterization of Le Corbusier's work as being "of the future." Albert Léon Guérard, a French professor who lived for many years in the United States, discussed the "future of Paris" in his book *L'Avenir de Paris,* published in 1929. Guérard was careful to point out that, while a "little encyclopedia" presenting the problems facing the city could prove very useful, his study was not a work of "'anticipation' à la Wells or...à la Le Corbusier."[77] While Guérard was likely unaware of this fact, an exchange did take place, somewhat indirectly, between the modernist architect and the *The War of the Worlds* author. In the early 1930s, H. G. Wells had participated in a BBC broadcast in which he called on "professors of prediction" to prepare the future. *The Listener,* a weekly magazine established by the BBC in 1929, published a series of articles by different personalities on the role of prophecy in modern societies.

Written in 1932, Le Corbusier's response, "Professeur de prévisions," later appeared in the collection of writings and drawings he brought together under the rubric of the "Radiant City."

In this essay on the future, Le Corbusier rejected the label "professor of prediction" to begin with. Giving readers an impassioned defense of his architectural and urban vision, he addressed the idea of anticipation head on:

> I am an architect...I make plans that take into account present realities...I make (in 1922) plans for "a contemporary city of 3 million inhabitants." All of my critics, without exception, speak of my "city of the future." I protest in vain; I affirm that I know nothing of the future, but I do know the present. "No," they reply with a cowardly strategy: "you concern yourself with the future," implying that "they" (everyone) concern themselves with the present. Falsehood: with all the modesty of a researcher, I cling to the present, the contemporary, today and "they" live "yesterday" and they live off of yesterday. That is the drama of modern times. Everything that Mr. Wells evokes pertains to today, not tomorrow.[78]

Le Corbusier called for a reading of Wells as the author of analytic, fictive projections of contemporary relevance and concern. His own work, like that of Wells, was less about "predicting" the future than engaging with a present that defaulted to "the future" because of contemporary resistance to conceive and implement change. Elsewhere in his writings, Le Corbusier underlined these sentiments. In *Urbanisme,* for example, the architect protested against certain responses to his 1922 "Ville contemporaine": "My friends...said 'All this is for the year 2000!' Everywhere, the journalists wrote 'The City of the Future.' Yet I had called it 'A Contemporary City'; contemporary because to-morrow belongs to nobody."[79]

This insistence on the idea of the "contemporary" did not, however, keep Le Corbusier from using the *figure* of the future in the representation of his ideas about space, work, and the city. Le Corbusier did not always refuse "the future" as vehemently as he did in response to critics who rejected the feasibility of his designs. In articles such as "La Cité future de travail" (The Working City of the Future) and "Paris sera-t-il la première grande ville moderne du monde?" (Will Paris Be the First Large-Scale Modern City in the World?) Le Corbusier linked his descriptions of a "city of the future" to the broader concerns of labor and the role of Paris in international affairs. Over the years, Le Corbusier also gave numerous talks and interviews on "the city of the future." In an "exclusive interview" published in *Beaux Arts* in 1938, the architect outlined his ideas for the "Radiant City." When asked to describe his image of the city of the year 2000, Le Corbusier expanded on his plans for this *contemporary* city: the machine, the separation of residential and industrial sectors, and construction upward to decrease ground-level density and enable the free flow of traffic, both pedestrian and automobile.[80]

In debates about the future "Frenchness" of Paris, participants from across the cultural and political spectrum fixated on the skyscraper. The skyscraper was a principal feature of Le Corbusier's designs, but plans for Paris that built upward were not his exclusive domain. Other architects projected constructions in the same vein. Some proposed the skyscraper in utopian designs of a future city, others, as a practical solution to the problems of pedestrian and automobile circulation. Even a critic of Le Corbusier such as Guérard found a place for height in his study devoted to "the future of Paris." Guérard was, however, a fan of the "Greater Paris" model that offered to alleviate the problem of density while "better respect[ing] the old Paris." Giving the city room to breathe provided a solution to the dilemmas of overcrowding, circulation, and hygiene. According to Guérard, new architectural forms might be permitted beyond the historical boundaries of the city without affecting the treasured monuments of the capital, making "extension" a form of "traditionalism."[81]

The question: "Will skyscrapers conquer Europe?" touched on issues of modernization, Americanization, military planning, and the role of Paris in international relations in the interwar years.[82] While visions of towering buildings had appeared in science fiction and architectural fantasies before the war, it was during the interwar period that the debate over the skyscraper really took off. For some, the "city of the future" meant "the combination of skyscrapers raised higher and higher, between which arteries of high-speed traffic [would] intersect at different levels."[83] As writer Pierre Lyautey noted at the time, "An important trial w[ould] soon be judged by public opinion, that of skyscrapers." According to Lyautey, "The verdict look[ed] uncertain."[84]

In an article entitled "Doit-on excommunier les gratte-ciel—Paris 1940?" (Must We Ban Skyscrapers-Paris 1940?) that appeared in the popular magazine *VU* in 1930, Lyautey and a number of architects and urban planners, including Le Corbusier, were asked to contribute their points of view on the future of the Parisian skyline and the role they imagined for Paris in a broader international context. The president of the Comité supérieure

2.3. Albert Laprade's photomontage of a skyscraper surrounded by Haussmannian buildings, 1931.
DAF/Cité de l'architecture et du patrimoine/Archives d'architecture du XXe siècle.

d'aménagement de la Région Parisienne and former president of the Conseil Municipal de Paris, Louis Dausset, responded to a series of questions concerning the future of the city and the question of skyscrapers. Other participants included the Dutch painter Kees Van Dongen, the architect Henri-Paul Nénot, and the publisher Bernard Grasset.[85] Respondents addressed the question of the marriage of "the chefs-d'oeuvre of [French] history" and "modern architecture" in the Parisian context and commented on a series of images produced by the government architect Albert Laprade (figures 2.3 and 2.4).[86]

Juxtaposing the historic monuments and buildings of the capital with towering constructions, these playful images expressed, at one and the same time, the anxiety and fascination with which French architects and urban planners considered the possibility of the transformation of their capital city. Humorous in their representation of the "city of the future," they suggested the incongruence of such constructions with the most loved sites of Parisian history and culture. They represented "the future" as a composite of two architectural presents: a French "historic" and an American "modern." Throughout the interwar years, numerous images like these appeared in magazines like *VU, Lectures pour tous, Miroir du monde, La Cité*

2.4. Albert Laprade's photomontage of a skyscraper next to La Madeleine, 1931. DAF/Cité de l'architecture et du patrimoine/Archives d'architecture du XXe siècle.

moderne, and *Sciences et voyages.* In these publications, the twenty-first century, even the thirtieth, could be conjured easily by creating a collage of some structural representative of the American metropolis, and a familiar Parisian site or monument such as Notre Dame, La Madeleine, or the Place de la Concorde.

Opening the discussion, the writer Pierre Lyautey asked, "First of all, what is a skyscraper? A horror that disfigures a landscape. But is a landscape disfigured in direct proportion to the height of its constructions?" Lyautey was quick to point to the height of the Eiffel Tower that, while tall, remained the "prize of Parisians." Lyautey pointed out that many lower buildings currently cropping up around Paris were even more ugly than the towers that others dismissed as unappealing. "The skyscraper cannot then be condemned for its height alone," he concluded.[87] As another French writer had observed in the magazine *Science et la vie* in 1925, the skyscraper seemed to embody "the ideal building for economical and rational comfort" in the modern world, one of many "applications of the science of habitation" and a site for the "scientific home."[88]

As far as Le Corbusier was concerned, the skyscraper constituted the "only response to the problems of increasing density and decongestion of the centers of major cities."[89] He also emphasized the ways that the skyscraper could work to protect Paris from "the air war" of the future. On another occasion, Le Corbusier claimed that,

> Only those cities which are conceived along the lines of the Radiant City are capable of emerging victorious from an air war. Because in the Radiant City, 100% of the ground is freed and only 5% to 12% of the surface has buildings on it; now, those buildings are "on *pilotis* [stilts]," which means that air circulates...that the wind will be able to dissipate the gas. Apartment buildings in the Radiant City are 50 meters high; thus a number of floors are situated above the gaseous mass; the inhabitants will take refuge on the upper floors and no longer in cellars made especially impervious to gas.

Le Corbusier also suggested these structures "be equipped with bomb-resistant armored platforms" and "shock-absorbing devices." Not only was the skyscraper a potential way out of the crowding and concentration of the city; towers were also potential points of defense against aerial attack.[90]

While Le Corbusier championed skyscrapers as a form of protection, others saw the structures as a serious threat. Louis Dausset rejected the skyscraper for Paris, stating such constructions "in the center of Paris are an impossibility.... To raise them, we would have to start by blowing up entire streets and creating vast open spaces all around. In doing this, we would destroy the traditional character of our capital." Dausset, like Guérard and others, preferred the model of "Greater Paris" one that would "leave intact the *chefs-d'oeuvre* of our traditional architecture."[91] Van Dongen made the preservationist argument that "everything would have to be demolished and rebuilt" in the city to enable the incorporation of an urban aesthetic that was decidedly un-French, catering to "American needs and living conditions [that] have no place in Paris."[92]

Resistance to construction upward was clearly caught in the fear of denigration of national culture and heritage. André de Fels, the deputy of Seine-et-Oise, maintained, "Paris must remain a horizontal city and should not become vertical like New-York." De Fels expressed his faith in a national aesthetic when he clung to the ideal that "the Paris of the twentieth century should not take its inspiration from an American city." De Fels went on to note: "It seems to me that the sky and climate so particular to France that gives rise to a whole play of shadows and light does not allow for the construction of the American skyscrapers."[93] Even attempts at compromise were vague, revealing an anxiety about the cultural uniqueness of the French city, rather than a rejection of height per se. De Fels, for example, suggested there might be some place for *gratte-ciel* in the city, perhaps as residences: "I can well imagine dwellings, something like skyscrapers, but with something essentially French that you find in smaller structures."[94] He did not go into great detail, however, about what that "something essentially French" might be. It was difficult to articulate what might make any tower (other than Eiffel's of course) fit in the French capital or cultural imagination.

The inspector general of the Services téchniques d'architecture et d'ésthétique du département de la Seine, Louis Bonnier judged advocates of the skyscraper harshly. In an article entitled "Les Transformations et l'avenir de Paris" (The Transformations and the Future of Paris) published in the magazine *La Construction moderne* in 1930, Bonnier considered the "city of the future" as he worried about the capital. Bonnier identified verticality as betrayal of the city in the guise of improvement when he wrote, "In the housing crisis, under the pretext of modernization...and progress, the snobs of Americanism seek to provide contemporary Paris with constructions 300 meters high, the height of the Eiffel tower, more than five times that of the towers of Notre Dame."[95] Critics like Bonnier insisted that Paris should not, at any cost, be transformed into a city like Manhattan or Chicago. He went on to explain that he could "understand skyscrapers in a city that was born yesterday, without a past, without history, without art, on a terrain that can support them." Paris, was not such a place, however, and Bonnier believed skyscrapers "would be absurd and impractical in the center of a city of art, violating all proportion, scale, harmony, whatever the value of these buildings on their own."[96] The specter of the American metropolis, with its towering buildings, loomed menacingly over the low rooftops and narrow streets of the French capital in Bonnier's words. It also appeared in the images Bonnier produced of an "Americanized" Paris (figures 2.5 and 2.6).[97] Like Laprade and others, Bonnier visualized the

2.5. Louis Bonnier's photomontage of skyscrapers near the Place de la Concorde and L'Église de la Madeleine, n.d. DAF/Cité de l'architecture et du patrimoine/Archives d'architecture du XXe siècle.

collision of two culturally distant cityscapes in the present, creating composites that could and often did stand for the "city of the future" in the French context.

For a number of French observers in the interwar years, the skyscraper functioned as the emblem of everything that was wrong with the "city of the future" and Le Corbusier figured frequently as verticality's principal champion in their eyes. Fears about the modernization of the city center often confused the architect with the culture and values of the United States. This, despite the fact that Le Corbusier himself rejected cities like New York and Chicago as poorly planned "nightmares."[98] At the same time, architects and

2.6. Louis Bonnier's photomontage of skyscrapers next to Notre-Dame, 1928. DAF/Cité de l'architecture et du patrimoine/Archives d'architecture du XXe siècle.

urban planners who rejected the skyscraper for Paris were willing to admit construction upward along the city's periphery, or in the suburbs. Bonnier, for example, wrote:

> Of course, our apprehensions concern the historic and monumental Paris that extends from the *Place du Trone* to the *Porte Maillot*...in the new suburbs, far from the *Chateaux* of *Versailles, Saint Germain de Maisons* or *Vincennes,* new constructions should be built at great height and surrounded by open spaces...but we should respect Paris, its past, present and its future.[99]

The suburban regions of Paris that were in the process of development and expansion were, like the American city, relatively without history. For Bonnier and others, there was an important distinction to be made between "the city of the future" and a "future" for Paris. The latter was a future continuous with and dependent on the architectural and urban past.

In the interwar years, much of the discussion of the future of Paris anticipated further territorial, political, and military possibilities while condemning more radical aesthetic and formal change as essentially un-French, a betrayal of the city and of the nation as a whole. The figures that sought to imagine France's urban future after 1918 struggled with the predominance of an aesthetic conservatism that venerated the past and resisted the abandonment of architectural tradition. Ambivalence about new styles and forms in the urban context reflected a desire to return to "Belle Epoque" values and ways of life and to defend the nation from a future that a variety of French cultural critics identified increasingly with the United States.[100] Suspicious of American innovation and power, certain French conservatives saw their worst fears embodied in the American metropolis, cities like New York and Chicago. The war had created new opportunities for and ideas about the improvement of French cities. At the same time, respecting the capital's historic significance while responding to the need for renovation and renewal proved challenging for those architects, political representatives, and municipal officials who sought to imagine the "city of the future" without suggesting the disappearance of those monuments and aesthetic features that seemed to make the city most "French."

Paris in Ruins

In 1927, the French filmmaker Jean Renoir shot a seventeen-minute short with leftover stock from the production of his film *Nana*. *Sur un air de Charleston* is set in the year 2028. In the film, a Central African explorer named Johnny Higgins departs on an archaeological visit to the ruins of a post-apocalyptic Paris. When he arrives in the city, Higgins stumbles upon a woman, accompanied by an ape, dancing the Charleston in the streets of the capital.[101] Frightened and unfamiliar with this "ancient dance" of the 1920s, Higgins runs from the woman. She chases him and then draws a telephone on the wall. The image transforms into a real telephone and several disembodied heads with wings appear, reassuring the explorer that the woman means no harm. The explorer and the woman dance together for a few minutes. Soon after, they leave together in Higgins's flying craft.

Renoir's fantasy of Paris as a "city of the future" made direct references to the filmmaker's own cultural experience and vocabulary. Though the film was silent, jazz was the soundtrack implied by the movement of its characters. Other traces of the interwar past appear in the film as well. The telephone, while not entirely the telephone of the 1920s, recalled the instrument that was transforming the world of human communication in the first part of the twentieth century. Even the severed heads suggested something about a future intelligence with a body that might not be quite whole.

The story that unfolded in Renoir's brief film was unusual, but not entirely unique. Published in 1924, André Reuze's novel, *Venus d'Asnières*, also focused on an African scientist's exploration of the "long-ago destroyed" capital more than one thousand years in the future. In Reuze's account, the archaeologist Traveling-Robinson outlines a history of the demise of European civilization in the twentieth century from the perspective of the thirtieth. According to Traveling-Robinson, a series of wars in 1914, 1918, 1938, and 1950 had pitted the "Francs" against the "Germains." These conflicts led to the use of chemical weapons in warfare and the annihilation of European civilization as a whole. By the twenty-third century, African civilization had evolved to world dominance. By the twenty-ninth, France had become part of a European "no man's land" and Paris a set of ruins to be excavated and studied. Traveling-Robinson's notes on the city include references to a bourgeois apartment, the destruction of the Louvre and the Bibliothèque nationale. Although the archaeologist cannot locate the Eiffel Tower anywhere, he does, like Renoir's Johnny Higgins, discover a "savage" young European woman who tries to seduce him.[102]

In both of these fictional accounts of the future, Paris was a city virtually dead, the remnant of a civilization long abandoned. Both narratives accentuated the disappearance of the "city of lights" by relying on an inversion of civilizations perceived as "primitive" and "advanced." In both the film and the novel, gender, race, and sexuality are mobilized as cultural tropes and traces of the future. Renoir and Reuze played with racist and sexist stereotypes from their contemporary cultural landscape: the assumption that Africans were less civilized than and subservient to Europeans and that women were temptresses whose bodies rendered them closer to animals and "savages." Figuring Africans as the explorers and scientists of a future humanity, these narratives of "postcolonial anticipation" represented the future in terms of a reversal of the imperial relationship between Europe and Africa and the transfer of authority, power, and knowledge to the once colonized. In the case of Renoir's film, for example, Higgins, the African, arrives in a futuristic vessel while the Parisian girl he encounters roams about the ruins of the city with a primitive ape.[103]

Although neither Renoir nor Reuze referred directly to the debates about the capital that had been taking place in France since the war, their representation of the "city of lights" as a city extinguished in the future expressed a broader cultural anxiety that Paris might not, ultimately, survive the twentieth century. For many interwar observers, Paris was incompatible with notions of a "contemporary" city, let alone a "city of the future." The idea of a Paris in ruins was rarely made explicit in discussions of the future of the city after 1918. At the same time, a range of perceived aesthetic and military threats made the expectation of the capital's disappearance a central theme of the culture of anticipation of the interwar years.

[Handwritten marginal notes:]

This chapter begins well, & w/ promise, esp. idea about building from ruins of war, & this idea spreading even to cities, like Paris, not damaged or destroyed.

But then gets very thin, w/ focus on Le Corbusier which is not particularly successful at advancing beyond what already know.

Would have benefitted from moving beyond a few speculations & blueprints to discussing of how idea of future city actually being implemented (or attempted) at level of real city planning (renewal).

CHAPTER 3

The Next War

In 1928, Lucien Febvre, one of the founders of the Annales School of history, published a brief essay entitled "Frontière, le mot et la notion" in the *Revue de synthèse historique.*[1] Febvre pointed out that the term *frontière* had had different meanings in French since the Middle Ages, referring to the architectural "façade of a building," as well as to "the front line of an army."[2] He traced shifts in the definition of the physical frontière of France, from a "bordering territory in movement" to the idea of a fixed limit. Febvre noted that the meanings of the words *limites* (limits) and frontières (borders) "tend[ed] increasingly to overlap" by the seventeenth century, becoming virtually interchangeable by the end of the nineteenth.[3] In the final section of his analysis, Febvre identified three French definitions of frontière current in 1928: a "strip of land of varying width on the extremities of a country," a "demarcation line," and a "defensive barrier."[4]

Febvre's historical investigation of the language of French territory and its boundaries had implications beyond the etymological. Various French rulers had, since at least the seventeenth century, claimed the "ideal" boundaries of France to have been set in place by natural phenomena: the Rhine, the Alps, the Pyrenees, the Mediterranean, etc. This doctrine of "natural frontiers" had served as the foundation of projects to unify France internally and to justify the territorial expansion of, first the *royaume* (kingdom), and then the French nation after 1789.[5] Underlining the connections between changes in vocabulary/usage and the military and political objectives of various incarnations of the French state over the past several hundred years,

Febvre argued that France's territorial limits were neither timeless nor self-evident boundaries determined by nature or destiny. His analysis showed that the idea of the frontière, including what he referred to as the "mask" of the nation's "natural frontiers," had undergone revision and redefinition a number of times in the past, with shifts in terminology accompanying and underwriting changes in the aims and interests of ruling authorities and their armies.[6]

While Febvre made no explicit reference to the specific politics of the frontière in the contemporary French context, the word and the concept had certainly been on the minds of a number of other French observers throughout the 1920s. After World War I, a devastating conflict in which so many destructive battles had taken place in France, French military strategists and political representatives expressed an urgent need for a new approach to the security of the nation's borders and territory. The war had reinvigorated long-standing anxieties and inspired new fears regarding all three of the "current" definitions of frontière that Febvre outlined in 1928: the vulnerability of particular "strip[s] of land of varying width" near the nation's borders, the possible discontinuity and instability of different lines of "demarcation," and the question of what type of "defensive barrier" might best protect the nation against enemy attack and invasion in the future.

The Treaty of Versailles had been signed in 1919. The French government would not make its official declaration of war against Germany until September 1939. In the twenty years in between, the "next war"—a conflict imagined in terms even more destructive than the "Great War"—loomed in France, despite the allied victory, despite hopes for a stable and lasting peace.[7] Contemplating the successes and failures of the last war as they attempted to prepare sufficiently for the "next," military officials negotiated the memory of battles recently fought as they attempted to prepare for the struggles that they considered likely in the years ahead.

Throughout the 1920s, French military officials considered a range of anticipated threats to the security of the nation. The series of offensive and defensive plans that they developed incorporated new and existing technologies of warfare, including fortification, tanks, and air power.[8] The military's rigid centralization and the lack of a sufficient, professionally trained fighting force would contribute to the inflexibility of France's eventual war effort from 1939 to 1940. Believing that the last war had valuable lessons to offer, interwar strategists maintained that firepower and "methodical battles" would be decisive in the "next war." These assumptions would lead ultimately to a general neglect of offensive mobility in their approach. By the 1930s, a defensive doctrine would come to dominate French plans for

the future and, in the decade before defeat, permanent fortification emerged
as the centerpiece of France's territorial defense system.[9]

In 1929, shortly after the publication of Febvre's essay, the French government voted a sum of nearly 3 billion francs to fund the construction of a
massive system of fortification intended to protect France's borders, a series
of installations that would be known as the "Maginot Line."[10] Named after
Minister of War André Maginot and constructed in stages from 1930 to
1940, this defensive barrier became a unique and powerful emblem of the
French frontière as a whole. The image of the nation as a fortress protected
and steeled against outside invasion by the "Great Wall" of the Maginot
Line emerged as an antidote to the fear of attack, invasion, and defeat.
Despite its limitations, the Maginot Line became a military and cultural
symbol of total impregnability. A project unprecedented in terms of its scale
and expense, it embodied like no other strategy of defense that had preceded
it a desire to shield the nation by sealing up its borders.

Deeply invested in preventing any recurrence of the loss of life, physical
destruction, and psychological trauma of World War I, the French military
in the interwar years had become focused on ensuring national territorial
integrity and guarding the "whole" of France from the particularly terri-
fying and devastating impact of another war against Germany. The trouble
lay in defining and protecting this national "whole." Questions about the
relationship between historic and anticipated fronts of war, the so-called
"natural frontiers" of France, and the shifting boundaries set by treaties and
agreements in peacetime made it difficult to fix the nation's territorial limits,
let alone guarantee their security in the future.

The "total" protection of France's borders was troubled by their instability and the eventual discontinuity of the barriers constructed on them.
Visions of a war of the future that emphasized the menace of aerial strikes
and the likelihood of attacks on civilians also challenged the fantasy of
the nation as fortress, offering radically different images of the "whole" of
France. In a war waged in and from the sky, the nation would be a surface
entirely vulnerable, its traditional military and political borders easily overrun. Airplanes and gas masks, features of the war of 1914–18, became the
fetishized traces of a war of the future, a conflict imagined in terms that rendered impossible any strictly territorial definition of the space of the nation.
Finally, the imperative to protect the "whole" national body intersected
with military and pronatalist anxieties about the physical and numerical
weaknesses of the nation's bodies in the wake of World War I.

The history of the Maginot Line has been written in many publications.
Scholars such as Roger Bruge, Judith M. Hughes, Barry Posen, Robert

Doughty, and Elizabeth Kier have examined in detail the complexities of French military planning in the interwar years, including the proposal and pursuit of various approaches to national defense. Their analyses have contributed to our understanding of the impact the experience of World War I had on French ideas about security and military engagement after 1918. These authors have shed considerable light on the logic of French strategy in this period, situating key military decisions within the contexts of domestic politics, economic constraints, the "problem" of population, and the relationship between France and its allies in the aftermath of World War I. Posen and Kier in particular have also considered French military doctrine in a comparative frame. Confronted in all of these studies is the crucial question of how and why the French defeat of 1940 happened as it did.[11]

In *La Nation*, the second part of the edited collection *Les Lieux de mémoire*, Pierre Nora asserts that the "national definition" of France in territorial terms has transcended differences between and within regimes, relying on the memory (and forgetting) of a complex past. Nora claims that territory has been essential in the French context given that "of all the old nation-states of Europe [France] has had the greatest number of kilometers to defend."[12] At the same time, Nora's understanding of the significance of territory as a *lieu* of national memory goes beyond that of a physical space that can be measured or demarcated. A number of Nora's collaborators in *Les Lieux de mémoire* show that the history of France as a physical territory is also the history of a cultural imaginary, a field of changing representations, as well as a set of concrete shifts in the shape and dimensions of a geographic area.[13]

Building on these historical foundations and insights, this chapter revisits the archive of French territorial defense planning in the interwar years. While the origins and consequences of military and government decisions during this period are matters of critical historical importance, my emphasis, like Febvre's, is on words and concepts rather than the evaluation of the success or failure of strategy and tactics. In the pages that follow, I examine the ways that military and civilian voices expressed their anxieties about the physical space and limits of the nation under threat of war and territorial invasion. Linked to the representation of French bodies and cities, ideas about the past and future of the nation at war provoked a profound and unprecedented interrogation of the stability of the frontière as a locus of French national self-definition. In this period, the projection of the "nation-territory" of France into the "next war" was, to use Nora's terminology, a *lieu* of both cultural memory and anticipation.

The "Whole" Nation

Soon after the Armistice, French military strategists began to entertain the
idea of turning the entire country into a fortress. The material damage
wrought by four years of battle created a new commitment to ensuring
that the "next war" would not be fought on French soil. Billions of francs
would need to be spent replacing the thousands of roads, buildings, canals,
and railway lines now in ruins. The regions affected had been key French
sources of coal, iron, and steel before the war. The hostilities had also left
vast stretches of agricultural land completely devastated.[14] "Total" war had
challenged ideas about the division between home and battle, military and
civilian fronts. The need to mobilize and protect all of the country's productive capacities and resources—its people, machines, and land—had complicated the definitions of military terrain, fronts, and targets.[15]

While the war experience had a significant impact on notions of national
territory and space, the idea of defending the "whole" of France was by
no means entirely new. It depended on the centuries-old idea of "natural
frontiers" that Lucien Febvre examined critically in 1928. The claim to a
national "whole" with natural boundaries was also linked to the representation of the nation in corporeal terms, a habit with a long history in France.
In the ancien régime, the words and concepts *state, body,* and *politics* were
bound up with one another in complex ways.[16] The sovereign's was a body
whose power and authority over the realm derived from God, a symbolic
body that could represent the entire kingdom. The king had had "two
bodies," one natural and the other sacred, and this political and religious
figuration had been essential to French royal authority for centuries.[17] The
political and cultural representation and control of bodies at once gendered
and classed was crucial to the "modernity" of the state and society that
emerged in and through the French Revolution of 1789.[18] Finally, organic
and medical metaphors were a powerful way of representing the nation and
its territory as a body that could be thriving or diseased in nineteenth- and
twentieth-century France.[19]

In the last third of the nineteenth century, the intersection of French
ideas about the state, the territorial boundaries of the nation, and the body
entered a particularly traumatic phase. After a humiliating defeat in the
Franco-Prussian War of 1870–71, France lost the northeastern departments
of Alsace and Lorraine, border regions that became part of a newly united
Germany. The annexation of these lands had, from the French perspective
at least, "deformed the outline" of France, opening a new chapter in the
representation of the national body.[20] As Jean-Marie Mayeur has argued,

this "territorial amputation caused French nationalism to reaffirm its foundations" and the region became the site of a "frontier memory."[21] Indeed, invested with the memory of invasion and defeat, these dismembered departments would continue to haunt the nation like territorial "phantom limbs." According to Mayeur, "Alsace be[came] the heart of France" and the recovery of this ceded territory signified metonymically the recovery of the entire French national body for more than forty years after 1870.[22] The *provinces perdus* achieved something of a mythic status during this period.[23] Combined with the bloody conflict of the Paris Commune that followed in 1871, the memory of defeat fueled feelings of national self-doubt and anxieties about external and internal enemies, military and industrial weakness, and national degeneration. While a war of *revanche* per se may not have been a priority for all or even most citizens after 1871, the lost provinces continued to play a significant role in the French political and cultural imagination in the decades ahead.[24]

A site of memory, this region also became a frontier of anticipation between 1871 and 1914. Throughout this late-nineteenth- and early-twentieth-century "interwar" period, French national defense efforts included the construction of a line of fortifications to protect the nation's remaining territory against any future German invasion. General Séré de Rivières, who proposed this set of defensive structures in 1874, intended them to guard the new territorial limits of France (limits that no longer included Alsace and Lorraine) and to match German fortifications at the time.[25] After the First World War, this region would continue to play an important role in discussions regarding the defense of a national territorial "whole." In the event of another war, these departments (regained in 1918) would not be protected within the nineteenth-century system of fortification noted above. Their security was a matter of symbolic as well as practical importance. Like the wounded soldier's body and the nation's capital, this borderland would play an important role in the interwar culture of anticipation, a *part* that could stand in for the future of the *whole* nation.

The return of Alsace and Lorraine to France came on the heels of a period of invasion and occupation that the French military and civilian population had also understood in literal and figurative corporeal terms. In wartime accounts and propaganda, the physical suffering of the nation's bodies and the physical invasion and occupation of the national body were inextricably linked from 1914 to 1918. From the onset of hostilities, French representations of German atrocities included testimonies and references to the murder, mutilation, rape, and torture of men, women, and children, as well as the destruction of homes, churches, and monuments.[26] Accounts during

THE NEXT WAR 83

and after the war figured the physical landscape as a body transgressed, wounded, and scarred. Added to the legacy of the northeastern departments once severed and now reattached, these recent experiences of territorial "violation" exacerbated the sense that the bodies and body of France needed to be protected from external enemies at all costs. Layered and complex, the cumulative memory of territories invaded, occupied, and annexed would greatly influence the anticipation of the "next war" after 1918.

Total Impregnability

In the early 1920s, the members of the French Conseil supérieure de guerre (CSG), or Superior War Council (reestablished after the war), began their discussions of how best to guard the nation's territory in the years ahead. In their meetings, letters, and reports, a number of contentious issues came up repeatedly: the idea of territorial "inviolability"; the relationship between military and political, present and future borders; and the necessity and nature of fortified installations that might defend France against an enemy offensive. The military would eventually make the construction of a system of permanent fortifications on the border a key element of their plans. Far from inevitable, the construction of the Maginot Line would come at the end of a long series of debates about the "next war." Between their initial meetings in 1920 and the presentation of a budget for the project to the National Assembly in 1929, the military would pose and attempt to answer serious questions about the future security and defense of the "whole" of France.

For the majority of military leaders after the war, it seemed that the insecurity of any part of the nation's territory could jeopardize the entire nation. In 1922, Maréchal Philippe Pétain, the "hero of Verdun," was adamant about the "need to prevent national territory from becoming the theater of operations" in the future. Pétain would be a key exponent of the imperative to protect French soil in the "next war." He argued that this objective, the foundation of military defense planning, had always been a matter of primary importance. Historically, territorial defenses had been "undertaken or studied in those moments when" the nation's military "realized, through recent experiences, the danger of supporting war on our own soil."[27]

According to Pétain, territorial "security" meant guaranteeing the "inviolability of the *sol national*." In order to achieve this security, military planning would have to include "consideration of the lessons of the last war [and] the likely conditions of a future war." If wars in the past had prompted discussion of defense, the war of 1914–18 had created a whole new set of security imperatives. As Pétain explained, "The last war demonstrated harshly that the invasion of any part of the country brought with it a proportional loss in the active force we were able to bring to the struggle, not to mention the economic disaster that followed." In "total" war, mobilization was not simply a question of calling troops to the front. The nation as a whole would henceforth participate in the war effort, exposed potentially to the violence and destruction previously reserved for the battlefield. Pétain pointed out that war now "demanded the mobilization of all of the resources of a country," and therefore "the need to prevent the enemy access to territory [had been] reaffirmed with a strength infinitely greater than in the past."[28] Fortification, Pétain suggested, could be an effective means of achieving this goal. Conceived appropriately, it could play a role in both defensive and offensive strategies in the future.[29]

A number of the maréchal's colleagues agreed. General Eugène Débeney, commander of the Ecole supérieure de guerre and director of the Centre des hautes études militaires, would underline Pétain's comments about the lessons of 1914–18:

> The last war showed the importance of territory itself in an advanced, civilized nation: industrial sites, agricultural exploitation, the riches of the soil, these [resources] are squeezed into narrow areas and their destruction in battle, even victorious, results in economic disaster, the consequences of which are felt harshly for years afterwards. In countries like our own, it is no longer a question of barring the routes of invasion or even zones of penetration, we must protect our territory.[30]

General Edmond Buat, the chief of the General Staff from 1920 until 1923, had already expressed his views on the matter during a CSG meeting two years earlier, insisting: "We cannot envision the abandonment of any part of our national territory."[31]

While the members of the French military hierarchy would agree that the defense of territory was a vital concern, there was nevertheless some debate over how much focus should be given to "inviolability" in the future. At another meeting held to establish the CSG's position on this issue, Maréchal Ferdinand Foch expressed his concern about this new and "perilous dogma." Foch noted that in the past, "the defense of territory was assured by the maneuvers of armies." Fortification and other forms of defense had served these ends rather than guaranteeing territory in and of themselves. Foch worried that the imposition of territorial inviolability as a primary goal might hinder the work of armies in the future, leading potentially to their downfall. An overemphasis on inviolability would constitute a "ren[unication] of the principles by which wars ha[d] been fought until now."[32] Recent experience had shown the importance of mobilizing the "whole" nation in times of war, but too great an emphasis on the defense of the nation *as a whole* might ultimately curb the capacity of its military forces to engage the enemy successfully.

The discussion of inviolability inevitably raised questions about the borders of the nation. In order to protect the "whole" of France in the future, it would be necessary to define it. In a report submitted to General Adolphe Guillaumat, General Buat expressed his belief that "the inviolability of the *sol national*" was "the beginning and end of wisdom." The idea was "simple and precise," a "timeless notion," and it was imperative that the "doors" of the nation be "closed" and "organized" defensively, even in peacetime.[33] An advocate of a continuous fortified line of defenses on the nation's perimeter, General Buat would argue that inviolability depended on "the integrity of the border." "In the most distant ages in history," he asserted, inviolability had been bound up with an "instinctive search for the natural border." A reliance on "natural frontiers" was not always possible, however, and the role of the army had been crucial where "nature was defective." In these cases, "military art had created artificial borders destined to achieve the same security."[34]

Defending the nation in the future by securing a set of "artificial" rather than "natural" borders was complicated, however. Given that any system of fortification would necessarily be built on French territory, how could such a system guarantee territorial security, let alone victory, against the enemy in the future? If the imperative of French military defense was to prevent the "next war" from taking place on French territory, then perhaps the "notion of the defense of the border at the border" was, as General Guillaumat had suggested earlier, "a monstrosity." Guillaumat worried about "the billions [of francs] spent that would be unavailable for the offensive" if such a system were to be implemented. The "next war" needed to be planned and fought *beyond,* rather than on or behind, the borders of the nation.[35]

Borders were also subject to change. In 1920, General Charles Mangin raised the issue of the border's future instability at a meeting of the CSG. Wondering whether it made sense to devote great amounts of time and money to fortification, Mangin asked, "Where will we build these fortified regions? On the border. But which border? The one we will have in fifteen years?"[36] Mangin's questions suggested that the current border of France, the security of which Buat equated with national territorial integrity, could not be guaranteed because its location could not be assured in the decades to come.

Foch had posed the question in terms that further highlighted the uncertainties of the future: "What will be the objective of the "next war?" What will the political situation be at that moment? What is it today? ... Will Germany attack us? If it attacks us, where should we defend ourselves?" Given the number of unknowns involved, Foch resisted the idea that the defense of France's current borders might guarantee the nation's territory in the years ahead. It was imperative to "seek out the front of war where it is and not where it is fixed in peacetime by treaties." Foch warned the other members of the CSG to "be wary of an abstract system which leads us to the error of digging ourselves into the soil." According to Foch, it was not reasonable to fortify behind the likely front of a future war. "Today we must defend ourselves at the Rhine," he insisted. "In fifteen years, if Germany crosses the Rhine, it will be in violation of the treaties and then we will have to run to the Rhine to make our barrier."[37]

At the moment when Foch and his colleagues grappled with the issue of the frontière's future location, Allied troops continued to occupy the Rhineland under the terms of the Treaty of Versailles.[38] That occupation further challenged the idea of guaranteeing territorial integrity by securing a political border located behind a likely future front. Even beyond the terms of this temporary French military presence on German territory, it seemed, to some military leaders, that the only effective way to protect the French border, and the "whole" of France it circumscribed, was to maintain the front of the "next war" well into enemy territory.

The problem of the current and future disjuncture between the nation's military and political borders would come up a number of times in the early 1920s. In 1923, Pétain would try to address these concerns, responding to three years of debate, studies, and reports on the subject. Pétain began by explaining what he saw as two main positions on defensive organization. While some of his colleagues (such as Buat) argued that this organization had the "single and unique purpose of permitting armies to block the enemy's access to the nation's territory," others saw it as a part of a larger "plan of operations." As Foch had before him, Pétain noted that the French army was "currently on the Rhine" and this made the situation more complicated.[39] Once again, history had its limited uses. Pétain was careful to point out that "when defensive systems were created in the past, the military border coincided with the political border." "Today," he observed, "our military border is in front of our political border."[40] Foch and others maintained that this state of affairs made the defense of the border itself unwise.

Pétain disagreed. "Fighting on the Rhine is one thing, assuring the integrity of national territory is another," he insisted. In order to truly guarantee territorial inviolability, something had to be done to protect the border itself. Regardless of plans for the fronts of the "next war," it would only be possible to build fortifications on or behind that border. According to Pétain, these were defensive measures that it would be "possible to realize more or less completely in peacetime."[41] Any strategies, whether offensive or defensive, intended for territory on the other side of the political border could only be determined and implemented at the (as yet unknown) time of mobilization for the "next war." The defense of the nation's borders was necessary in the event of the failure of whatever offensive plans might be executed beyond their limits. Inviolability, in other words, was a temporal as well as a spatial concern.

The idea of building fortifications to secure the nation's territory was an element of these discussions from the outset and presented an important opportunity for military leaders to look to the past as they tried to anticipate the "next war." Over the course of several meetings and reports, these officials debated what sort of fortifications they should construct where and with what strategic intentions. In 1922, the military created a Committee of Territorial Defense (CDT). Outlining a brief history of fortification, the agenda for the CDT's first meeting noted that fortification had been used in the past to protect individual cities and then to "cover both border cities and borders themselves." As of the last war, it made sense to refer to the "the entire country" as "a fortress under siege."[42] While the use of local and regional systems of fortification had continued to develop and expand over the years, the protection of sites within the nation would, from now on, be relocated to the borders. The demolition of the "outmoded" walls surrounding cities like Paris and Strasbourg were the most salient examples of what historian Antoine Prost reads as the postwar "enlargement of the idea of the siege."[43] The displacement of security from the nation's interior to its territorial limits had practical and symbolic implications at the local and the national levels.

The image of the nation as fortress ran throughout these discussions of territorial defense planning. During the CDT's first meeting, General Emile Hergault declared, "The question is to know if we will transform all of France into a fortress," suggesting that the committee consider "surrounding France with defenses that guarantee a maximum of resources."[44] Maréchal Joseph Joffre, the CDT's chairperson, also referred to "the *Nation*" as a "stronghold." "Without exception, all of the resources of the country would contribute to its defense" and therefore the goal of the military was to "protect all of France." General Buat concurred, claiming, "In fact, on the defensive, a nation like France is like a fortress under siege."[45] Buat called for a "return to…a system of a continuous surrounding wall," arguing that "all of the territory should be covered by a system of bastions."[46] Although he would characterize fortification as "a return," the system Buat envisioned for the "next war" would depart significantly from the defenses of the nineteenth century. As the general would explain elsewhere, the fortified system of Séré de Rivières "ignore[d] the principle of the inviolability of territory because it accept[ed], *a priori,* that the enemy surround an entire zone and that the battle, with all of its devastating consequences, be waged on national soil."[47] According to Buat, this flaw had contributed to the devastation of 1914–18. A wall around the border would be needed in the future.

The idea of the fortifying the "whole" nation was not entirely feasible, however. Buat would not hesitate to refer to the "national fortress" that France could become in the face of the "next war."[48] He nevertheless conceded that "the general notion…of a wall…is an ideal plan of which we will execute this or that part."[49] Having asked if all of France should be transformed into a fortress, General Hergault also acknowledged the existence of "a chasm between the conceptualization and the realization," insisting that "there is nothing wrong with conceiving of a wall and executing fragments in practice."[50] The CDT had begun its work in 1922. The military established a Committee of Frontier Defense (CDF) in 1925. In 1927, yet another body, the Committee of Fortified Regions (CORF) focused on the planning and construction of permanent fortification on key segments of the French border. A narrative of the conceptual and practical shifts in French military defense policy in this period can be traced in the successive names of these three decision-making groups. With each change in vocabulary, from the consideration of *térritoire* (territory) in general, to a focus on the nation's *frontières* (borders), to the fortification of specific *régions* (regions) as a privileged defensive system in preparation for the "next war," this crucial aspect of French military strategy became more focused, emphasizing specific regions or parts of the nation rather than the "whole" of France.

Despite the general acknowledgement that a continuous defensive barrier was neither desirable nor practical, a number of military leaders would repeatedly express their discomfort with the strategic ideal and the image of a *muraille,* a wall or rampart, of France. If Joffre claimed that "all of France" required protection, he had also warned, "We will only condemn our selves to defeat if we build a new Great Wall of China."[51] The "fortification of France as a whole" required investigation and the military would, inevitably, "make choices [and] establish a set of priorities."[52] Acknowledging the need to "choose the regions to organize and...not build everywhere," Joffre maintained "no one is asking that we build a continuous fortification running the entire length of our borders. We must look at those regions where we must help nature along."[53] In 1920, Guillaumat had cautioned his colleagues, "We will let ourselves be attacked by our adversary [if we] end up building a Great Wall of China on our border."[54] He later referred to this wall as "a dream, financially speaking and perhaps dangerous from a military point of view."[55] Guillaumat was particularly concerned about the illusion of impregnability the idea of a "Great Wall" seemed to invite and its impact outside the military. In a letter to Pétain in 1922, Guillaumat questioned what he perceived as a desire "to situate ourselves on a defensive terrain," taking particular exception to the language of a "Great Wall of France."[56] The general's concern was that this image would "more often than not be misunderstood and misinterpreted, particularly in government circles when the question of fortifications is raised there, for budgetary and other reasons."[57]

Invoking the Great Wall of China, an ancient, continuous barrier, Guillaumat, Joffre, and others dismissed the idea of a national fortress as anachronistic and unrealistic. Such a fantasy had no place in French defense strategy and preparation for the "next war." While they had emphasized inviolability and the imperative to secure the "whole" nation, these military leaders also qualified their plans for the protection of that national whole as practical, partial, and discontinuous. As they worked through questions about territory, borders, and defenses, the image of a "Great Wall" of France was nevertheless a powerful and recurrent trope. In their insistent return to this image of total impregnability, French military officials contributed to, even as they resisted, a growing myth about the nation's security in the future.

By the late 1920s, the fortification of the border became an even more important strategy of defense than it had been in years previous. The French government had, at the Hague Conference of 1929, agreed to a final evacuation of Allied troops from the Rhineland in 1930, five years ahead of the original schedule set out in 1919. Once that evacuation was complete, the nation's military and political borders would no longer be dislocated from one another as they had been since the end of the First World War. The defense of the border at the border made more sense under these circumstances. In December 1929, France's elected officials voted 2,900,000,000 francs to the project of territorial defense, including the construction of the system of fortification that would be dubbed the "Maginot Line." Before these funds were approved however, representatives from across the political spectrum voiced their concerns about the future security, inviolability, and fortification of the French frontier. As they did so, the theme of invasion (remembered and anticipated) was a central feature of the speeches they delivered and the questions they posed about the financial and strategic value of different defense strategies.[58]

On December 10, 1929, André Maginot, the minister of war, spoke in defense of his proposed military expenditures for 1930, including the funds required to build the fortified system that would eventually bear his name. In his remarks, Maginot underlined the need for France to prepare its territorial defenses "even in peacetime," noting that the imminent evacuation of the Rhineland only made matters more urgent. The minister also explained that the plans that had been devised "accentuate[d] the defensive character" of France. The relationship between France and its allies depended in part on the avoidance of any semblance of French aggression toward Germany. The perception that the military might be planning an offensive war could also ignite domestic concern among a wider public eager to avoid another conflict on the scale of the First World War.

The minister was careful to acknowledge that while military and political officials were in basic agreement about the "principle of the defensive organization" of the nation's territory, there was significant disagreement about the "means" of achieving and guaranteeing security. Maginot outlined in broad terms the "doctrinal controversies" that had pitted military and political officials against one another for almost a decade in debates over the tactics and matériel that would best serve the French cause in the "next war."

Focusing on the defense of the nation's borders, Maginot signaled the compromise that had emerged after years of study and discussion between proponents of different types of fortification. "In the end," Maginot explained, "we could not have permanent defensive structures everywhere, as some might have wished."[59] A system of continuous fortification was "too costly." Invoking, once again, the image of the nation as fortress, Maginot was clear that "even out of concern for effective security, no one could entertain the idea of building a sort of wall of France all along our borders."[60] The continued denial of the abstraction was, in some ways, testimony to its imaginative power. The idea of a "Great Wall" appeared again and again as the perceived antidote to the deep-seated fear of invasion and the imperative to prevent its devastating consequences in the future.

The commitment to a security that had been defined repeatedly in terms of the protection of the "whole" nation resulted in the partial realization of a discontinuous system of concrete installations barricading the border regions deemed most vulnerable to attack and invasion in the future. Despite disclaimers and adjustments to initial plans, the metaphor of a national fortress remained an important part of the military imagination and the rhetoric of its system of defense within and beyond military circles. Time and again, representations of the Maginot Line depicted the system as if it shielded all of France. The line's confident slogan, "Ils ne passeront pas" ("They shall not pass"), echoed the 1916 Battle of Verdun, an episode that epitomized the defense of French soil against a foreign enemy. The "Maginot Line" became the "Great Wall of France," seeming to protect the *whole* country from invasion as it purported to seal off the most vulnerable *part* of the border with Germany.

In 1939, an anonymous French officer, "Colonel X," published his account of the Maginot Line, *La Ligne Maginot: Bouclier de la France* (The Maginot Line: Shield of France). The title of the colonel's account indicated his perspective on the fortifications' capacities and, perhaps more importantly, their symbolic value. The line was a "shield," "a deadbolt blocking invasion and the routes of access," to the entire nation "and a belt of iron." The colonel emphasized the ways the system had "allowed for the rallying of the French forces in total security." The fortifications had a high "moral value" and the colonel underlined how important it was for the French population and for the "men who defend it" to "have confidence in its strength."[61]

In 1940, shortly before the French defeat, the commander-in-chief of the French ground forces sent a memo to the minister of information (Military Bureau) entitled "Faits et chiffres conçernant la ligne Maginot" (Facts and Figures concerning the Maginot Line).[62] Three and a half pages long, the memo outlined the "nine years of construction [that] had enabled the erection of a protective barrier at the border." It emphasized the existence of "a line of fire without lacunae" that was "an effective obstacle." A system of great "continuity" and "cohesion," the fortifications "blocked the traditional route of invasions forcefully." As the memo pointed out, the line was also an engineering feat of awesome proportions. The underground sections "represented a volume equivalent to...a large canal linking Paris to Bordeaux." The *ouvrages* above ground had required a mass of concrete equal to the volume of the Grand Pyramid of Egypt whose construction spanned a generation." The weight in steel of the installations was over "six times the weight of the Eiffel tower." Finally, the range of fire of the line's weapons, "put in line, end to end, would form a band longer than the distance from the North Pole to the Equator."

The memo attributed the successful blockade of German aggression since the beginning of this latest war to the "existence of this Wall of France," characterizing the strength of the system in the same hyperbolic terms as the imagined "Great Wall" and national fortress that it had come to represent. The slippage between these fantastic projections and the actual fortifications located in this sector of the border recurred throughout this eleventh-hour praise of the line as "a coherent system, of formidable strength, that covered our borders on the eve of the conflict." In its final words, the memo gestured, once again, to the ideal of the "Great Wall," declaring, even at that late date, "France is unceasingly perfecting the rampart; the work continues."[63] It was a ringing endorsement of the fortifications not long before their capitulation.

Total Vulnerability

A massive system of permanent fortification appeared to some French observers to be an unsuitable strategy because it did not cover all of the vulnerable points on the border. The idea that the "next war" might be a conflict of rapid, mobile forces on the ground and in the air challenged the idea of protecting the "whole" of France in even more profound ways. During the December 1929 Chamber of Deputies debates on defensive planning, Pierre Cathala, the Radical deputy for Seine-et-Oise, expressed his concerns in terms of an opposition between the past and the future: "I have the feeling that at the present time, the battle we are preparing is the one that we have just waged during the war of 1914–18."[64] Permanent fortification seemed to Cathala to belong to "the school of war...the study of the facts of the past." Warning his colleagues about "the preparation of chemical warfare that is, for Germany, the secret and veritable formula for the struggle of the future," Cathala insisted, "in reality, the life of the army should be oriented towards the future, given that its main objective is the preparation of national defense for future conflicts."[65] Cathala articulated his distrust of a system of permanent fortification in terms of a "dualism between historical facts and the necessity to look toward the future...a dilemma from which we have not freed ourselves."[66] Other representatives challenged aspects of the proposed plans as well, raising questions about the nature, location, and overall value of fortification. Addressing Maginot directly, Pierre Cot, the Radical from the Savoie, asked, "Are you sure of your concrete Mr. War Minister?"[67] Cot pointed to the existence of routes of invasion other than those "secured" by the proposed fortifications. Some of Cot's colleagues wondered about whether territorial limits would even play an important role in the "next war." "Borders will be useless in a new war because it will

be a war of airplanes," claimed Emile Faure, the Republican socialist from
Indre-et-Loire.[68]

Members of the chamber from across the political spectrum expressed
a range of financial and technical concerns about the nature of the defenses proposed. They also wondered about the contradiction of pursuing
such elaborate military preparation at a time when the French government
claimed to be seeking peace and disarmament. A program of such proportions could jeopardize the "whole" of France economically speaking and
even a defensive system might give the appearance of French aggression in
the international realm. While representatives from all parties raised these
issues, those on the political left were particularly vocal in their objections.
René Burtin, the Socialist representative from Saone-et-Loire, referred to
the permanent fortifications proposed for the border as "anchored ships"
that would provide only an "illusory protection." "These fortifications,"
Burtin suggested, "will let the enemy pass." Responding directly to the
alleged impregnability that was crucial to the image of the Maginot Line,
Burtin followed his provocative statement with an outline of a "new war"
he believed would take a very "different form" from the war of 1914–18.
Highlighting the likelihood of aerial bombardment, nighttime attacks, and
the use of toxic gases, Burtin also warned his colleagues about the threat
of biological weapons that would be "more formidable than chemical
warfare."[69] According to Burtin, "none of these eventualities [were] imagined." "What will become of your fortifications in a war like this?" Burtin
asked.[70]

As the construction of the Maginot Line got underway in the early 1930s,
military and civilian representations of the "next war" proliferated in France.
Many of these representations of the future reiterated the fears and doubts
that had already been raised in the 1920s. One of the most forceful critiques
of the course being pursued by the French military came from Lieutenant
Colonel (later General) Charles de Gaulle, the man whose name would become synonymous with the French resistance after the defeat of 1940. In
1934, de Gaulle published a detailed study entitled *Vers l'armée de métier*,
a book that would eventually be translated into English as *The Army of the
Future*.[71] While the original French title did not include the word *future*, the
anticipation of the "next war" was certainly a focus of this military manifesto on the need for a professionally trained, highly mobile military force
in France. De Gaulle's analysis was divided into two parts: "Why?" and
"How?" Each part of the study was further divided into sections treating
the issues of protection, technique, policy, composition, employment, and
the military high command.

De Gaulle began his analysis with a discussion of the natural frontiers and the "body of the country" as the key to understanding the war and the army of the future: "As looking at a portrait suggests the impression of the subject's destiny to the observer, so the map of France tells our fortune." The lieutenant colonel went over the physical geography of the nation, highlighting the Rhine "which nature meant the Gauls to have as their boundary" and "the northeast frontier" as a "breach in the ramparts…the age-old weakness of the country."[72] "The Franco-German frontier is an open wound," claimed de Gaulle, returning to the image of the national body as a whole that had suffered and remained vulnerable to attack.[73] "Gaping wide open, exposing her defenseless body to blows, deprived of all respite and all refuge, where then can our country find her latent protection except in arms?" he asked dramatically.[74] In de Gaulle's estimation, the "army of the future" would need to be a professional force capable of moving quickly in its execution of offensive tactics. It would make use of the latest technologies and would not remain committed to the defense of a continuous front on the nation's borders. *The Army of the Future* included illustrations of tanks and airplanes and argued that thousands more of these weapons would be required to win another war against German forces that would be more formidable in number. Massive fortification was a mistake, the result of an "eagerness to rely on the past in order to picture the future."[75] While this approach could hold "some advantages," it could also hinder military planning for the "next war." "It is true," de Gaulle pointed out, "that at all times France has tried to obscure the breaches in her frontiers by fortifications. She is still doing the same."[76] At the same time, the lieutenant colonel was clear in his disapproval of the decisions that had resulted from too much emphasis on the fortified "defense of the border at the border": "Our future strategy can no more limit itself to the strict defense of our territory than our policy can be confined to watching over frontiers."[77]

In his 1930 study, *Le Danger aérien et l'avenir du pays* (The Aerial Threat and the Future of the Country), Lieutenant Colonel Arsène Vauthier had declared that modern "aviation called into question the notion of the border" altogether.[78] According to Vauthier, before the possibilities of air travel, national defense had been dependent on the protection and security of the physical border between the nation and other countries, including the natural boundaries of water, mountains, and forests. As long as battles had remained fixed to the ground and sea, the core of national defense rested on protecting borderlands and coasts. The threatening promise of aviation demanded a new spatial understanding of "the entire region exposed to the assault of enemy aircraft as an aerial border."[79] Vauthier lamented what he perceived as the neglect of the aerial threat in France relative to other European countries, insisting that the possibility of air attack should be an important concern for the entire French population, well beyond the military. This meant that civil defense on the part of the French population would be crucial in the "next war." The possibilities of the air war of the future represented a danger to the country as a whole.

In the preface to Vauthier's book, Maréchal Hubert Lyautey urged readers to pay attention to Vauthier's analysis of "the worrying unknown of the war of the future," pointing out that the threat of aerial warfare "was the only true novelty of the last European war."[80] Vauthier warned that aerial attacks could seize the nation suddenly, that "peace could end abruptly, even without a period of political tension."[81] He worried that France was not "ready...to see enemy planes, carrying one or two tons of payload or more...set fire to Paris, Lyon, Rouen, Lille, Nancy, Reims, and Troyes and inundate them with noxious gases and explosives." Insisting, "the entire future of the country is at stake," Vauthier predicted that "the entire civil population will be placed abruptly on the warfront, despite the efforts of ground army troops, despite all obstacles and all fortifications."[82]

Just as it had become the focal point of military fortification, the northeastern border of France figured as the principal point of departure for the hypothetical aerial attacks Vauthier anticipated.[83] Using this point of origin, it was possible to calculate the times of night when different targets within France's borders would be attacked.[84] In a series of illustrations, Vauthier showed that aviation brought with it a whole new spatial configuration in which the frontier, no longer "a line," would now have to be understood as "a surface."[85] Given that the threat of aerial attack mooted the defense of the traditional borders of France, the second part of Vauthier's study focused entirely on preparation of the inside, rather than the outline of the nation. The lieutenant colonel underlined the importance of equipping cities within France's borders with antiaircraft weaponry, as well as preparing forms of passive defense, such as shelters, that would protect the civilian population from bombardment.

In 1936, the French colonel Albert Grasset warned readers of *La Petite Illustration* (a supplement to the weekly magazine *Illustration*) that "all of [France's] territory" would be "exposed to foreign aerial attack" in the "next war."[86] The Republican-socialist senator Paul Bénazet also expressed his concern that France was not adequately prepared for the future. In his 1938 study, *Défense nationale: Notre sécurité* (National Defense: Our Security), Bénazet lamented the fact that, while France had, in the past, occupied the number one position in terms of aerial force, the failure to keep up with recent technological advances meant that much French equipment had become outmoded.[87] According to Bénazet, French inferiority in this regard reflected more than budgetary concerns or a weak birthrate. French factories had not been sufficiently modernized to build up-to-date aircraft, in Bénazet's assessment. While he appreciated the value of land fortifications, he warned that such installations "only defend us against one form of sudden attack."[88]

The idea that the fortification of the nation's borders offered only one, extremely limited form of protection found its way from the debates of generals, political leaders, and military experts to a broader popular culture in France in the interwar years. In 1931, the French weekly *VU* published a special issue on "La Prochaine guerre" (The Next War), a panorama of the dangers of aerial warfare (figure 3.1).[89] The magazine included articles by experts such as Vauthier, as well as fictional accounts anticipating the outbreak of a future conflict beginning in 1932, 1936, or later. In photographs and photomontages that were playful, but ominous, the "next war" represented in *VU*'s pages was one in which the "whole" of France was completely vulnerable. If a future war could strike suddenly at the heart of the nation, as Vauthier had warned, systems of fortification and boundaries like the political borders of France would be virtually irrelevant. The "whole" of France would, as Vauthier predicted, be transformed into a war zone. The images in the magazine emphasized the transformation of civilian life, depicting invasion not as an intrusion or violation of the edges of French territory, but as a total occupation and transformation of all the activities and spaces of national life. Featuring masks and protective clothing, these "scenes from the war of the future"—a woman and man "flirting," the Civic Guard helping the wounded at La Madeleine in Paris, and the Eiffel Tower exploding—were scenes in which the targets of military attack had become most immediate (figures 3.2, 3.3, and 3.4).

On the opposite end of the spectrum of defense from a nation sealed at the border, its body guarded as a whole, stood the intimacy of the gas mask, a barrier to protect the individual body of each French citizen. The gas mask was a defense against a form of invasion in which existing definitions of the frontière that Lucien Fevbre outlined in 1928—a "strip of land," a line of "demarcation," and a "defensive barrier"—seemed irrelevant. This was a genre of attack so insidious that it would defy traditional definitions of the space, territory, and targets of war. The gas mask figured as a central icon of threat and "passive defense" in visions of a war that would strike swiftly at the core of the nation and the lives of all of its citizens. Just as the Maginot Line had the metaphoric power to represent total

3.1. "Numéro spéciale: La Prochaine Guerre." Cover illustration, *VU*, 1931. Trucage, A. Noel. Courtesy of the Ryerson and Burnham Libraries, Art Institute of Chicago.

3.2. "Flirt," from "Scènes de la guerre future" *VU*, 1931. Photo, Universal. Courtesy of the Ryerson and Burnham Libraries, Art Institute of Chicago.

3.3. "La Garde civique porte secours au premier blessé place de la Madeleine." *VU*, 1931. Trucage, A. Noel. Courtesy of the Ryerson and Burnham Libraries, Art Institute of Chicago.

3.4. "Tour Eiffel (1889–1932)." *VU*, 1931. Trucage, A. Noel. Courtesy of the Ryerson and Burnham Libraries, Art Institute of Chicago.

impregnability, the gas mask had the metaphoric power to represent total vulnerability.

The Nation's Bodies

It was difficult indeed to represent the future of the nation as a whole in the interwar years. Military strategists had tried to isolate the "next war," to seal up the borders of the nation in order to protect its "body" into the

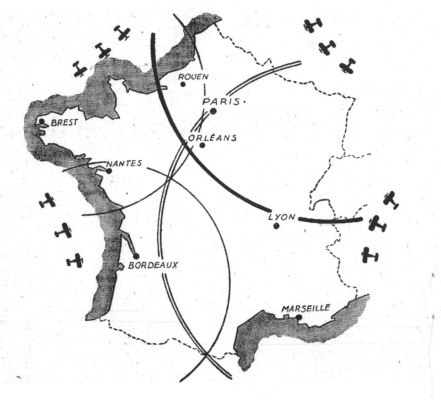

3.5. "Aerial weapons threaten France throughout its territory." *La Petite Illustration*, 1939.

future. But new technologies and weapons had complicated the definitions of the frontière, generating territorial and corporeal analogies and metonymies that ricocheted throughout the discourses (both military and civilian) of security and defense in the interwar years.

In the summer of 1939, just a few months before France entered the war against Germany, a range of publications alerted the French population to the methods and strategies of "passive defense." The popular weekly *Illustration*, for example, published an entire issue of *La Petite Illustration*, devoted to "La Défense passive" (Passive Defense). Throughout the pages of this issue, the French population could learn about the possibilities of air and gas attack, as well as the appropriate responses to potential war emergencies. Illustrations and maps depicted possible attack scenarios (figure 3.5) and offered strategies for dealing with the effects of gas (wearing protective gear, closing windows, and seeking refuge in underground shelters). The movie house, the family home, the school, and the factory—all of these sites would become points of defense in a nation at war.[90]

The image on the cover of "Passive Defense" (figure 3.6) exemplified the challenge of defining the nation and its security in territorial terms, including competing versions of the "whole" of France in the interwar years: a single figure, equipped with a gas mask and protective clothing—the new face of war—took up most of the space of the outline of the French nation. Both of these bodies were targets, fronts and territories to be protected and defended. The significance of using a single French body "entirely" protected to stand for the "whole" of France went beyond linking the threats of aerial and gas attack to the problem of the nation's frontier. The idea that the strength and vitality of the national body depended on the strength and vitality of its individual citizen bodies had appeared in French political discourse and pronatalist propaganda since the French defeat in the Franco-Prussian War.[91] A low French birthrate, combined with the unprecedented loss of life between 1914 and 1918, increased exponentially existing French anxieties about depopulation and national weakness. The connection between the nation's bodies and the national body was linked in important ways to the ideologies of gender and race following World War I. Fears about a declining citizen body contributed to concern over the breakdown of traditional gender roles and the potential impact of immigration (European and from outside Europe) on the racial makeup of the French population.[92]

Population was, inevitably, a matter of serious military concern. In 1922, General Frédéric Hellot of the CSG had pointed to a particular French demographic inadequacy that rendered fortification a military necessity. Like many of his colleagues, Hellot underlined the imperative to "do everything possible to keep the enemy from violating [France's] national territory, exploiting its resources, destroying its riches, letting terror reign in the hearts of its people." According to Hellot, "Fortifications allow us to save our forces along part of the front." This "savings" was particularly important "for a nation in a situation like France's vis-à-vis Germany." Hellot claimed the ratio of French to German forces to be "2:3," noting, "demographic trends in the two countries do not encourage us to hope, unfortunately, that this situation will improve in the future." It was therefore essential "to call upon the resources of fortification to increase [the nation's] chances" of surviving and winning the "next war."[93]

A number of military strategists conceived of permanent fortification as "a valuable resource [that] enables the economy of men" and "a financial sacrifice that must be made to compensate for the weakness of our national

LA
PETITE ILLUSTRATION

LA
DÉFENSE
PASSIVE

PROTECTION DES POPULATIONS CIVILES CONTRE LES ATTAQUES AÉRIENNES

3.6. "La Défense Passive." Cover illustration, *La Petite Illustration*, 1939.

birth rate."[94] The construction of fortifications on the border represented the protection of the French population and of soldiers' lives. It was a *prosthetic* strategy congruent with the refusal to revisit the slaughter and brutality of the last war by replacing and supplementing human bodies with concrete in the "next war." After World War I proposals to reorganize the French armed forces included the reduction of the length of military service in France to one year in keeping with the peace and a larger imperative to prevent future loss of life on the scale that had been witnessed between 1914 and 1918. Legislation to this effect had been passed in 1928.[95] Concerned about protecting soldiers, the officials of the CSG also acknowledged that fortification represented compensation for a lack of prepared, fighting bodies in the first place.

An important aim of the system the military constructed was the protection of troops from contact with enemy fire. Bodies, however, were essential to the nation and the "next war" would not be possible without them. In a report submitted to the CSG in 1923, General Guillaumat had warned it was a mistake to let loose the notion "that a material system of any kind might be substituted for the hard work and preparation of soldiers."[96] Foch had also expressed his concern, noting, "The defense plan of a country could not be based on fortification, inert matter that is only worth the troops stationed there."[97] At the same time, however, depictions of the Maginot Line emphasized concrete over soldiers, underlining its role as protection in the "next war." In 1923, Lieutenant Colonel Louis Chauvineau reiterated the problem of French numbers, concluding that "only permanent fortification c[ould] prevent disaster" at the outset of the "next war."[98] "Along a permanent front," Chauvineau argued, "it is not the fortification, but the soldier who should be held in reserve. Fortifications should oppose the brunt of initial enemy attack." Chauvineau went as far as suggesting that the soldier "would be virtually a spectator of the battle between enemy fire and concrete" in the early stages of a conflict, buying time for the full mobilization of the nation's forces.[99] Fortification in general, and the Maginot Line in particular, had virtually supplanted the *poilu* (a colloquial term meaning "hairy" used to refer to the average soldier) as the central icon of French military strength and resistance.

In 1927, General Joseph Maurin of the CSG cautioned his colleagues not to "forget that the continuity of a fortified front was a fatal obligation— Only this continuity, given the relative weakness of our numbers, can withstand the blow of armies much more numerous than our own."[100] General Filloneau suggested that by pitting concrete against the "exposed assailant... many soldiers and human lives can be saved." Filloneau's elaboration of the advantages of fortification implied that the installations held possibilities that rendered them even more useful than the troops stationed there. He emphasized that concrete fortification was "constantly ready since it has been constructed during peacetime." Unlike the living soldier, fortification held an "immediate usefulness, given its firepower…the trench and surrounding system [would] be useful to it, but not indispensable." According to Filloneau, the new system of defense was one in which "permanent fortification becomes the first instrument used in battle."[101] Fortification had taken the place of the traditional soldier up to a point, not only to preserve his life, but because concrete could provide a more effective system of defense than one comprised of bodies.

The perceived relationship between a weak French population and the fortification of the nation that appeared in military discussions also found expression in pronatalist representations of the failure of French families to protect France through reproduction. The March 1939 issue of *Natalité,* the official organ of the Alliance nationale contre la dépopulation (National Alliance against Depopulation) included a pamphlet that illustrated yet another perspective on the future of the French frontière. Entitled "La dénatalité, c'est l'éffondrement de la défense nationale" (Depopulation leads to the collapse of national defense), the pamphlet had been sent out to "3000 journalists and writers" in France, as well as to "all members of parliament." In a first run, the alliance circulated at least 42,000 copies.[102] The pamphlet's illustrations included a rather unusual map of the border region in the northeastern part of France that was, by this time, the site of the Maginot Line (figure 3.7). On this map, the French border with Germany was divided into a number of sections. The accompanying text claimed: "If the defense of the border were equally divided among all families, here is how France would be defended." In the "Sector of large families," with five or more children, a "numerical superiority" would ensure the "victorious counter-attack of our troops." In the "Sector of middle-size families" with three or four children, there would be "sufficient troops; the enemy would not pass." In the "Sector of families with one or two children, however, "Our troops would be crushed…the Maginot Line would be pierced quickly." And finally, in the "Sector of homes without children," not fully recognized as "families," "the German army would flood into France across our empty trenches."[103]

The pronatalist mapping of population as fortification placed every French family on what seemed the most likely front of a future war. In the interwar years, the superimposition of what appeared to be worrying statistics on French family size and reproduction laid out as a discontinuous, flawed

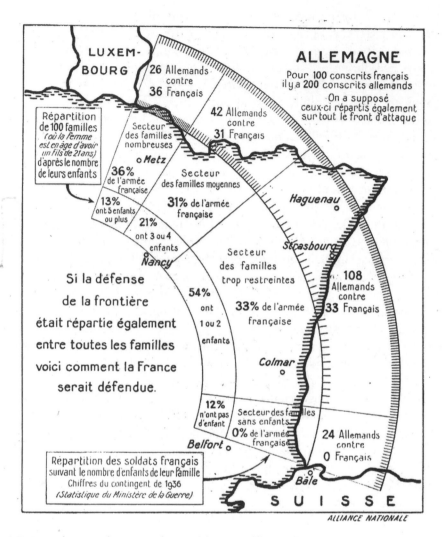

LUXEM-BOURG

26 Allemands contre 36 Français

ALLEMAGNE

Pour 100 conscrits français il y a 200 conscrits allemands

On a supposé ceux-ci répartis également sur tout le front d'attaque

Répartition de 100 familles *(où la femme est en âge d'avoir un fils de 21 ans)* d'après le nombre de leurs enfants

Secteur des familles nombreuses

o *Metz*

36% de l'armée française

13% ont 5 enfants ou plus

21% ont 3 ou 4 enfants

Nancy

42 Allemands contre 31 Français

Secteur des familles moyennes

31% de l'armée française

Haguenau o

Strasbourg

Si la défense de la frontière était répartie également entre toutes les familles voici comment la France serait défendue.

Secteur des familles trop restreintes

54% ont 1 ou 2 enfants

33% de l'armée française

108 Allemands contre 33 Français

Colmar o

12% n'ont pas d'enfant

Secteur des familles sans enfants

0% de l'armée française

24 Allemands contre 0 Français

Belfort o

Répartition des soldats français suivant le nombre d'enfants de leur famille
Chiffres du contingent de 1936
(Statistique du Ministère de la Guerre)

Bâle o

S U I S S E

ALLIANCE NATIONALE

3.7. "Dénatalité." *Natalité. Organe bimestriel de propagande de l'Alliance nationale contre la dépopulation,* 1939. Courtesy of the Service historique de l'armée de terre, Vincennes.

system of fortification against outside attack, served as a compelling emblem of panic. The frontière had become the practical and symbolic focus of French territorial security. Using the trope of the fortification of the Franco-German border to represent the nation "underdefended" by low rates of reproduction, pronatalist propaganda traded on the obsession with absolute territorial integrity and inviolability that had been the focus of French military, political, and cultural attention since the end of World War I. The alliance's map depicting the frontière contorted the metonymic identification of the northeastern border with "whole" of France in yet another way: in this case, the inadequacies of the population of France as a whole could be visualized most effectively by representing this national weakness and military insecurity in terms of the penetration of the part of the border that represented, simultaneously, the nation's vulnerability (as a historic route of invasion) and its alleged impregnability (as the site of its most impressive system of fortification). To suggest that a failure of French families to reproduce adequately rendered that border insecure not only cut to the quick of anxieties about whether or not military defense strategies including fortification could protect the French population; it implied that the nation's protection, beginning with its borders, depended on the strength of its (civilian) families. It was the strength of the home rather than the battle front that would determine the fate of France as a whole.

So — what else is new?

The Border Consumed

In the early months of 1940, the French weekly magazine *Match* published a series of reports and images from the front. Understandably a cause of tremendous fear and anxiety, the war that had begun in 1939 was also the object of popular fascination and a certain degree of spectacle. Offering civilian readers a glimpse into military life, and reassuring those at home of the well-being of soldiers stationed at the front, magazines like *Match* and *Illustration* contributed to an image of the French nation sufficiently prepared for battle. Coverage before and during the war focused on the French troops stationed at the Maginot Line. From the mobilization on, the French press reported visits to the Maginot Line by famous personalities, depicting daily life in the underground fortifications. This coverage included *Match*'s own "Noel à la ligne Maginot," a special focus on Christmas 1939.

Images of military installations and reports from the Maginot Line that emphasized "human interest" stories were not the only evidence of "frontière fever" in France in the months before and during World War II. Advertisers traded on the idea of national defense in their own ways, underlining the themes of territorial strength and protection. An advertisement for Palmolive shaving cream invoked the "tagline" of the so-called *drôle-de-guerre* (phoney war): "Rien à signaler" (Nothing to report).[104] While reports from the front used the phrase to refer to a lack of action in the early months of the war, the Palmolive advertisement featured three women exclaiming

"Nothing to report on his cheeks or his chin!" The surface of a man's skin could be perfectly smooth, a zone of tranquility analogous to the border of the nation (thus far) secured and free of bloodshed. An advertisement for *Banania* touted the hot beverage as a kind of "Défense passive pour votre corps" (Passive defense for your body). "Overwork, irritation, insomnia, alarms, worries, all of these things risk compromising your health," it read. "Put your organism in a state of passive defense."[105] Another ad claimed *Banania* was a vital "D.C.A.," or "Défense contre l'anémie" (Defense against anemia).[106] Yet another promised that, while babies were vulnerable, parents could avoid losing anymore sleep by seeking out "the security" of Nestlé's. A baby's body could become "an impregnable fortress!" steeled against the "countless enemies…watching for the slightest slackening of resistance."[107] Just as the Maginot Line guarded the nation's frontier, Nestlé could help fortify individual French babies against attack.

These advertisements all appeared in issues of *Match* from January until April 1940. They were neither the first nor the last advertising images to deploy the theme of military security and defense in France or elsewhere. Indeed, the 1931 issue of *VU* that I discussed earlier included an advertisement for Ovomaltine, a "fortifying" beverage (figure 3.8). The caption read: "The happiness we have to defend." Produced years before the *Match* ads noted above, this image from the magazine's special issue on the "next war" testified to a civilian preoccupation with defense that long predated the war's outbreak. Considered in isolation, these examples might be dismissed as expressions of an obvious and understandable popular preoccupation with enemies, fronts, and fortification. But if we look at their appropriation of military vocabulary and imagery as part of a broader French cultural fixation on the frontière and its protection, these popular images take on a much deeper significance. Indeed, they become cultural artifacts of a very specific moment in the history of the representation of the space and bodies of the nation in France. The emphasis in these ads on the surface and strength of the civilian body, from the nourishment of healthy babies to the iron levels of fortified adults, echoed the military debates and strategies intended to guard the nation and its borders in the interwar years.

These images and slogans also revealed an intricate set of connections between physical and cultural entities that had become inextricably linked by 1940: the territory of the human body and the territory of the nation. The protection of the vulnerable civilian body was crucial to the discussion and representation of possible future military attacks on French soldiers and civilians. An interesting variant on the theme of republicanism (the nation one and indivisible), this metaphoric relationship between the individual

3.8. "Le Bonheur qu'il faut defendre." Advertisement for Ovomaltine. *VU*, 1931. © Associated British Foods. Courtesy of the Ryerson and Burnham Libraries, Art Institute of Chicago.

and national body expressed anxiety about new forms of warfare that could render every piece of national territory—and even every single body in the nation—a possible front of the "next war." One could only hope that those fronts remain, as Palmolive promised, unbroken surfaces, with "nothing to report." Finally, the fortification of civilian babies in particular was an image that exploited historical anxieties about natality and national strength in France. Military and political officials, as well as pronatalists, had already identified the weakness of the French population in numerical terms as a crucial military disadvantage in the planning and preparation for war. The use of military phrases in advertisements for everyday products may have been intended only as playful metaphor. Nonetheless, these cheerful promises of calm, resistance, and strength bore the traces of real fears and anxieties that troubled the French cultural landscape during the interwar years: borders could be multiple and unstable, the fortified system protecting the nation could only ever be partial, and every French civilian body had become, at least potentially, a genuine military target.

In his 1986 study, *L'Identité de la France* (*The Identity of France*), historian Fernand Braudel declared, "The frontier has always devoured the history of France."[108] Braudel worked with Lucien Febvre, the historian whose analysis of the *frontière* I examined at the beginning of this chapter. Like Febvre, Braudel recognized the significance of territory and its limits to the history of the French state, its military conflicts and defeats, and a national identity rooted in soil as well as culture. The interwar years, as I have argued here, constituted a unique moment in that history, a moment when contests over the very meaning of the "whole" of France and its defense expressed deep anxieties about the fate of the nation in the years and decades to come. While the border may have preoccupied and "devoured" France's past, some of the imagined configurations of the "next war" implied that the future might, in its own turn, devour the border.

So – how does this chapter connect w/ first 2 chapters?

CHAPTER 4

The Future Is a Foreign Country

In January 1920, a new play by Eugène Brieux began its run at the Théâtre de l'Odéon in Paris.[1] A Parisian playwright born in 1858, Brieux was a member of the Académie française and the author of a number of dramatic works including *Blanchette* (1892), *L'Engrenage* (1894), *La Robe Rouge* (1900), and *La Femme Seule* (1912). When the full text of his latest play, *Les Américains chez nous* (The Americans In Our Midst), appeared in a February 1920 issue of *La Petite Illustration,* the following note appeared on the front page: "This play is dedicated to the women of the United States who tended to our suffering." Referring to the thousands of American nurses who had served in France during the First World War, Brieux signed his dedication: "A humble and respectful tribute in gratitude from a French man."[2]

Set in the French countryside just after the end of the war, *Les Américains chez nous* centers on the Charvet family: Henri, his sister Henriette, and their father, Monsieur Charvet. Henri returns home from the war after falling in love with Nellie Brown, a volunteer nurse from Illinois. Having hoped Henri might marry a wealthy, local French girl and take up a medical practice in the area, Henriette is devastated when she learns of her brother's plans to marry Nellie and move with her to the United States. George Robert Smith, a U.S. Marine, also figures in the play. As the domestic scandal over Henri's engagement erupts, Monsieur Charvet is involved in negotiations with Smith over the sale of land that has been in the Charvet family for centuries.

Over the course of Brieux's three acts, public and private exchanges between the play's characters lead to the discussion of cultural differences between France and the United States. Stereotypes of French and American women and men, Brieux's characters stage the love/hate relationship between their respective nations. Nellie is a practical, willful woman of the "New world." She arrives at the Charvet residence unannounced, she is forceful in her interactions with Henri (addressing him only in English), and she insists they return to her native Chicago. Her presence in the Charvet home reveals divergences between French and American gender norms, including ideas about the role of women in marriage and the family. Henriette is Nellie's alter ego in the play. The embodiment of a traditional French femininity, she is deeply devoted to her family and respectful of her ancestry. Beyond the domestic scene, Smith's legal and property entanglements also highlight tensions between French and American approaches to business and financial matters. Workers in Smith's employ complain about his factory methods and "Taylorism," his disregard for French values and conventions.[3]

In *Les Américains chez nous,* the encounter between characters and cultures is complicated throughout: Henri is in love with his American fiancée, but she disturbs his family and wants to take him away from his home. Smith and Henriette have little in common, but the attraction between them grows. Other characters in the play resent the presence and influence of Americans at the same time that they are unable to refuse the aid and financial investment these foreigners offer. The dramatic tension between France and "America" comes across most starkly in the exchanges between Henriette and Smith. In one scene, for example, Henriette becomes very emotional over the felling of an old oak tree, lamenting the erosion of tradition in service of "hideous utility."[4] In another, Smith proposes to raze a hill of great historic significance to the Charvet family. Henriette expresses her dismay at the American's willingness to dispense with the past. "And all of our memories?" she asks him. Smith suggests she "let them fade. Replace them." "With what?" pleads Henriette. "With plans," Smith retorts.[5]

At a number of moments like this one, *Les Américains chez nous* staged a set of binaries that held tremendous rhetorical power in France throughout the interwar years: a clash between French and American "values" and approaches to life, the struggle between "tradition" and "modernity," the pull between an idealized past and an uncertain and sometimes threatening, future. In the play, Brieux figures France as a nation saturated with history. Fearful of and resistant to American methods and proposals for change, French society seems (like Henriette Charvet) to be weighed down by memories. Embodied by Nellie and Smith, "America" appears in the play as a set of attitudes and behaviors: an unshakable belief in technological innovation, a commitment to productivity and profit, and a disdain for the habits and ways of the past, Brieux's conclusion to this dramatic meeting of cultures is neither perfectly happy nor entirely heartbreaking. Henri, having decided to "prepare the future" in France, rather than abroad, does not go to Chicago with Nellie.[6] Henriette and Smith fall in love and get married. From the ashes of one culturally mixed union, another is born.

Depicting "America" as alternately appealing and frightening to its French characters, *Les Américains chez nous* was a theatrical contribution to a protracted history of representations of the "New world" as the cultural "Other" of the "Old." Indeed, French ideas about "America" had been conflicted for centuries before Brieux's play opened on the Parisian stage for the first time. As scholars such as Jean-Baptiste Duroselle, Tony Judt, Jean-Philippe Mathy, and Philippe Roger have demonstrated, the subject of "America" has been a preoccupation of French thinkers since the eighteenth century.[7] Focusing their attention on the phenomenon of "anti-Americanism" in particular, these authors have also shown that, for many French observers, thinking about American society, politics, and culture has been, and remains, a way of thinking about France itself. Economic and political shifts in both France and the United States have, at different historical moments, shaped a range of sympathetic and hostile cultural representations of each nation in the eyes of the other. Varied in its forms and contents, the perception on both sides of a significant "cultural distance" between France and "America" has been a persistent feature of the historical relationship between the two nations for more than two hundred years.[8]

While the authors I have cited above have done much to illuminate our understandings of how the French have perceived "America," they linger only briefly if at all on the ways that "America" has become inextricably bound up with how many French observers understand and define "the future." This habit has a history, and the interwar years constituted a crucial episode in that history. In the introduction to this book, I suggested that an analysis of representations of the future in France from 1918 to 1939 might reveal a great deal about the cultural landscape of the present in the interwar years. The first three chapters of this study focused on the future imagined in ideas about the body, the home, the city, and the territorial borders of the nation. During this period, these physical entities, spaces, and limits all functioned as privileged sites for the projection of France forward in time. Referring to international ideas, influences, and perceived threats, these visions of a "prosthetic" everyday life and labor, a "city of the future," and a "next war," expressed anxieties about the preservation of a distinctly

French national culture and its possible contamination by outside forces. "America" has already figured in discussions about the working and resting bodies of French men and women, and in debates about the transformation of Paris in the future. As the previous chapter has shown, the "German enemy" also played a major role as an anticipated menace, particularly with respect to the fear of another war of invasion. In a final chapter on language, I will examine some of the ways that political and cultural internationalism could further inspire interwar anxieties about the demise of "Frenchness" in the future.

This chapter considers the future's nationality from yet another perspective. In the pages that follow, the culture of anticipation was, once again, a discursive field whose architects were preoccupied with traces and disappearance. In this case, the trace of the future was the United States of America itself, an entire nation that could be visited and observed in the present. Throughout the interwar years, a number of French novelists, academics, and journalists suggested that the future of France was always already American, belonging to a foreign country elsewhere in time as well as space. In multiple descriptions and analyses of the civilization across the Atlantic, these authors framed the "cultural distance" between France and the United States as a difference in time. Using "the future" as a rhetorical device to frame their evaluations of the differences between France and "America," they also used "America" as a way of understanding and thinking about the future.

Perhaps the most famous of these commentators was Georges Duhamel, a French physician, writer, and winner of the prestigious Prix Goncourt in 1918. Published in 1930, Duhamel's *Scènes de la vie future* took France by storm, becoming the most widely cited and debated text in a critical mass of writing on "America" in the interwar years. Translated into English in 1931 as *America the Menace: Scenes from the Life of the Future*, Duhamel's account made the equation between "America" and "the future" most explicit.[9] *Scènes* was not the only reading that forged a link between the two in the French cultural imagination during these years, however. Before and after Duhamel traveled to the United States, many other French observers also considered the implications of American methods and ways of life for Europe as a whole and for France in particular.[10] Following the publication of *Scènes,* several writers made direct references to Duhamel's account in their own depictions of "America" as a "danger," a "menace," and even a "cancer."

The French authors whose accounts I explore below often turned to the language and images of science fiction as they sought to describe their physical and cultural experiences of "America." Like a fantastic voyage to outer space, the passage from France to the United States seemed to give these authors the opportunity to travel through time. The representation of the journey as a crossing from past to future was a recurrent trope in their portrayals of "America." Arriving in New York, many French visitors lingered on the American metropolis as the incarnation in the present of a "city of the future." The streets of urban centers such as Manhattan and Chicago became landscapes of anticipation in these travel narratives. These readings of American architecture and cities would, in turn, feed the debates over the fate of the French capital that I explored in chapter 2. The vertiginous height of skyscrapers, the speed of rushing vehicles, and the spectacle of mass cultural consumption and entertainment all featured in these depictions of American cities and their inhabitants. American women in particular figured as the provocative, independent emblems of a chaotic future "civilization without sexes."[11] Reproducing a centuries-old image of the "New world" as a space of possibility and change, freed from the burdens of history, many of the authors I examine here also fixated on the youthfulness of American society and culture. Reflecting on France as they considered the United States, these cultural time-travelers expressed anxieties about the anachronism of their own *civilisation* in the face of a future that they imagined was already taking place on the other side of the globe.

A Brief History of "America" in France

"America" did not suddenly become a "menace" in the interwar years. In the wake of the American Revolution, the new republic across the Atlantic had seemed to many French thinkers and reformers to show tremendous "promise."[12] In the first half of the nineteenth century, French images of American culture, however, were based on relatively limited contact and consisted largely of folklore and caricature regarding the proximity of Americans to the land, the innocence and virtue of their ways of life.[13] For many French observers, the "New world" had for some time appeared to be a static society, a noncivilization that did not, because it could not, pose a significant cultural threat to France. The perception that Americans were somehow "removed from the vicissitudes of history" fed characterizations of "America" as an innocent and quaint society.[14]

In the latter part of the nineteenth century, however, French observers began to express a range of anxieties about "America." The rising industrial strength of the United States, combined with concerns about its actual and possible imperial ambitions, contributed to a growing sense that "America" might ultimately pose a threat to Europe.[15] The U.S. declaration of war against Spain in 1898 would launch a new phase of concern in France over what began to be referred to as the "American peril."[16] While many Americans continued, to some extent at least, to look to Europe for their sense of "history," this relationship of cultural dependence began to shift in the early years of the twentieth century. Culture, like political and economic relations, was subject to a balance of power that no longer seemed to be tipped by default in Europe's favor. In 1930, the French writer André Siegfried would reflect on the psychological impact this change had on France by the interwar years. As Siegfried noted, "Lincoln, with his Bible, his Aesop's fables, his classical taste, was still a figure within our reach. But if we admire [Henry] Ford, we feel him to be distant from us and, deep down, he frightens us."[17]

French fears about the spread and influence of American culture went hand in hand with anxieties about the demise of European traditions and civilization as a whole. Lacking experience and depth, "New world" society seemed preoccupied with accumulation and ostentation rather than the nourishment of the intellect. Even French republicans who felt a basic affinity for American political values expressed concern over the fate of the individual and the leveling effects of the varieties of mass culture in the United States. This aversion was particularly strong on the part of those observers who worried about the implications of American-style cultural democracy for the role of the intellectual as a mediator and arbiter of taste and ideas.[18] Representing the nation *outre Atlantique* in terms of economic and political strength on the one hand and cultural weakness on the other, the French thinkers who contributed to this imaginative figuration tended to view the United States in rather monolithic terms. While a suspicion of American culture and values played an important role in the intellectual life of other European nations, it was in France that a sense of cultural superiority vis-à-vis the United States developed most intensely.[19]

Whether enthusiastic or pessimistic about the possibilities for the future that the United States seemed to promise or threaten, a number of French commentators by the early twentieth century had already begun to see in American society and culture a vision of the future of "modern" civilization. Some French advocates of political, economic, and cultural change and reform saw in the United States a model of advancement and a potential for emancipation from centuries of "Old world" inertia. For many others, however, the United States became the emblem of everything that could go wrong with "modernity" in the future.[20] As historian Pierre Milza has noted, "By the end of the [nineteenth] century, the America of trusts and skyscrapers incarnated a modernity that fascinated some and worried others...who rejected a lifestyle and system of values that seemed to be the fruits of a technological progress out of control."[21] The United States was for these anxious observers, a worrying alternate present to contemporary France.[22]

The First World War cemented and intensified French uncertainties about the kind of future "America" might represent. Following the entry of the United States into the conflict in 1917, the presence of hundreds of thousands of American military and medical personnel on French soil provided an unprecedented and profound experience of cultural contact between the two nations. Confronted with these *Américains* in France during and after the war, French men and women responded alternately with enthusiasm for and wariness, even resentment, of the military, economic, and political power wielded on the European continent by the United States.[23] The feelings of fraternity and gratitude expressed in dedications like Eugène Brieux's in 1920 would not ultimately outweigh a growing anti-American sentiment in France. After a long and bitter military conflict, France had emerged victorious but devastated and in serious financial debt to its military ally across the Atlantic. The economic strength and political isolationism of the United States in the wake of the war only fueled the currents of resistance in French society to a variety of American industrial methods and cultural phenomena.[24] While Fordism, Taylorism, Hollywood cinema, and jazz found many admirers in France, these emblems of "modernity" *à l'américaine* could also generate serious anxieties about the erosion of values and traditions and the future of "Frenchness."[25]

Scenes from the Life of the Future

When Georges Duhamel visited "America" for the first time in 1928, he followed in the footsteps of a number of other French travelers and writers who had made the United States a focus of their attention since 1918. In the decade after the war, a number of French military and political officials including René Viviani, Marshal Ferdinand Foch, Edouard Herriot, and André Tardieu traveled to the United States with a view to sorting out financial and diplomatic matters and strengthening ties between the two nations.[26] In 1928, the trade unionist Hyacinthe Dubreuil spent more than one year working in the United States and studying American industrial practices and methods. Published in 1929, Dubreuil's *Standards: Le Travail américain vu par un ouvrier français* (*Robots or Men?: A French Workman's Experience in American Industry*) became the most widely known account focused on techniques, production, and management.[27]

By the late 1920s, other French commentators such as André Siegfried and Lucien Romier made their own important contributions to perceptions of "America" in France. Deeply concerned with the future of Europe as a whole, both authors also considered the specific impact of American culture and society on France. Trained in political science in Paris, André Siegfried traveled extensively throughout the world, visiting the United States several times from the late 1890s through the mid-1920s.[28] By the end of the decade, Siegfried had become one of the foremost French authorities on Britain and the United States. Published in 1927, his *Les Etats-Unis d'aujourd'hui* (*America Comes of Age*) was a detailed study of contemporary American society that included analysis of the politics, ethnic and race relations, and economic development of the United States. In an effort to understand this powerful nation so emblematic of the "new world" that had emerged after the war, Siegfried posed serious questions about the respective histories and possible futures of the civilizations on both sides of the Atlantic.[29] Like Siegfried, Romier also made it clear that Europe's future would be tied, in some very important ways, to the mass production and consumption of "America." In titles like *Qui sera le maître, Europe ou Amérique?* (*Who Will Be Master, Europe or America?*), Romier expressed his ambivalence about American models and approaches. While both authors recognized an unmistakable set of challenges for France, they also allowed for the possibility that the best aspects of European civilization might be preserved through measured reforms and responses to mechanization and mass culture.[30]

Georges Duhamel's journey to the United States in the late 1920s must be understood in connection with the French writers who preceded him in the postwar years, many of who framed their own observations in terms of the future of France. Other authors also published travel narratives within months of the appearance of *Scènes*. Paul Morand, who had traveled to the United States a number of times in the 1920s, published *New York* in 1930.[31] Sent on assignment to New York several times between 1926 and 1929 for *L'Ami du Peuple*, Paul Achard shared his impressions in *Un oeil neuf sur l'Amérique* (A New Look at America) published the following year.[32] Both of these works would be reviewed alongside Duhamel's, creating a cohort of publications within a very short time span that only drew more attention to each individual author and his work.[33]

Duhamel's encounter with the "New world" must also be considered in relationship to the experiences and ideas he brought with him as he crossed the Atlantic. Born in 1884, he had served as a military surgeon during the war. Duhamel drew on his experiences of the conflict when he wrote *Vie des martyrs* and *Civilisation,* the novel that won him the French Prix Goncourt in 1918.[34] Deeply affected by the destructive forces and acts he had witnessed during the war, Duhamel returned to the theme of civilization again and again in his oeuvre, expressing a profound suspicion of claims to human advancement that relied on too simplistic an equation between technology and progress. Duhamel's analysis of America society reflected this ongoing fascination with the problems and the fate of human civilization as a whole.[35]

In the preface to *Scènes,* Duhamel declared: "Of all the tasks common to the men of my time none is more urgent than that of incessantly reviewing and correcting the idea of civilization."[36] Preoccupied with the question, the works of Romier and Siegfried certainly confirmed this observation. Duhamel began his discussion of the United States by looking back on his experience in the war, noting that while the "problem" of civilization was one to which he had "devoted a good part" of his writing, it was one which he had not yet "solved."[37] In the cultural analysis that followed, Duhamel would evaluate, "not the American people ... but American civilization."[38] Duhamel was not a tourist, interested in "America" for its own sake. He believed that "America [wa]s the protagonist, the herald, and the prophet," of a civilization that would take the world "toward one of those periods which figure as dreary gaps in the history of the mind."[39] Previewing what he determined was the dismal era ahead, Duhamel provided French readers with a scathing depiction of American society as a whole.

In chapters that moved from the treatment of the cinema, prohibition, sports, and advertising to the slaughterhouses and streets of Chicago, Duhamel surveyed the American "life of the future," denouncing this "counterfeit of civilization."[40] Referring to the word "future," historian Pascale Ory has noted that "the adjective in Duhamel's title, [was the] key to his entire argument, the engine driving his passionate rejection of that [American] model of civilization."[41] Indeed, Duhamel's account was as much a meditation on the idea of "the future" as it was a study of "America." Early on in *Scènes,* Duhamel remarked, "An enthusiastic respect for the word 'future' and for all that it conceals" was "among the most ingenuous ideologies of the nineteenth century." At the same time, he expressed his suspicion of the "intoxication" that convinced people that the future would "be the home of every kind of perfection, and of every sort of prosperity."[42] "I do not care much for the game of anticipation," Duhamel declared. While he admitted that the future is inaccessible, that it "has on its side the great strength and virtue of not yet existing," Duhamel nevertheless insisted this would "not prevent [him] from watching it come and judging it impartially."[43]

Toward the end of *Scènes,* Duhamel, claimed that "the future" was, in fact, the true subject of his analysis: "America? I am not talking of America. By means of America, I am questioning the future; I am trying to determine the path that, willy-nilly we must follow."[44] This concern with a future that seemed inevitable ran throughout the observations and events he recorded in *Scènes.* In addition to the book's title, chapter headings such as "Approaching the World of the Future" and "Notes and Sketches Illustrative of the World as It Is to Be," reinforced Duhamel's temporal figuration of "America" in relationship to France. In scene after scene of American life, Duhamel described the "living images of the future." "America" was the *trace* of a destiny that could be examined and judged. Addressing one of his hosts, Duhamel warned of the dangers lying ahead: "In short, you are the slaves of America, as, following your example, the whole world will some day be the slave of itself."[45] Discussing Prohibition, he insisted to another American friend, "It represents not only the spirit of America, but the spirit of our future world."[46] The future was a foreign country where "even the fruit, even the eggs seemed to taste of machinery."[47] Duhamel reflected nostalgically on traditions and ways he was certain would disappear, mourning *in advance* the loss of the "little pubs of France, with [their] low-ceilings, warm, smoky little rooms where three poor devils, packed tightly round a tiny iron table, can tuck away Burgundian beef, swap stories, play the flute, and be cheerful, blessedly cheerful."[48]

Having arrived in French bookstores in early April 1930, *Scènes de la vie future* went through several editions rapidly as readers could not seem to get enough of Duhamel's account.[49] Reviews appeared in a number of newspapers and literary journals across the political spectrum in France including *Le Figaro, La Croix, Paris presse, Le Monde, L'Humanité, L'Echo de Paris, Action française, Avenir, Comoedia, Le Journal des débats, L'Oeuvre, Liberté, Feuilleton du temps,* and *Nouvelles littéraires.*[50] Reviewers characterized the work as "an event," noting that buyers were "snatching" copies from bookstores in France.[51] "Here it is, the book we've been waiting for!" exclaimed André Rousseaux, a regular contributor to *Le Figaro. Scènes* had "hit France like a bolt of lightning." Duhamel's volume was more than just a travel narrative; it was an "act."[52] According to Rousseaux, Duhamel's account was a vital contribution to French society's understanding of itself and an invitation to change cultural course. "American civilization," he noted, "is a deforming mirror in which certain of our flaws appear ridiculously exaggerated. This civilization invites us to look at our own reflection, not to admire it, but to examine and reform ourselves."[53]

Others who responded to *Scènes* expressed their praise and critiques of Duhamel's "roman de civilisation."[54] A reviewer for *L'Echo de Paris* hailed *Scènes* as "truthful, eloquent and vibrant," "a courageous book," the work of a "master" who "does not allow himself to be indoctrinated or intimidated."[55] Another contributor to *Le Figaro*, Abel Hermant, wrote that "[the book] haunts me, like a nightmare."[56] Maurice Constantin-Weyer of *L'Action française* called the book "perhaps the best study to appear on the United States since the admirable works of Jules Huret."[57] A journalist for *Le Figaro*, Huret had published a series of articles and two volumes on the United States in the early twentieth century.[58] Writing for *Le Monde*'s "Chroniques de cinéma," Georges Altman endorsed Duhamel's take on Hollywood while admitting that certain films might be worth watching. In the final analysis, however, Altman claimed: "We are with [Duhamel], as will be everyone who wishes to defend the human spirit against the pestilence of the dollar."[59] Not all of Duhamel's readers were so impressed, however. According to Rousseaux, Duhamel's book had caused a "war...between writers who were either cinema lovers or detractors of the screen."[60] Taking issue with the harsh critique of American film in *Scènes*, *Liberté* columnist Philippe Dastre accused Duhamel of *cinémaphobie* and of surpassing "the limits of a reasonable writer."[61] Writing for *Oeuvre*, journalist André Billy had mixed feelings about Duhamel's "hard" and "violent" critique of "America." While he agreed with many of the ideas in *Scènes*, Billy also admitted that the book's "tone" at a number of moments made it read like a "pamphlet."[62]

Duhamel's attack on American society marked a distinct watershed in the French representation of both "America" and "the future," leaving its mark for decades to come. In the years after the publication of Duhamel's critique, other French writers would refer to *Scènes* as one of the most important French cultural texts on the United States, essential reading for anyone interested in "the future" itself. It quickly became impossible to travel to the United States and to write about that journey without making some gesture toward Duhamel's account. *Scènes de la vie future* became to the twentieth century what Alexis de Tocqueville's *Democracy in America* had been to the nineteenth, shaping, since the moment of its initial publication, a distinctive French mode of writing about "America." When *Le Figaro* conducted a survey of French intellectuals' views on America in 1931, a number of the French thinkers who responded made direct references to

Scènes. Journalist Gérard de Catalogne compiled and later published selections from the more than 250 letters submitted to the newspaper by a number of individuals including Julien Benda, Robert Brasillach, Paul Morand, and André Siegfried.[63]

Duhamel was not, of course, solely responsible for the proliferation of French writing on "America" in the early 1930s. In addition to the authors who had formulated their thoughts in advance of the publication of *Scènes,* events outside the intellectual world also shaped this wave of French interest in the United States. Global in its eventual implications, the stock market crash of 1929 raised serious questions about the American economy, casting a shadow over the "progress" associated with American technological innovation and methods of production. The immediate French responses to the crisis included a certain assuredness about France's security from its effects. This short-lived confidence reflected hopes that France would be saved by the very methods and economic differences that had seemed to place it in an increasingly inferior position relative to the United States on the world market. What appeared at first like a strictly American problem quickly became a global crisis that did not leave France untouched. While a number of the authors noted above fixated on the abundance and prosperity of the United States, the economic crisis and its worldwide ramifications reinforced existing anxieties about the future so many observers had come to identify with the "New world."[64]

The Journey and Arrival

Many of the authors who made the journey from France to the United States in the interwar years saw travel itself as a form of research, a fundamental means of understanding the world and appreciating the differences between human beings and their societies. In the introductory remarks to *Scènes,* Duhamel emphasized the importance of travel as a means of cultural study and observation. In his preface, Duhamel claimed, "Whoever travels in space travels also in history."[65] A journey to a far-away land could feel like a voyage backward in time. As far as Duhamel was concerned, however, "America" was a future space and, as such, a more disturbing destination than an "ancient" site such as Greece or Egypt. If travel could be a learning experience, it could also make the traveler feel "ill at ease...farther astray in time than in space." "The past disconcerts us less than the future," Duhamel wrote, adding, "the educated adult inhabitant of Western Europe finds himself more at home among the troglodytes of Matmata than he does in certain streets in Chicago."[66] When André Bellesort reviewed *Scènes* in the *Feuilleton du Journal des débats* in 1930, he seconded Duhamel's sentiment: "Chicago made the same impression on me...I would prefer to live like a troglodyte than to inhabit that horrible forest of buildings."[67]

Already on the way to "America," Duhamel remarked on the "enormous stretch of white-capped space," the literal and figurative ocean between worlds familiar and strange. A few days after his ship had departed from the Canary Islands, "touch[ing] land for the last time," the author observed that "the voices of the Old World became inaudible."[68] Following a difficult and disorienting experience clearing United States security checks and a mandatory, government medical screening, Duhamel entered the foreign country with a dramatic sense of his own journey through time: "I took four steps, each one of which left me a decade or so older, and found myself in the land of the future."[69]

Other writers also understood their travels in temporal as well as spatial terms. Using the imagery of science fiction and time-travel to frame their depictions of the voyage, French authors of the interwar years produced and reproduced an imaginative identification between "the future" and "America." Viewing themselves as hybrid explorers, part Christopher Columbus and part Jules Verne, these writers sought the rediscovery of the "New world," a land where the future of France, and of civilization as a whole, might be witnessed and explored.

In *Le Grand mirage—USA*, published in 1929, the writer Lucien Lehman depicted his arrival in America with wonder. "When the traveler, coming from Europe, contemplates the immense harbor of New York from the deck of an ocean liner," Lehman explained, "he cannot help but admire its grandeur and exceptional beauty...it is a marvel of nature." Noting the "towers of Babel that banish the sun for most of the day," Lehman described New York as a city that "despite oneself, sends one's imagination running wild."[70] Lehman was right. The approach to New York, urban emblem of the "New world," was a recurrent trope that appeared in a series of French travel narratives that reenacted the story of European contact in futuristic terms.

In *Un oeil neuf sur l'Amérique,* Paul Achard wrote: "The voyage to America is the only voyage to make in our time."[71] Identifying the United States with the whole of the contemporary world, Achard insisted: "What cannot be denied, is that the twentieth century bears the mark of America....the twentieth century is American." Describing the thrill of crossing the Atlantic to see the civilization on its other shore, Achard noted the "direction in which the 240 million eyes of the United States are turned: the future."[72]

To visit and look without prejudice upon America was to "experience Jules Verne."[73] The moment of arrival in New York inspired Achard to praise the "infinite" possibilities of America.[74] Excited by the approach to Manhattan, he was "joyous to see that on a planet that had become exact and without surprises, a wonderland still existed."[75] Achard marveled at the splendor of the American metropolis, stating: "I have to say that the geometric immensity of New York and other large American cities gives off an intense beauty, a distinct harmony...full of grandeur."[76]

André Maurois experienced amazement similar to these other writers when he traveled to the United States to take up a teaching position at Princeton University in the 1920s. "Maurois" was the pen name of Emile Herzog, a Jewish writer from a wealthy Alsatian family. Trained as a political scientist, Maurois, like Siegfried, had been an interpreter for the British Army during the First World War. The author of numerous works, he had become famous for his *Silences du Colonel Bramble,* a humorous novel based on Maurois' experiences during the war that he published in 1918.[77] Maurois produced two significant studies of the United States, *En Amérique,* published in 1929 and *L'Amérique inattendue,* published in 1931.

Having read Aldous Huxley on the ship that carried him across the Atlantic, Maurois had come to believe that, eventually, "the world will be Americanized."[78] Maurois remembered approaching the port of New York for the first time in 1927. "What is that fortified hill in the distance?" he had asked a friend. "That's no hill, my dear Frenchman," his friend replied, "It's New York." Maurois "was expecting a few skyscrapers towering over a human city." Instead he "found Metropolis, city of giants." Maurois recalled "the rare older houses still standing," noting that they "seem[ed] like children's toys."[79] In a description that recalled the journey itself, Maurois likened the entire city of Manhattan to an "enormous ocean liner, gliding softly towards infinity."[80]

Confronted with "America," Maurois turned to fantasy. Contemplating the future of this metropolis that he found so extraordinary in the present, Maurois imagined New York several decades beyond his own visit:

> 1970—Yes, said the American to the young French man with whom he had just had lunch on the terrace of the 100th floor at 1100 Park Avenue. Yes, in my childhood, New York was a very strange city. There were small houses of 30, 40 storeys high. In this very place, there stood a curious house. All the traffic circulated on the ground; the elevated roadways were as yet unknown.[81]

Of course, Maurois was even more comfortable with anticipation as a mode of writing than some of his fellow travelers. Alongside his other works of fiction and nonfiction, Maurois published titles such as *Deux fragments d'une histoire universelle,* the futuristic novel set in the 1990s that I discussed in chapter 2.[82]

For French observers, the American city was nothing like cities in Europe, especially Paris. As R. P. Gillet, a contributor to the *Revue de Paris,* noted in 1931:

> A Frenchman who arrives in the United States, even for the second time, is first of all struck as much by the differences in appearance separating him from an American as by the human similarities that bring the two together. When, for example, one arrives in the sprawling city of New York and sees the profile on the horizon of those huge 50, 60, even 80 storey buildings...one is disconcerted. The sudden view of such vertiginous height is surprising and shocking given our...love for measure.

Coming from Paris, Gillet had been overwhelmed by the "sprawling city" with its "torrents of cars and buses."[83] For Maurois, the comparison between the French capital and the American metropolis was a question of time. "In Paris," he remarked, "a busy man counts his hours; but in New York, he counts his minutes."[84]

In *New York,* published in 1930, the journalist Paul Morand also marveled at "Manhattan which, after gentle Europe appears to be a factory, and is in reality nothing but a boutique."[85] Morand quoted Paul Adam, another writer who had observed that, next to New York, "Paris seems like an archaeological site, an outdated city of meticulous artisans." New York was a city that did not "rest on its laurels" the way that cities in Europe tended to do.[86] Figuring the cultural distance between France and the United States in temporal terms, Morand reminded his readers, "We forget that New York was like London and Paris...twenty years ago....We go to New York," he insisted, "because for the last ten years, in terms of politics, diplomacy, commerce or finance, we cannot understand anything going on in the world without knowing the city." Referring to a gap between urban and rural France, Morand claimed, "We journey [to New York] like a peasant goes to the market with his eggs; we go there like farm maids run to work in the county-seat 'because there is the cinema every night' (and what cinema!)."[87] For Morand, New York was "a city that never stops or relaxes," where "fashions last one week," where "everything moves quickly [and] the wind blows at one hundred kilometers per hour, shaking the skyscrapers."[88] Citing an observation made by Jean Cocteau that "you go to New York to have your palm read," Morand described Manhattan as a city "supercharged with electricity."[89] New York was a city of the future, "what all cities will be like tomorrow."[90] For this French writer as for so many others, science fiction was a crucial point of reference. "It is not the shadow of Stuyvesant that looms over the Manhattan of 1930," Morand remarked, "it is the Doctor Ox at Quinquendam in Jules Verne."[91]

Ferdinand Bardamu, the protagonist of Louis-Ferdinand Céline's 1932 novel, *Voyage au bout de la nuit* (*Journey to the End of Night*), also emphasized the journey to and arrival in "America" as profoundly dislocating to a French visitor.[92] Bardamu was stunned by that "moment between two civilizations when one finds oneself struggling in a vacuum." His disorientation illustrated the complexities of cultural distance and time that a number of other French writers also noted in their descriptions of the United States.[93] In Bardamu's words, travel could change a man's life, providing an "inexorable glimpse of existence as it really is." A displacement at once spatial, cultural, and temporal, a voyage could make the traveler "see things, people and the future as they are—that is to say skeletons, nothing but ciphers."[94] Bardamu's first sighting of New York resembled other interwar depictions of a chasm between France and the United States. Awed in the face of this American city that "went straight up in the air," Céline's main character recalled "home [where] cities lie on their sides." The American metropolis "didn't relax at all; it stood there very stiff, not languid in the least, but stiff and forbidding."[95] In the city itself, Bardamu felt as if he "was crumbling to pieces," dizzied by the "tornado of sensations." Bardamu lingered on his confusion, expressing his amazement at "those few lucid hours... when you are leaving the customs of the last country behind you and the other, new ones have not yet got their hold on you."[96]

If the cities of the "New world" astounded and disturbed French travelers real and fictional, cars and women seemed to be some of the most unsettling features of the urban landscapes of "America." In *Scènes de la vie future*, Duhamel came to a startling realization while speeding around the streets of Chicago in an automobile. It was perhaps one of the best illustrations of his discomfort with American culture:

> My eyes, tired of the hoardings [*sic*] with their advertisements, turned to the inside of the car, and I suddenly saw in it the symbol of the world of the future. What better symbol of it could there be than this madly rushing machine, turned loose at full speed between two

pasteboard landscapes, steered by a charming woman with manicured nails and beautiful legs, who smoked a cigarette while traveling between fifty and sixty miles an hour, while her husband, seated on the cushions of the rear seat, with a set jaw, scribbled figures on the back of an envelope.[97]

Elsewhere, Duhamel commented on the superficiality of American culture by focusing on women's bodies, their "legs, the lovely legs with their beautiful contours, obviously mass-produced…sheathed in glistening, artificial silk."[98]

Other writers also made the connection between the women, cars, and speed of American society and culture. Maurois recalled the fast-paced, "deft nymph who drove me home in her Ford. Red lights. Green lights."[99] If "America" embodied "the future," the autonomous woman seemed to embody "America." Writing for *Illustration* in 1930, Gaston Rageot pointed to "le problème féminine" (the female problem) in his article "Une visite aux Etats-Unis", remarking on the American woman's reputation for beauty and independence.[100] In "Pour ou contre la civilisation américaine," (For or Against American Civilization) the 1931 *Le Figaro* survey on the American "menace" that I discussed above, Gérard de Catalogne expressed his worry that "the authority of the [American] woman over her children will lead to the breakup of the family." De Catalogne was particularly concerned about the implications of the Nineteenth Amendment to the United States Constitution that had granted women the right to vote in 1919.[101] While the French Senate had shot down any such legislation in 1920, (in addition to passing new laws against contraception and abortion), the Americans had allowed women to enter politics.[102] In a nation where the problem of depopulation fed conservative anxieties about the confusion of traditional gender roles, a "future" emancipation of women could easily signal the "end" of French civilization.

The tendency to represent "America" in futuristic terms had a life beyond monographs and novels devoted to the "New world." Popular and scientific magazines such as *Illustration*, *VU*, *Miroir du monde*, *Sciences et voyages*, and *Science et la vie* featured articles focused on the United States before and after the appearance of *Scènes*. In these publications, "America" appeared again and again as a "source" of information about technological innovation. Writing for *Mercure de France* in 1931, G. Hanet-Archambault, for example, was convinced that the "French newspaper of tomorrow" would definitely be American.[103] This seemed to "go without saying" for, according to Hanet-Archambault, "the French newspaper of today already

[was]."[104] The future of French journalism lay in the "modern information *à l'américaine*": the by-line, the humorous cartoon accompanying articles, a news and information system pumped out by agencies using the "methods of production found in factories: rationalization, serial production, assembly-line work...[all] driven by commercial gain."[105] In the media, an inevitable American invasion would determine the news of tomorrow, "sweeping aside the entire current [French] system."[106]

The French popular science weekly *Sciences et voyages* frequently used the latest news from the United States as the basis for predictions about the world of "the future." In 1933, an article by "Arthenay," one of the magazine's regular contributors, asked the question, "How do the Americans conceive of the world of tomorrow?"[107] The two-page spread provided a panorama of everyday Americans' visions of the future. Rather than conducting a survey of French views on the matter, the magazine published this imported set of opinions and representations of changes to the home, transportation, technology, and society. Projecting an image of American domestic life as a scene of maximum comfort, Arthenay pictured a soundproofed, centrally heated and air-conditioned interior space where everything would be "automatic."

The author went on to anticipate the expansion of the media and the development of television, an emergent technology that promised to bridge the gap between public and private space. An apparatus that would link households to the world outside, the television could also become a key intermediary connecting citizens to the state. In the future, information would reach the individual through television broadcasts and participation in the political process would be mediated by television. In the end, however, the anticipation of future transformations would somehow lead Arthenay back in time. The ultimate expression of mass politics in a technologically advanced society, the "televised election" would, he argued, effect a "return to a state of politics not so different from the ancient democracies in which all citizens participated directly in the life of the polis."[108]

A Land of Martians and Children

In "Conseils à un jeune Français partant pour l'Amérique," the final section of *En Amérique*, André Maurois offered some basic advice to a young man traveling to the United States for the first time. While Maurois acknowledged how alien "America" could seem to a French visitor, he reminded his reader, "You are going to America, not the moon."[109] At the same time, there *was* something "extraterrestrial" about American culture for some

French writers. In 1931, André Siegfried went as far as describing former President Woodrow Wilson as "a fantastic character, with the allure of a Martian escaped from a Wells novel."[110]

In *La Vie sur Mars* (Life on Mars), published in 1924, the French meteorologist and astronomer Abbé Moreux asked, "Is Mars inhabited?...If we believe the cosmologists," Moreux suggested, "Mars is considerably older than Earth." "Born earlier in a much smaller world," he continued, "has life there evolved more rapidly than here at home?" Moreux suspected the Martians had "attained...a more advanced state" of civilization than humans. "Do they think like we do?" he asked. "Are they interested in literature, science and religion?" Turning to conflict and war, Moreux inquired:

> Do they fight amongst themselves, like Earthlings do...how far have they developed the means to kill each other? Have they, like the Germans, invented asphyxiating bombs, the bombardment of peaceful cities, the systematic destruction of houses of worship? Out there, do they have maritime nations who, while always ready to preach disarmament, continue to maintain formidable war fleets?[111]

Like Moreux's, meditations on extraterrestrial civilizations often allude to the contemporary cultural and political concerns of their authors. Theories on the nature of alien life forms frequently depend on the assumption that these beings are older, and therefore more advanced than those on Earth. "Progress" in these formulations is typically regarded as a function of age. In the interwar years, the scientific hypothesis that the planet Mars, for example, was much further along in its physical evolution suggested that its inhabitants (Martians) would have reached a more advanced state of civilization. Beyond scientific investigations of extraterrestrial life, this notion informed a range of French fictional narratives about Martians, the inhabitants of Venus, and even a race of Moon people. In one author's imaginary conversation with a Martian astronaut, for example, the reader learns that "the inhabitants of Mars are no longer in the period of class struggle." "Given the progress already achieved on Earth," the author muses, "we can imagine the improvements of a civilization 10,000 years older than that of the Earth."[112]

In the case of alien civilizations, evolution and advancement depended on history and the accumulation of a society's or a species' experience. This assumption that an "older" life form was likely to be more advanced stood in striking contrast to the opposite assumption applied here on Earth that the "New world" must hold the keys to the future. While imagining the civilizations of "outer space" provided an opportunity for some French authors to speculate about the future of humanity, the "other space" of "America" functioned as the terrestrial equivalent of an alien culture and civilization that seemed destined, for better or for worse, to transform the "Old world." For a number of interwar authors, "America" represented "the future" because it was a "younger" society.

According to André Siegfried, American culture was "liberated from the past."[113] This freedom from history is what made "America" the symbol of a "new age of humanity, in the same way that we speak of the Stone or Bronze Age." This future was "an unavoidable destiny...made up not only of a new technique, but a new politics and system of values."[114] In *Les Etats-Unis d'aujourd'hui,* Siegfried used the young/old metaphor to discuss industrial and natural resources in America and Europe. He referred to America as a *cadet,* the "prodigious young rival" of Europe, noting that the development of standardization and models like Fordism only reinforced the "youthfulness" of the American economic system.[115]

In 1931, R. P. Gillet observed that America "did not have centuries of intellectual development behind it."[116] Paul Morand described "Europe" as a "mother" who "had sent the children she wished to punish to New York over the course of history."[117] "America is like a precocious child," Maurois suggested. "It is like those adolescents, the sole inheritors of a vast fortune, whom the elders invite begrudgingly to the meeting table."[118] In his discussion of American women and young girls, Maurois lingered on the age metaphor, once again claiming America has "a young face." He saw Americans as "a people who is twenty years old, while we are forty." American culture had the "flaws and virtues of adolescence," combined with the hope and strength of youth.[119] Gérard de Catalogne referred to America as "a nation of little boys who do not want to grow up."[120] Returning from his visit to the United States, Gaston Rageot commented, "Americans switched from one extreme to another, like children go from giggles to tears."[121] The politician Charles Pomaret also represented the cultural divide between France and the United States in terms of generation, expressing his concern that world "hegemony will be handed over to the younger continent, freed from European tutelage."[122] For Pomaret, America's freedom from history was an important part of what made the nation a "menace" and a "peril...perhaps a fatal peril" for France:

> The United States conquering Europe and the world? Everything points to this. The values, taste and habits, the spectacles of Europe are today under the influence of and dependent upon America. And we can neither work in our office, nor go down into the street, nor enter a public

place without something reminding us of our own subjection, without a telephone receiver, an automobile advertisement, the name of a cocktail or a movie poster reminding us that the world's motto is from now on "Made in America."[123]

Emphasizing the novelty of American society, Paul Achard insisted, "There is no question of copying America or Americanizing. This would be ridiculous. The Americans have been cut out of whole cloth, something much easier than patching up the old."[124] Achard envisioned a back and forth between French and American culture. Asking himself whether he would "spend [his] entire life in America," Achard responded, "No, because life in France is good...but I would return happily tomorrow, given the chance, and I'd stay easily for a few months a year." Achard thought this kind of exchange might enable "a mix of our two civilizations: the young that admires the old, but wishes to remain young, and the old that is charming, but horrified when you call it old." Although Achard appreciated elements of both the "old" and the "new" civilizations represented by France and the United States, he nevertheless made it clear which one had the upper hand. "Only the young one understands that life is short and that we must make haste," Achard remarked. "The old one," on the other hand, "has us living as if there are centuries awaiting us...and this, because there are many behind us." In the end, Achard characterized Europe as "that poor old [civilization] that has trouble keeping up with the century." America was not necessarily better off, however. "Afraid of resembling the old," the nation "ha[d] immersed itself in its extreme opposite, an excess of speed and mechanization."[125]

Whether or not the Americanization of France was inevitable, it seemed that French *civilisation* was out of step with the contemporary world, a living anachronism. And a truncated sense of time, tied to its lack of experience, marked American civilization. Even those authors who suggested that "America" was not so young tended to equate the future with that foreign country. While Morand insisted "New York is not young; it is older than Saint-Petersburg," he nevertheless concluded, "Its adventure will be our own. Defending ourselves against the novelties of Broadway would be like refusing the pre-established order known as the future."[126]

Other interwar commentators also attempted to resist the identification of America with novelty and youth. Though Duhamel claimed he had seen "the future" across the Atlantic, he also insisted "America is growing old; it is even growing old quickly."[127] In *Le Figaro*'s 1931 survey on the United States, author Robert Brasillach argued that the problem of American culture was particular to his generation, a generation that had grown up on its various exports. Responding to "the great, dramatic movement that M. Duhamel [had] unleashed," Brasillach suggested that "the real danger of America is the danger of conservatism." Brasillach claimed his aversion to "America" was not a "reaction against the future, but against the past." American culture was a relic, a set of "old furnishings and photo albums" to be "relegated to the attic."[128]

Authors like Duhamel and Brasillach perceived a fundamental incompatibility between "Frenchness" and "America." Other European societies in the interwar years also suggested possible futures for France: the Soviet model after 1917, as well as the varieties of fascism in Italy, Spain, and Germany. "France has no other recourse but to become American or Bolshevik," claimed the French writer Paul Adam in 1929.[129] "Ford or Lenin?" asked André de Fels, the deputy for Seine-et-Oise in 1930.[130] In 1931, the French journalist Gérard de Catalogne would remark, "Europe, Russia and America are the three poles of attraction at play in determining the future of nations."[131] Discussions of military danger and the "next war" focused, understandably, on Germany. As one contemporary French writer insisted, "The immediate danger for us is not being Americanized, but being Germanized."[132] For French military strategists the principal menace to France existed, not across the Atlantic, but across the Rhine; the most pressing threats to France were territorial, not cultural or economic.

In discussions of the French future in cultural terms, however, French authors focused on the United States.[133] Despite the fear of a possible German military invasion of France's territorial borders, the United States appeared poised to transform France via cultural imports such as Hollywood cinema and business approaches like Fordism. This invasion would take place in the name of technological "progress" rather than through outright military conquest.[134] While Russia constituted another important point of reference in French considerations of social, economic, and political change, Americanization figured uniquely in considerations of "the future" because it took the form of a gradual rather than a revolutionary or violent break with the past.

After 1918, it seemed that there could be no way for France to keep up industrially, technologically, or economically with the United States. Following from this set of anxieties, French cultural custodians abandoned the idea of the reinvention and evolution of French culture forward in time. They rejected the imagination of the French nation in terms of "the future," taking up instead the position of a "superior," historic culture under threat. The absorption and elimination of a "traditional," European civilization embodied in France and "French" ways of life into an imaginary all-consuming,

culturally and economically powerful America appeared as both *unthink-* ⎞
able and *inevitable.*

The Agony of the Globe

> It seems to us that France as a nation is in a state of decadence
> and that it might soon be in agony.
>
> —ROBERT ARON AND ARNAUD DANDIEU, *Décadence de la nation*
> *française* (1931)

In 1935, one French writer tried to imagine what would happen if
"America" fell off the face of the Earth. In his novel, *L'Agonie du globe* (The
Agony of the Globe), science fiction author Jacques Spitz detailed a fantastic
sequence of future events in which the "New world" was cast into oblivion,
never to be seen again. He outlined the details of a European separation
from American influence and power, the severing of all diplomatic, economic, and cultural ties. Spitz conjured this fictional scenario at a historical
moment when a number of French observers engaged in conversation and
debate about the future of France as the center of European civilization.

Set in the 1940s, Spitz's narrative proceeded from a series of catastro-
phes—earthquakes, tidal disturbances, and other natural disasters—that
would create a rift of space between the "Old world" of Europe and Asia and
the "New world" of the Americas. Temperatures would drop in a Western
Europe deprived of the warm currents of the Gulf Stream. The opening of a
"Grand Canal" of space between the two hemispheres would have tremendous economic repercussions: "One could no longer think of the exchange
of raw materials and products of mass industry: machines, automobiles, etc.
The world market [would be] divided in two."[135] The Americas would lose
all control over investments made in Europe. The social and cultural impact
would also be great as Americans in Europe found themselves cut off from
their homeland. First travel, then communication between the hemispheres
would become increasingly difficult and, eventually, impossible.

Diplomatic and political concerns would arise in all directions. As the
distance between the two hemispheres increased, becoming physically un-
bridgeable, a "European Commission" on relations with the "New world"
would have to be set up. As the other half of the globe drifted further into
space, away and out of reach, organizations that had coordinated international relations between the hemispheres would become useless, unneces-
sary. European headlines would read: "The End of Ties with America,"

"America Has Been Eternally Silenced," "Alone with Ourselves," "The Heavens Have Closed Again," "The Last Page in the Adventure of Christopher Columbus."[136] The American hemisphere would eventually become a satellite, like the moon, and later the "New world" would be completely destroyed, leaving only debris, a few stray islands floating through space. The "Old world [would] once again become the entire Earth, the third planet revolving around the sun."[137]

Spitz articulated a European "revenge fantasy" that many of his fellow French citizens might have appreciated in the years after 1918. The Europeans in Spitz's fictional account did not mourn the loss of America. Rather, they celebrated their liberation from the "yoke" of America's influence. This included the renegotiation of territorial and financial holdings on both sides of the world. In one proposal, European colonies (such as French Guiana) would be exchanged for a renunciation of American investments and business interests in Europe as neither would be possible to control from such a distance. Spitz noted that the resolution of "an old question of debts incurred during a war that had taken place around 1915, at the beginning of the century," would fall under the rubric of this exchange. In the future Spitz described, the economic and political balance of power that followed the First World War would remain a crucial point of contention. Spitz highlighted the jubilation felt by many Europeans in response to the new freedom from this and other obligations a definitive separation might bring. This celebration exhibited itself most profoundly in the "joyous demonstration" accompanying the scene "on the Old continent" when "the last Ford motorcar that had crossed the Atlantic was driven to the cemetery."[138]

The fantasy that Spitz indulged in his novel suggested a future that might indeed belong to Europe, and to France in particular. Spitz's future world represented a kind of European "restoration" rather than a future evolution toward European global domination, however. The only way to rid the globe of the tightening grip of the "New world" on human civilization would be to turn "the last page in the adventure of Christopher Columbus," that is, to create a world free of any trace that "America" had ever been "discovered." Only an incredible catastrophe could bring about such a transformation. Spitz's imaginative tale betrayed a sense of inevitability that ran throughout the French culture of anticipation of the interwar years—the only way to avoid a future dominated by the United States would be to eliminate an entire hemisphere, taking a profound, agonizing step back in time.

CHAPTER 5

The International Language of the Future

In *A Short History of the International Language Movement*, published, in 1922, Professor Albert Léon Guérard, a French expatriate living in the United States, traced the development and use of a variety of national and so-called artificial languages, languages invented to facilitate human communication and to encourage peaceful cooperation between different nations and cultures.[1] Guérard's history proceeded from an analysis of linguistic traditions and movements in the past to the projection of a world to come. Entitled, "Anticipations," the final chapter of *A Short History* began: "Let us imagine, then, that the...League of Nations, acting upon the report of a competent committee, has formally adopted a scheme which, for the sake of neutrality, we shall call Cosmoglotta. What will happen?"[2]

Guérard imagined a not-so-distant future in which "'Cosmoglotta" would gain equal footing with the two, three, or four languages officially used by the League of Nations.[3] According to Guérard, Cosmoglotta would not be employed at either the local or the national level. Reserved for international relations and exchanges, it would become a kind of "Latin of democracy," facilitating European unity in particular.[4] While battles still in recent memory in 1922 had divided Europe in a number of ways, Cosmoglotta could help to relieve international tensions by facilitating clearer communication in all domains. Like the territorial boundaries that could seem less and less relevant in an age of advanced military technology, so too would political, cultural, and linguistic borders gradually give way to more openness and exchange between different nations. In terms of language,

Guérard saw this community extending outside the European continent, predicting, "After a few years, it is probable that all business would be conducted exclusively in Cosmoglotta" eventually bringing about an "emancipation from Babelism."[5]

At the same time, Guérard wondered about the impact of Cosmoglotta's reach on national languages, literatures, and cultures:

> Will the day ever come when Cosmoglotta is no longer an auxiliary, but a truly universal language? Will our existing tongues gradually be reduced to the position of home dialects...still the vehicles of local literature, but hopelessly outdistanced in the race by the one great instrument of government, science, commerce? Will the leveling influences of modern civilization gradually conquer [the] last strongholds until the languages of Dante, Shakespeare, Cervantes, Goethe, Victor Hugo, fade into classic unreality and popular oblivion, like the speech of Homer and Virgil?[6]

While Guérard predicted "even a Cosmoglottic literature will be developed," his answer to this series of questions was a resounding "no." As far as he was concerned, "the idea of a Universal Empire, and even of a Universal Republic" had long since been abandoned. In Guérard's imagined future, each inhabitant of the world would have "two fatherlands, the country of his allegiance and the common home of the race." Each world citizen would be fluent in both "his mother tongue and the common, neutral medium of all." Cosmoglotta would help to create, "a universal federation wherein no originality would be stifled, but all would be freely and peaceably harmonized through justice and love."[7]

Guérard insisted that *A Short History*'s concluding thoughts on the future "need[ed] no apology," given that they were based on reasonable extrapolation from experience. "Prophecy is the sober trade of the promoter," he claimed, calling on his reader to join him in the kind of anticipation he perceived as vital to human progress. In his words, "Lesseps would not have dug the Suez Canal if he had not expected that boats would use it, nor Zamenhof devised Esperanto if his eyes had been obstinately turned backwards."[8] Here, Guérard referred to Ferdinand de Lesseps, the French diplomat who played a key role in the building of the Suez Canal, and Ludovic Zamenhof, the Polish physician who had, in the nineteenth century, developed Esperanto, the most widely known of the invented languages Guérard discussed in the pages of *A Short History*.[9]

Despite the fact that Guérard referred to "Cosmoglotta" "for the sake of neutrality" in his anticipation of world affairs, he drew on the history of Esperanto as the basis for his projections about the development of an international language in the future. Indeed, throughout his writing on the subject, he remained enthusiastic about the potential of Esperanto to improve human relations. In *A Short History*, Guérard referred to Esperanto as "the linguistic manifestation of the spirit of the modern world, practical and idealistic at the same time, the spirit of free co-operation without privileges and without violence."[10] Though Guérard hoped that any "new language" would learn from the evolution of Zamenhof's invention, he nevertheless identified Esperanto, in particular, with progress and peace. "The bond of union of the 'Esperanto people,'" was, in his words, "the embryo of the pacific world-state of the future."[11]

Guérard liked to meditate on the future. Less than a decade later, he would publish *L'Avenir de Paris*, the analysis of city planning and architecture that I discussed in chapter 2 of this book. *A Short History* engaged with the past, present, and future of an emblem of French culture no less important than the nation's capital: the French language. In the case of plans and designs for Paris, Guérard would object to the irreverence with respect to the city's history that he saw in proposals such as those of the architect Le Corbusier. Guérard was not interested in the preservation of the past for its own sake, however. In the case of both cities and languages, change on certain fronts could be beneficial, even essential.

In a 1925 study entitled, *Beyond Hatred: The Democratic Ideal in France and America*, Guérard returned to the idea of an international language, cautioning readers that a conservative attachment to linguistic tradition (in France and elsewhere) could be an obstacle to the progress of peace and understanding between nations and peoples. "Our historical languages," he wrote, "with all their charm and splendor, are the embodiment of much ignorance and loose thinking. If there clings about certain words or phrases a fascinating fragrance of the seventeenth century, there clings also an odor of seventeenth-century prejudices."[12] "An auxiliary language is needed," Guérard argued. Such a language "will not abolish frontiers: it will transcend them, and deprive them of their hateful features." The adoption of an international language such as Esperanto would "be the symbol of the new industrial and democratic civilization" freed from "the capricious historical lines of another age."[13]

Guérard thus shared some common ground with the architect whose urban plans he criticized in *L'Avenir de Paris*. In his writings on human cities and societies, Le Corbusier had noted the "continuing lack of a universal language" as "tangible proof" that the "revolution of the machine" he anticipated eagerly was not yet complete. Le Corbusier looked forward to a linguistic evolution "which would break down the cardboard barriers erected along frontiers that from now on are overrun—nighttime barriers in a brightening field."[14] For both of these writers then, the use of an international language was an important feature of the positive futures they envisioned.

The future scenario that Guérard outlined in his musings on "Cosmoglotta" was not so far off from a very real set of contemporary debates about international, and specifically linguistic, community. During the interwar period, existing states and nationalist movements continued to assert their sovereignty against supranational schemes and the imperial ambitions of powerful states within and outside the European continent.[15] A vital emblem of national identity, language became an important international agenda item in the years that followed the war. In a significant break with tradition, the allies who met at the Paris Peace Conference of 1919 decided that English (in addition to French) would be an official language of the proceedings, of the written agreements negotiated there, and of the proposed League of Nations. In the league's initial meetings in Geneva in the early 1920s, delegates from many nations, including France, entertained proposals for the official recognition of other national languages in addition to French and English. And in 1922 (the year of A Short History's publication), the League of Nations was, as Guérard suggested, reviewing a "report" by "a competent committee," one that considered seriously the possibility of endorsing Esperanto as an international language.[16]

While the international language movement had preoccupied the minds of some proponents before the war, it was during this early phase of the league's activity that Esperanto, in particular, seemed most likely to receive the international recognition and support its advocates had long been seeking. Linked as it was to a range of pacifisms and internationalisms, from liberal democratic, to socialist, to communist, Esperanto garnered new adherents and opponents after 1914. Promoters of the language hoped that its gradual adoption by the league's member nations would represent linguistically the league's transcendence of the kind of national divisions that had led historically to conflict and the horrors of war.[17] Ultimately, however, hopes like those Guérard expressed for "Cosmoglotta" would never be realized. While the international language reflected a spirit of world unity for some delegates, for others it appeared to contradict an important principle of the league: the respect for the sovereignty and individuality of particular nations, their territories, and cultures.

The positions and investments of a number of French participants (both government officials and private citizens) in these discussions about language, nation, and internationalism were especially significant. In the early postwar years in particular, a number of French writers, educators, scientists, representatives of the business community, government ministers, and diplomats debated the possibility of adopting Esperanto as an auxiliary language for the purposes of international commercial, political, and intellectual exchange. Esperanto appeared to be a language "of the future" in both practical and symbolic terms. An invented, planned language, Esperanto seemed to lack history because it had not emerged from a particular national tradition. It could thus be understood as either a welcome or a threatening break with the past by enthusiasts and detractors respectively.

Over the course of the last four chapters in this book, I have explored French representations of the bodies, cities, wars, and civilization of the future through the analysis of cultural objects and artifacts that appeared to bear their traces: prosthetic appliances, skyscrapers, military fortifications, and "America." This chapter examines the idea of an international language as yet another key site of the culture of anticipation of the interwar years. The pages that follow deal with a relatively brief period after the war. From another perspective, however, this final chapter takes perhaps the widest view of any in this book, considering France as a nation struggling to negotiate memory and anticipation in an international political and cultural field that the war had altered in radical ways.

The "Battle of the Languages"

When the heads of the Allied states convened for the Paris Peace Conference in 1919, it was immediately apparent that they were not all on the same page. Their differences were aggravated, moreover, by the fact that their pages were not all written in the same language. These representatives had a number of important issues to sort through together: questions of disarmament, the redrawing of the European map, the status of colonial holdings, financial reparations, and the controversial "war guilt clause."[18] Before any of these crucial items could be addressed, however, it was essential that these leaders arrive at some sort of agreement about the form negotiations would take and the procedures they would follow. On January 5, 1919, the French government submitted its proposed plan of procedure for the months ahead.[19] In a series of preliminary meetings beginning on January 12, the "Council of Ten" (consisting of representatives from Britain, France, the United States,

Italy, and Japan), met to discuss its contents.[20] The plan was divided up into a few key sections covering the representation of belligerent and neutral states, the leading principles and order of questions to be examined, and the organization of the conference. This last section laid out a number of rules of order, including the following proviso: "The French language is acknowledged as an official one for the discussions and resolutions of the Conferences."[21] While the plan allowed for the use of other languages in meetings and texts, French translations would be required and French alone would be accorded official, textual status. This privileging of the French language over others resulted in what the American journalist Ray Stannard Baker referred to as "the battle of the languages," a heated debate over which official languages participants would recognize, particularly in the text of any resulting agreements.[22] Indeed, language became the question of the day in the Council of Ten meetings that took place on January 15, 1919.[23]

The French foreign minister Stéphen Pichon began the discussion with a reading and explanation of the article regarding the official language of the conference. While Pichon acknowledged that delegates should be allowed to speak in their own languages, and that texts in multiple languages might be published, "only one text could be the official one" and this should be the French. "In recent times," Pichon noted, "French had always been accepted as the diplomatic language."[24] History was, in fact, largely on Pichon's side. As Professor Antoine Meillet, a leading French linguist and the author of *Les Langues dans l'Europe nouvelle* (Languages in the New Europe), had explained in 1918, "French had become the language of diplomacy at the beginning of the eighteenth century."[25] Pichon went on to list a series of treaties and conferences in which French had been used first and foremost, from Paris, to Berlin, to The Hague, to "Peking." While "English...was perhaps more widely spread and widely known than any other language," French was the language of precedent. On this basis, Pichon insisted that, "should a dispute arise as to the correct interpretation to be given to a particular statement, the French text should be recognised as the official text."[26] In the conversation that followed, the French- and English-speaking representatives (of Britain and the United States) took up opposing sides, the former insisting on the recognition of only one truly official language (their own) and the latter arguing for the recognition of both English and French on equal terms.[27] In the justifications they offered for their respective positions, these representatives struggled in their own ways over the tension between experience and expectation, between a respect for historical precedent and tradition, and the desire to create a "new" world in the aftermath of the war. Their "battle of the languages" was in some sense, a battle over understandings of the kind of international future being planned at the conference. For the French in particular, the debate over language seemed to imply that their nation's authority and power on the world stage was in decline.

British prime minister David Lloyd George was the first to object to Pichon's claims. He assured his colleagues that while "he was in no way prejudiced on the subject of the French language,...the official language of 160 to 170 million people to be represented at the Conference was English." Lloyd George proposed that both English and French be acknowledged as official languages. United States president Woodrow Wilson "agreed that they all recognized the historic claim of the French language." Wilson pointed out that "there were very few languages that excelled it in precision and delicacy of shading." Nevertheless, "English was the diplomatic language of the Pacific."[28] Both Lloyd George and Wilson claimed an official place for English on the basis of the large number of English speakers *around the world.*[29] The French prime minister Georges Clemenceau would later reflect on the Paris Peace Conference and its challenges in *Grandeurs et misères d'une victoire* (1930). In his discussion of the war and the difficult peace that followed, Clemenceau would take the time to mention the loss of "the diplomatic pre-eminence of the French language" that was the eventual outcome of this dispute in 1919.[30] He noted then French president Raymond Poincaré's dissatisfaction on this front.[31] In his own defense, Clemenceau would later declare: "All the same I fought hard for the claims of the French language."[32] And so he had. In response to Lloyd George's and Wilson's arguments on behalf of English, Clemenceau "said that he was greatly embarrassed."[33] While "he fully admitted that the English language was a most widely spread language and had brought with it great activity and liberal institutions," he maintained that "the French language possessed the great advantage of extreme precision, which was useful in the case of official documents."[34] In an attempt at compromise, Clemenceau proposed that French, English, and Italian be recognized as official languages of the Peace Conference, with the French version of texts holding true in cases of dispute.

Linguistic protocol was more than just a practical matter of translations and textual verifications. It carried great symbolic meaning for the representatives assembled. Pichon reminded President Wilson that he "had recognized that French had a historical privilege in this matter." He went further, "appeal[ing] to [Wilson] in order that, at the end of a War in which France had suffered so heavily, she should not find herself by the very first act of the Conference deprived of this ancient prerogative."[35] Later, Pichon would underline his point dramatically, stating that "even Bismarck, who was no friend of France, had raised no objection to the use of French in the Treaty of Berlin."[36] Clemenceau had already offered an amendment to the French plan of procedure "in a conciliatory spirit," by including "two other official languages in addition to French, [and] only reserving for the last the text that could be appealed to in exceptional cases of disputed interpretation."[37] Historical privilege and precedent, wartime suffering, and compromise— these would all be crucial themes for the French throughout the negotiations that would take place in the months ahead.

It was at this point in the discussion that President Wilson linked the pro-posed bilingualism to a vision of the future, to the progress of peace and democracy throughout the world. Wilson noted that while he "felt nothing but admiration and affection for France...he felt obliged in this matter to omit sentiment."[38] While much had been said about the historic claims of the French language, Wilson insisted that this had been an essentially *European* tradition. "This case," however, "did not affect only Europe: the rest of the world had come into the arena."[39] According to Wilson, "this Conference concerned the future and not the past. The documents prepared by it were not merely to be useful to historians, but were to be the basis of the life and of the action of Governments in the future." Wilson "wished the future to think that this Conference had done its best in a practical spirit, and placed in the hands of posterity the most useful instruments that could be devised." But Wilson's understanding of the future was not the only one in the room that day. Clemenceau insisted that he too "wished to make a new world and to do new things, but (it was perhaps a trite observation) the future was attached to the past, and had its root in it."[40] For a number of important reasons, bilingualism's break with tradition went too far for the French prime minister. A decade before Georges Duhamel crossed the Atlantic, Clemenceau and Wilson embodied the temporal figuration of a cultural distance between France and "America" as the opposition between an obsolete past and an irreverent future.

The introduction of English as a second official language at the Paris Peace Conference (and in the official business of the proposed League of Nations) was, in the end, more than just a preliminary administrative de-tail. Other decisions and compromises made in Paris in 1919 would lead to disappointment and even resentment for the parties involved. Many of the issues on the table, such as reparations, for example, were arguably much more significant in terms of their economic and political implications. Still, the new bilingualism marked an important shift. For the French in particu-lar, this loss could be linked to deeper wounds. In 1922, Guérard would note that "many Frenchmen...found it difficult to understand why France, who had poured her blood and gold for the common cause, should be asked to give up a proud and cherished tradition, amounting almost to a vested right, and a precarious part of her spiritual patrimony."[41] By the time that Antoine Meillet published the second edition of *Les Langues dans l'Europe nouvelle* in 1928, the controversy over bilingualism had settled down. Meillet nevertheless deemed it worthwhile to discuss this episode in his revised text:

> It was a French general that had commanded the allied troops at the final victory. But when the necessary treaty negotiations between the allies began, it turned out that the British and American delegations did not know French....and almost all of the preliminary discussions took place in English. By a singular—and absurd—innovation, the Treaty of Versailles had been drafted in two languages....The ending of a war in which France had played the primary military role thus ruined the privilege that had made French the sole diplomatic language.[42]

While English may have dominated in Paris in 1919, however, it did not in fact supplant French in the assemblies of the League of Nations that followed. French apparently continued to hold position as the primary language of diplomatic discourse in these meetings in the years ahead. Herbert Shenton, a Syracuse University professor of sociology cited statistics to this effect in 1933. More than a decade after the granting of official status to the English language, Shenton observed, "Although the League is legally bilingual, a situation exists in practice which amounts to virtual control by French."[43] Shenton noted that in 1920, the English language was used by six countries where it was not the national language, while French was spoken by twenty-four. According to Shenton's statistics, as late as 1927, English was spoken by two countries in the league where it was not the national language, while French was spoken by twenty-five. The legal bilingualism of the league did not loosen the hold of the French language. On the contrary, French seems to have gained strength over English following the introduction of the second official language.[44] Clemenceau and others had mourned a privilege that would not, in the end, fade so quickly.[45]

Despite the indignation of the French representatives at the Paris Peace Conference, French would remain the de facto official language of the league. There were some practical reasons for this. President Wilson had been a strong presence in Paris in 1919, helping to form an English-speaking bloc of the powers assembled. But the United States was not one of the nations officially represented in Geneva. The U.S. Senate had failed to ratify American participation in the league. American delegates to the league would have increased the percentage of English speeches delivered before its assemblies. Not only were their English-speaking voices absent; they were not available to lend the encouragement of numbers to those other delegates who might have adopted English as their language of choice had it reflected a more powerful set of political and economic interests.[46]

The French representatives at the Paris Peace Conference wanted a future that would be respectful of tradition, one that would make amends for the material and moral damage France had suffered during the war. Their attachment to historical privilege and protocol set the tone for French governmental responses to the question of official and international languages in the years ahead. After 1919, it was neither the introduction of English, nor the possibility that other national languages might be granted official status alongside French and/or English that would ignite the greatest controversy. In fact, as Shenton's statistics suggest, the introduction of multiple languages could actually encourage the use of French as a common linguistic denominator for international discussion and documents. Once official bilingualism was no longer open to debate (once it became a fact in principle, if not entirely in practice) French anxieties about the future would focus on another linguistic competitor. While English had challenged French in Paris, it was Esperanto that would pose a problem in Geneva.

An Imagined Linguistic Community

At the First Assembly of the League of Nations that met in Geneva in 1920, representatives from a number of member nations submitted a "Draft Resolution Concerning Esperanto." The motion read as follows:

> THE LEAGUE OF NATIONS,
> Well aware of the language difficulties that prevent direct intercourse between peoples, and of the urgent need of finding some practical means to remove this obstacle and help the good understanding of nations,
>
> Follows with interest the experiments in the official teaching of the international language, Esperanto, in the public schools of some Members of the League,
>
> Hopes to see that teaching made more general throughout the world, so that the children of all countries may know at least two

languages—their mother tongue and an easy means of international communication,

And asks the Secretary-General to prepare, for the next Assembly, a report on the results reached in this direction.[47]

In accordance with the rules of procedure, the Assembly referred the matter to a subcommittee for further discussion.

One of the key figures behind this initial proposal was the international lawyer Henri Lafontaine, a Francophone delegate from Belgium who had won the Nobel Peace Prize in 1913. A socialist who served for many years in the Belgian Senate, Lafontaine was a committed internationalist and a supporter of Esperanto. He had also been one of the founders, in 1910, of the Union des Associations Internationales, or the Union of International Associations (UIA), a nonprofit, nongovernmental research and information organization dedicated to the encouragement of a global, civil society. Based in Brussels, the UIA brought together more than two hundred different international nongovernmental, nonprofit groups.[48]

Like Lafontaine, the other delegates who supported the promotion of Esperanto saw the use of an international language as a means to a diplomatic end. In his study, *Imagined Communities: Reflections on the Origin and Spread of Nationalism,* Benedict Anderson argues that "all communities are imagined," and they "are to be distinguished, not by their falsity/genuineness, but by the style in which they are imagined." Anderson focuses on the nation as "an imagined political community... inherently limited and sovereign."[49] He also points to "the fatality of human linguistic diversity" as the guarantee that individual nations will continue to exist as distinct entities.[50] In the early stages of the League of Nations, the proposal that Esperanto be encouraged as an international, "auxiliary" language would attempt to challenge that "fatality" while respecting national sovereignties.

The league's Committee No. 2 on Technical Affairs (including Lafontaine as one of its members) met to discuss the draft proposal above, submitting its report several days later. In that report, the committee "recogniz[ed] the serious linguistic difficulties which impede direct relations between the peoples." The committee stated that it was enthusiastic about the possibility "that an international language... be taught in all the schools, a simple and easy language... which would serve the future generations as a general means of international communication." The committee felt that "it would be desirable, however, to begin by undertaking an inquiry based on existing facts." Its report noted that the World Congress of International Associations had already sanctioned the language the previous year. It also acknowledged "that a widespread popular movement is beginning to take shape in Asia," as well as parts of Europe and Latin America. At the same time, "the Committee...thought that the Assembly should not undertake responsibilities beyond its competence." Its members had therefore agreed "it was necessary to suppress a paragraph in the proposal [cited above]...and change it to a simple recommendation." The passage beginning "Hopes to see that teaching..." was eliminated from the motion as a result.[51]

When the committee presented its report to the Assembly, some debate ensued. Lafontaine began the discussion with some opening remarks about the proposal under consideration:

> We are all aware of the difficulties arising from the multitude of the world's languages and we are acquainted with the efforts which have been made for a long time towards establishing an auxiliary language common to all. That common language has a history attached to it and is employed in various countries. Those who have signed the Recommendation indicate the countries where the use of Esperanto has already attained considerable success. This Recommendation is supported by representatives of the various continents of the world.

According to Lafontaine, it was not the purpose of the "proposers of this motion...to ask the Assembly to transform itself into an academy." He recognized the usefulness of English and French in the affairs of the Assembly, stating: "Here we have made use of two languages and the great majority of the Members of the Assembly speak at least one of them." "This, however, will not always be the case," he warned.[52]

Representing France, Gabriel Hanotaux was one of the first delegates to respond.[53] "The question of languages," he claimed, was an issue "not yet ripe for discussion." "What in reality is asked of us," he argued, "is to approve the use of a new language." Hanotaux challenged the evidence of Esperanto's success. "It cannot be maintained," he insisted, "that the use of Esperanto is so widespread throughout the world that the adoption of the principle that it should be studied or the passing of a recommendation in its favor would make easier the actual conditions under which we deliberate." "Esperanto is not really known by more than a certain number of specialists," Hanotaux claimed, "and certainly by no nation in the world."[54]

Hanotaux continued, referring back to a discussion that had taken place earlier during the Assembly: "Several days ago we regretted not to be able to admit...the Spanish language, which is the tongue of a considerable number of mankind. Are we today going to begin to study a special language with which other artificial languages, which are no better known, dispute the claim to be in future universal?"[55] Indeed, a number of delegates (from Spain, Cuba, Venezuela, Columbia, Argentina, Peru, and Chile) had submitted a proposal to grant Spanish official status in the league.[56] The Assembly had eventually decided that speeches might be delivered in any language, but that the cost of translation and publication of documents in languages other than those officially sanctioned (English and French) would be the responsibility of individual delegations and not of the league.[57]

Hanotaux's defense of Spanish seemed noble enough at first. It quickly became clear, however, that the French delegate had another agenda. Hanotaux's objections on behalf of Spanish ultimately served as an opportunity to remind those assembled that French was the best candidate for an international language of diplomacy. Warning his colleagues not to follow the "new path" of Esperanto "imprudently," Hanotaux went further:

> At least allow me as a member of this Assembly, and a member of the Académie Française, to press the claims of a language which has a past, which has an essential spirit of its own, which has been used by great writers, which is known throughout the world, which has been an admirable vehicle of ideas and which has the right to defend its position against new creations that may develop perhaps at some far-off future date.[58]

Hanotaux framed his objections in terms of a temporal continuum: French was the language with "a past...defend[ing] its position against new creations." Esperanto was a language without history, one whose future development was uncertain and "far-off." Hanotaux seemed to be responding directly to Lafontaine's earlier assertion that Esperanto was a "common language" with "a history attached to it." For the French delegate, nationality and history were inextricably linked and both of these values were best embodied by the French language.

Leaving aside the official bilingual policy of the league, Hanotaux spoke as if French privilege was in danger yet again. He was not entirely mistaken about this. The league had approved two official languages, but French was still the language of the majority of the speeches delivered at its meetings. Esperanto thus posed a challenge to a persistent French linguistic privilege that the introduction of English had failed to shake in its entirety. Clemenceau and Pichon had not, in the end, been able to resist the claims (based on population and widespread use) that had been made by the English-speaking powers in Paris in 1919. Hanotaux, however, could on different grounds, resist this latest bid by a language seeking international status. Hanotaux's complaint that Esperanto was "not really known by more than a certain number of specialists and certainly by no nation in the world" was strategically savvy. Given that it was the league's mission to act collectively in international affairs while respecting national sovereignty, it would be difficult to justify the encouragement of any movement that might be read as undermining that sovereignty. Hanotaux had moved that the question of international language be deferred and the Assembly supported his motion.

Esperanto's French History

The question of an international language would come up again at the league's Second General Assembly in 1921. At this assembly, delegates in favor of Esperanto pushed the league to order a more extensive inquiry into the subject. The league's secretary-general Sir Eric Drummond agreed. Seeking information about the teaching and use of Esperanto in various countries, the Secretariat circulated a letter and questionnaire on the subject to member governments and also notified a number of Esperantist groups internationally.[59] This included the Universal Esperanto Association (UEA), an organization founded in 1908. In the months that followed, the UEA helped to organize an international conference in Geneva, bringing together promoters and teachers of the language from across the world. Drummond even gave a speech welcoming the Esperantists gathered at the conference.[60]

The Secretariat of the league submitted its report, *Esperanto as an International Auxiliary Language,* to the Third Assembly in 1922.[61] The report concluded that the use of an international language could be an excellent means of improving relations between the league's members. The Secretariat's body of evidence seemed to "show that in scientific, commercial, philanthropic, tourist and, even more in working-class circles, there is a feeling that it is urgently necessary to escape from the linguistic complications which impede international relations and particularly direct relations between peoples."[62] According to the report, "it [was] obvious that the problem of an international language [was] both a practical and a linguistic one."[63]

The Secretariat's report acknowledged the significance of both history and nationality to any consideration of the language question. It acknowledged French as "an admirable literary language...that plays a leading part in diplomatic relations in Europe." Despite French "claims to universality," however, the report cautioned that "it would touch on too delicate a question to

attempt to establish the supremacy of one national tongue over all others."
While it was true that "an artificial language lacks the prestige conferred by
centuries of long historical and literary tradition," this very neutrality could
work in its favor. An artificial language would not only transcend national
differences but according to the report, it was possible that such a language
"may be easier to learn than a national language whose grammar is full of
irregularities." At the same time, an artificial language "could never become
more than a secondary language, limited to exceptional relations between
persons of different nations." It "could not compete with languages which
have an historical tradition."[64]

The report specifically recognized Esperanto as "the most widely spoken
artificial language" in the world. While the league Secretariat was careful
to state its respect for national languages, the report did describe Esperanto
as "a living language." The Secretariat noted that the language had been
spreading for more than thirty-five years and that it was "possible to express
feelings in it." This was, in fact, a language with a history. Esperanto had
"begun to attain a style," and "some writers and speakers…use[d] it with
force and elegance."[65] In its final pages, the report highlighted "the unanim-
ity and equality produced…by the use of a common language." Esperanto
placed "everybody on the same footing." The Secretariat concluded with
great hopes for the future:

> Language is great force, and the League of Nations has every reason
> to watch with particular interest the progress of the Esperanto move-
> ment which, should it become more widespread, may one day lead to
> great results from the point of view of the moral unity of the world.[66]

The Secretariat's report also examined the development of Esperanto in a
number of the league's member nations, including France. Zamenhof himself had published French editions of his Esperanto textbook and dictionary
that were well received in France.[67] Esperantists were present at the *Exposition universelle* in Paris in 1900, and France had become an important
site for the development of the movement by the early twentieth century.[68]
In 1905, the French government made Zamenhof an officer of the Légion
d'honneur. The first Universal Esperanto Congress was held in France that
same year. According to the league report, "the principal leaders of the Esperanto movement before the war were almost all French University men."[69]
French organizations, such as the Société française de l'Espéranto, created
in 1903, encouraged the spread of the language both within and beyond
France in publications such as *Le Monde espérantiste* (established in 1908)

and *France-Espéranto* published by the Office Central Espérantiste in Paris (established in 1915).[70]

Although a French delegate (Hanotaux) had voiced the strongest objections to the international language, the report provided evidence that his position did not represent the views of the nation as a whole: some of the most important figures in the Esperantist movement were French, and some of the most important figures in French intellectual life before, during, and after the First World War were, in fact, Esperantists. The cooperative and international ideals behind the language appealed to those who saw the breakdown of political and cultural differences as the route to a future entente between nations. The internationalism at the heart of the artificial language movement made Esperanto a particularly appealing project to those pacifist intellectuals (often, but not always, of the political Left) who saw the movement as an opportunity to develop stronger ties with colleagues and comrades around the world.

It was Eugène Adam, a Parisian laborer who, in 1921, formed an organization to unite the Esperantist workers of the world, the Sennacieca Asocia Tutmonda (SAT) or the "Association of Non-Nationalists." Adam had fought in the First World War as an ambulance driver and had learned about Esperanto during his service. After 1917, he had also become an ardent supporter of communist revolution. An internationalist on all fronts, Adam or "Lanti" (a nickname from the French *l'anti* or "the one against") became the editor of *Le Travailleur Espérantiste* (The Esperantist Worker).[71]

The Esperantist cause also found advocates in a number of French writers, many of who had fought in the war and, as a result of that experience, had pledged their resistance to the forces of militarism and nationalism. This included key members of the internationalist, pacifist movement known as Clarté, a movement that sought to bring about a social regeneration via the collaborative efforts of an international intellectual elite.[72] Henri Barbusse, the prize-winning author of *Le Feu* (1916), perhaps the most famous French novel of the war, was a leader of the Clarté movement in France. Barbusse had emerged from the conflict devastated by the violence and hatred he had witnessed and committed to creating a better world. His pacifism and internationalism were clearly expressed in both his enthusiasm for Esperanto and in his adherence to the French Communist Party after its formation in 1920. He also served as an honorary president of a SAT congress and contributed to *Le Travailleur Espérantiste* (in Esperanto).[73] In 1921, Barbusse wrote a preface to *Cours rationnel et complet d'Espéranto*, one of the standard textbooks of the international language published by the SAT. Barbusse used words and phrases like *great awakening, renaissance,* and *progress* in his thoughts on Esperanto's potential in the contemporary world. The war had brought about so much pain and strife, and Barbusse believed strongly that a "common language [wa]s the first tool that all the proletarians and the sufferers" harmed by class and militarist conflicts could use to move toward a better world society.[74]

Romain Rolland, another Clarté member and a winner of the Nobel Prize for Literature in 1915, also favored the use of an international language. Rolland's wartime experience had ignited in him an intense pacifism. After 1919, he committed himself to the development of an "intellectual's international," a movement to help prevent future violence and conflict.[75] Rolland voiced publicly his support for Esperanto shortly after the war, in two letters (dated June 25, 1919 and April 14, 1920) addressed to Eugène Adam/Lanti of the SAT.[76] In these missives, Rolland wrote that he "believe[d] absolutely in the need for an international language." He advocated the "mandatory" teaching of Esperanto in "all of the primary schools of Europe." "Without this," he insisted, "there will be no serious or lasting international rapprochement.... Let Esperanto give hearing to the deaf...!" Rolland exclaimed.[77] He criticized the French socialist press for remaining too tied to party matters and neglecting the "great international questions of a general interest—not exclusively socialist, but human." According to Rolland, the international language issue was a crucial one that needed to be addressed if the communist "International" itself was to be more than "just a word."[78]

Esperanto could appeal to French businessmen as well as to elements of the nation's literary elite. According to the League of Nations' 1922 report, the Paris Chamber of Commerce also supported the teaching of Esperanto in business schools in France. Having conducted a study of the language in 1920, the chamber had issued its own report in 1921, concluding that Esperanto could be very useful in international trade.[79] At the same time, however, that report also cautioned that Esperanto's use should not interfere with the use and appreciation of French. Early in the report submitted by the chamber's Commercial Educational Committee, its author, André Baudet, noted, "It is indispensable that this language should not be established to the detriment of the French language, to which we are deeply attached."

Baudet insisted that Esperanto "be regarded as a tool, a 'code' to be used as a method of interpretation." He pointed out that the "Committee... attached great importance to the name 'auxiliary' with which it would wish the international language to be always qualified, as national languages must not be affected in any way." Baudet went on to underline the "respect [for] native languages of other nations, also rich in literary masterpieces." The whole point of a "universal language" was that it should "not be a national language." "The choice of any one national language," Baudet argued, "would arouse strong opposition on the part of the other nations." There-fore any "universal language must be an artificial language."[80] An interna-tional language had to be understood as both "auxiliary" and "artificial." While figures like Gabriel Hanotaux rejected Esperanto because it did not represent any particular *nation,* it was this very disconnection that made the international language an important emblem of a more peaceful inter-national future.[81]

Finally, Esperanto also made a good deal of sense to numerous French scientists who saw the language as a practical tool for the dissemination and exchange of technical and theoretical knowledge. For example, the Association française pour l'avancement des sciences, the Association gé-nérale des ingénieurs des travaux publiques de l'état, as well as the Sec-tion française d'océanographie all endorsed the use of the language. Several members of the French Académie des Sciences signed a petition in 1921 supporting the teaching of Esperanto in technical schools, the use of the language at international congresses, and in publications. Its supporters encouraged the development of a scientific vocabulary in Esperanto that might facilitate international exchanges between members of the various branches of the scientific community.[82] In December 1921, on the front page of the newspaper *Le Petit Parisien,* Charles Richet, winner of the Nobel Prize in Physiology and Medicine in 1913, and one of the petition's signatories, waxed enthusiastically about the great hopes he had for Espe-ranto and a "new era in human relations":

> One day, maybe soon, we will be amazed that a humanity that could have given itself a common language so easily, hesitated to take this small trouble. Our grandnephews will be beyond stupefaction when they read about the infantile allegations that have been made in op-position to this immense progress...retrogrades, men with glasses and wigs, the heirs of those who balked at the rotation of the Earth, the circulation of the blood, railroads, automobiles, aviation.... They have not understood. We must forgive them.[83]

For Richet and others, Esperanto was a language of the future. To resist its spread was to fight progress itself. Once again, the image of a future "look-ing back" on the present could be a powerful rhetorical device for observers, whether enthusiastic or hostile, of change.

Banned in France

The league Secretariat was careful to point out in 1922 that, despite a broad and active base of French support for the language, Esperanto did not have *official*, state approval in France. What accounted for the disjuncture between France's numerous Esperanto advocates and the French government's opposition to the language? To answer this important question, it is necessary to consider more closely the context of domestic politics and the broader foreign policy of France with respect to entities like the league during the immediate postwar years. In the early 1920s, the *Bloc national*, a center-right alliance that had come to power in France in 1919, set the agenda and policies for the nation at home and in the international realm. Intensely nationalist in orientation, the bloc sought a postwar continuation of the wartime *union sacrée*. Politically united in opposition to the forces of socialism and communism, the coalition also pursued a rigid policy with respect to the terms of the Treaty of Versailles and the question of German reparations payments.[84]

From the First Assembly of the League of Nations, the French government had expressed its uneasiness about international cooperation on certain issues. France had always held a privileged position in cultural and intellectual affairs, and it seemed at first as though the league's involvement in this domain could only amount to interference beyond its mandate. French delegate Gabriel Hanotaux's stance on Esperanto in 1920 had been a striking example of this resistance to the idea of cultural internationalism.

The French government had soon realized, however, that cooperation on this front might actually promote France's interests, contributing to national security by supplementing more traditional forms of diplomacy with a "cultural arm." If the league were going to concern itself with culture, it would, in fact, be prudent for France to take a leading role rather than allowing some other nation or nations to achieve predominance in this area. Furthermore, any increase in the international profile of the French language, and French cultural and intellectual achievements, could only reinforce educational and other domestic efforts to promote national unity and pride. The French government therefore became quite active in the promotion and organization of the league's two main cultural entities: The International Committee on Intellectual Cooperation (ICIC), which would hold its first session in September 1922, and the International Institute of Intellectual Cooperation (IIIC), which would be set up in Paris in 1924.[85]

The protection of French interests in the international realm was linked to defensive political and cultural policies at home. On the domestic front, the bloc sought to shield national culture from international threats. Shortly before the League of Nations Secretariat produced its report on Esperanto, the French government had issued a ban on the teaching of the international language in the nation's schools.[86] On June 3, 1922, Léon Bérard, the French minister of public instruction, circulated a memorandum prohibiting "all propaganda in favor of Esperanto."[87] Bérard acknowledged the petitions in favor of the international language issued by various French organizations and associations. He also noted that "for some time" it had been brought to his attention that both students and teachers in French schools seemed to be increasingly inclined toward Esperanto. Indeed, France was a center of Esperantist activity and schoolteachers had become an important constituency in the movement. Given this interest, Bérard concluded "that the time [had] come to examine the Esperanto question in relation to public education."[88]

Bérard was "absolutely convinced that Esperanto had no place in education." "A language," he claimed, "must be both widely used and possess a literature worthy of the name in order to be taught in our classrooms. Esperanto has neither one, nor the other." For Bérard, the projections being made by advocates of the international language were wrongheaded and "chimerical." While Bérard acknowledged its "practical advantages" for "commercial relations," he could not envision the language having more than "the value of a telegraphic code." "French will always be the language of civilization," Bérard insisted.[89] The minister's ideal future was, like Clemenceau's had been, rooted in the past rather than in any radical break with tradition.

There were "dangers" attached to Esperanto according to the minister. "The development of Esperanto" was "detrimental to the teaching of living languages." Bérard also believed the "international organizations with headquarters outside France" that promoted Esperanto had ulterior motives that went beyond "simplifying linguistic relations between people." While he did not cite any specific evidence for his claims, Bérard was confident that these organizations were working actively to eliminate the very "raison d'être of a national culture," destroying "the Latin spirit and French genius in particular." Esperanto was an enemy of the French language and the nation as a whole. Bérard therefore urged the officials under his ministry to emphasize "the importance...of living languages" in their schools. He also asked these principals and supervisors to "warn" their instructors against sharing any "Esperantist propaganda" with their students. Finally, Bérard made it clear that school premises were not to be rented or used by any groups "who would use these to organize courses or conferences related to Esperanto."[90]

In the Esperantist community, the response to Bérard's condemnation of the international language was swift. "M. Bérard... is openly declaring war against us," claimed *Le Monde espérantiste*. Bérard was a "reactionary" and his memo was "stupid," "an aberration."[91] By November 1922, the French Ligue des droits de l'homme denounced the memo officially as an unjust repression of educational freedom. The league's founder, Ferdinand Buisson, felt strongly that Bérard was using the ban on Esperanto to undermine the political Left in France.[92] While Bérard would protest that his memorandum was not "inspired by any political agenda," it was clear from his comments about the language and its organizations, that this was not the case.[93] As a member of the conservative Bloc national government, Bérard was carrying out the broader political agenda of the coalition. His proscription expressed that government's commitment to the preservation of tradition and its deep anxieties about the erosion of French culture.

Bérard's ban would only last a short time. In 1924, the parties of the center-right in France were defeated by a left coalition known as the *Cartel des gauches*. This new government overturned the prohibition against Esperanto and subsequent French governments would not revisit the hostility of these early postwar years.[94] The position of the French government from 1922 to 1924 was extremely significant, however. These were decisive years for the spirit and practices of internationalism, and the official French opposition to Esperanto had important effects, from Paris to Geneva.

The League of National Languages

In September 1922, delegates to the Third Assembly of the League of Nations discussed the Secretariat's report on Esperanto, engaging in yet another round of debate over the international language. This time, the Brazilian delegate, Raul do Rio Branco expressed his worry that the league "might be attacked on the ground that it was acting as a kind of super-State" if it promoted the artificial language. Rio Branco advised caution: "Language was one of the strongest elements in nationality, and it was necessary to exercise the greatest prudence before tampering with it." Echoing comments made by Hanotaux and others, the Brazilian delegate insisted, "The best way to encourage international sympathy and to know other people was to study foreign languages." Furthermore, "Esperanto had neither history nor literature."[95]

During this most recent round of debate, the French delegate, Georges Marie Reynald played a key role, ensuring that the question of an international language would receive careful scrutiny before the league as a whole made any resolutions. The Assembly decided, on Reynald's recommendation, to refer the question to the league's International Committee on Intellectual Cooperation (ICIC).[96] Comprised of a number of international representatives, this committee had been given a mandate to deal with matters of education and culture, as well as the exchange of philosophical and scientific ideas between nations. In 1923, its members included a Norwegian zoologist, an Indian professor of political economy, a Dutch professor of theoretical physics, and two French scholars of international renown: the philosopher Henri Bergson (who served as the committee's chair) and the physicist Marie Curie.

The ICIC dealt with the question of international languages at its second session held in Geneva from July 26 to August 2, 1923.[97] In addition to the ICIC's official members, a number of other experts attended these meetings. These included Julien Luchaire, France's inspector general of public instruction (under Minister Léon Bérard).[98] It is worth noting that Luchaire presented a "Resolution on Mutual International Assistance for the Study of Modern Languages, Literatures and Civilisations" just prior to the committee's discussion of "questions relating to the teaching of Esperanto and the problem of an international language." Though perhaps not deliberately, the priority of these agenda items reflected the French insistence on national rather than artificial languages.[99]

Early on in the discussion, Gonzague de Reynold, a Swiss professor of French literature declared: "An auxiliary language might be useful for commercial purposes and for the tourist, but this question was of no interest to the Committee on Intellectual Cooperation."[100] Reynold, who regarded the league Secretariat's 1922 report with skepticism, insisted that delegates already had at their disposal two adequate "auxiliary" languages: English which was "chiefly the economic auxiliary language," and French, "the auxiliary language of intellectual and diplomatic life."[101] Reynold outlined a series of recommendations, reiterating points that other delegates had made many times: the league was "not competent to express an opinion in favour of any particular natural or artificial language" and should, instead, do its best to promote "the study of modern languages...as the surest means of maintaining in each country the intellectual 'elite' and of promoting mutual comprehensions between the various nations."[102]

Luchaire spoke up soon after Reynold. While he accepted that "an artificial language was useful if it allowed people from different countries to communicate one with another," he did not believe that Esperanto would really enable intellectual exchange. "The danger of an artificial international language," Luchaire argued, "would be in the belief that through it the necessity for learning living languages could be dispensed with. In this case, instead of assisting the promotion of goodwill, the artificial international language would alienate it."[103] Luchaire's position was in keeping with his government's general policy on the language question.

After a number of other members shared their views both in support of and in opposition to the idea of an artificial language, the committee's chair Henri Bergson offered his thoughts to close the discussion. In his remarks, Bergson argued that a "free play" of "intellectual and moral forces" should decide the question of Esperanto rather than any recommendation of the Committee on Intellectual Cooperation or the League of Nations as a whole. According to Bergson, "The object of the League of Nations was to bring nations together, and here there was no question of that purely mechanical rapprochement which consisted in facilitating communications." Bergson insisted that "the facilities offered by an artificial language in this direction would not, any more than the telegraph or the railway, influence spiritual rapprochement." If people wanted to understand one another, they could either live amongst one another or study their languages and literature from a distance. According to the philosopher, "language was imbued with the spirit of the people who spoke it." Bergson believed that when people from different nations learned one another's languages, "sympathy...was an inevitable result...even when circumstances might create a clash of interest." Given that "the whole object of [an] artificial language was to make superfluous in practice the study of living languages," this "rapprochement" could never be facilitated by the use of Esperanto or any other artificial system. National languages had to be preserved and it was vital that a body like the League of Nations support these. Bergson concluded that it was "henceforth the business of the League of Nations and of its Committee on Intellectual Cooperation...to encourage the study of living languages, and not that of an artificial language."[104] When he finished his comments the committee put the question to a vote, deciding "by 6 votes to 1, with 3 abstentions, that it ought not to recommend an artificial language."[105] The General Assembly did not pass any resolutions against Esperanto, but no significant future efforts were made to revive the proposal that the language be used in the league.[106] In 1925, the league sanctioned Esperanto as a "clear language" in telegrams.[107]

Bergson's statements on Esperanto were the culmination of several years of French opposition to the international language.[108] Representatives of the French government in the early interwar years faced the dilemma of imagining a peaceful, cooperative, international future while protecting what they believed to be a fundamental pillar of French national identity: the French language. Following the Paris Peace Conference, the future, whether in the form of linguistic diversity or linguistic unity, seemed to come at the expense of the historic privilege of French. French delegates to the League of Nations resisted Esperanto at every turn, just as French officials had tried to resist English as a second official language in 1919. While proposals that favored Esperanto had typically included statements about the respect for national languages, these attempts at reassurance did not soothe fears about the effacement of cultural differences between member nations. An emblem of a universalism that was too uncomfortable for the French political and cultural conservatives in power in the early 1920s, Esperanto was neither natural nor national enough.

In 1921, Paul Gsell published the collection *Les matinées de la Villa Said: Propos d'Anatole France,* a series of conversations he had had with France over several meetings at the Nobel Prize winning author's home in Paris.[109] In one episode Gsell recorded, France received a guest named "Capitaine X," an avid Esperantist. After singing Esperanto's praises to France, X informed the author that one of his novels had already been translated into Esperanto. He had come to seek France's permission to translate others from the latter's oeuvre. France said that he "did not want to rebuff a friend," but that he would rather the Captain not make such a request. "What do you have against the language, *Maître?*" X asked.[110] France insisted that while he harbored no hostility against Esperanto, he doubted that the language could really capture or convey human thoughts and emotions. France went on to explain his position:

> Come, my dear Captain, imagine that you receive a lovely doll as a gift. Her big, soft eyes would be shadowed with long, heavenly curved lashes. Her mouth would be a delicious pink, like the flesh of cherries. Her hair would be like rays of sunshine. She'll laugh. She'll talk with you. She'll call you "*Mon chéri!*"
> Would you love her?
> Imagine yourself on a desert island with her for a long time and, all of a sudden, a real woman appears, even a fairly ugly one, but nevertheless a real woman. Would the doll be the one you'd address your madrigals to?
> Your Esperanto is the doll.
> The real woman is the French language.

And this woman is so beautiful, so modest, so bold, so touching, so voluptuous, so chaste, so noble, so familiar, so crazy, so wise, that we love her with our entire soul, and we are never tempted to betray her.[111]

France's perspective was one that a number of French observers of Esperanto had shared, though they had not always expressed their resistance with such flourish. National languages (and the French language in particular) were organic and alive; Esperanto was an invention. Anatole France described the international language's synthetic nature in corporeal terms that were intensely gendered and sexualized: language was a lover not to be replaced with a doll, a device, no matter how beautiful or seductive.

Like the technologies and appliances I discussed in the first chapter of this book, Esperanto could be regarded as a kind of cultural prosthesis: artificial, inorganic, and mechanical. For those who believed an international language could help to bring about a world without conflict and war, Esperanto was a cultural *prosthesis* in a positive sense, the *trace* of a brighter, more harmonious future. For others who equated Esperanto's spread with the diminishing status of the French language—and with the waning political and cultural power of France in international affairs—Esperanto appeared to be the linguistic *trace* of the future *disappearance* of (French) nationality altogether. Once again, the landscape of the future, like the physical and psychic landscapes of the recent past, appeared to be a terrain of loss. The French body might become less human for better or for worse, Paris might be improved or ruined, territorial borders defended or overrun, civilization advanced or destroyed. An artificial language could be read as a threat or a promise that the future would be international rather than French...it would speak another language.

The Future's Remains

A nation is therefore a large-scale solidarity, constituted by the feeling of the sacrifices that one has made in the past and of those that one is prepared to make in the future. It presupposes a past; it is summarized, however, in the present by a tangible fact, namely, consent, the clearly expressed desire to continue a common life.

—ERNEST RENAN, "What Is a Nation?" (1882)

"The future" is an elusive subject for a history.[1] At any given moment it has simultaneously too much content and none at all. Consisting of a multiplicity of imaginative visions, predictions, and projections, it never "happens," has never happened. It is therefore difficult to know how best to close a study of the "culture of anticipation" in the interwar years. Many histories end with outcomes, reflections on the years that came after the period under study. In my case, this approach would lead me to a discussion of the outbreak of the Second World War in 1939, the French defeat of 1940, and the years of occupation, collaboration, and resistance that followed. It might even serve as an opportunity to explore the period on the other side of that conflict, looking back on the entre-deux-guerres as a rehearsal, a precursor, and a testing ground for ideas about and approaches to machines, cities, military conflicts, and international influences that have had an impact on postwar, that is to say post-1945, France. How does the landscape of the interwar help us to understand the internal rifts of the "dark years" that followed? What were the postwar legacies of this ensemble of political divisions and the cultural formations that went with them? These are the sorts of questions that look to "the future" from the interwar years, but with the hindsight of the historian who knows of various outcomes, who seeks to explain the origins of some events and the impact of others.

As I tried to make clear at the outset, however, the evaluation of aftereffects has not been the purpose of this project. I have tried instead to respect the integrity of the futures under investigation rather than evaluate them in light of what has since been realized or proved illusory. As such, this book has attempted to stay close to the "present tense" of the future between 1918 and 1939, to link its imaginative variations to the preoccupations of the years *in between* rather than to the events that unfolded in their wake. In some cases, the futures planned or expected included the prediction of another military conflict, anticipating the "interwar" itself.

I set out to write a book about the culture of anticipation from 1918 to 1939 as a way to push the envelope of our understanding of France after the First World War. I chose the future as a category of historical analysis and a way of reading with the intention of breaking with the histories of memory and commemoration that have dominated the study of twentieth-century France. But the future has brought me back to memory many times over the course of these five chapters. In the cases I have outlined, "the future" appeared in many forms: as a set of strategies and plans actively constructed and pursued, as a series of possible events expected with either eagerness or anxiety, as a temporal "next" on a continuum from the past, through the spaces, places, ideas, and movements of the present. The five zones of inquiry that appear here were not the only ones available to me, but they did emerge from my explorations as cultural and political sites saturated with anticipation: the body, the city, military defense, the idea of *civilisation,* and language. In the "present tense" explored above, the future often figured as a label, a way to denote something that seemed to break with the present, a premonition of changes not yet complete but apparently underway. Certain objects achieved futuristic status in the French cultural imagination during these years. A range of intimate machines and appliances, skyscrapers, airplanes and gas masks, American cities and ways of life, Esperanto—all became traces of possible worlds to come. Representations of these traces appeared in a variety of science fictions, from literary stories and images, to urban plans, to cultural critiques, to military strategies, and international diplomacy. The visions and projections I map here were inevitably dependent on everything that had come before, everything that various French observers imagined as their national cultural "tradition" and historical experience. While many architects of "the future" or self-appointed guardians of "the past" represented these temporalities as binary opposites, the cultures of memory and anticipation were inevitably imbricated. Collective anticipation, like collective memory, was structured around traces, loss, and disappearance. A cultural form with a set of privileged themes and objects, anticipation was, inevitably, implicated in the memory and forgetting of experience and the *lived time,* to return to Minkowski's formulation, of the present.

That ideas about the future should depend on the experience and recollection of the past, its more and less accurate representation, is perhaps not surprising. But there is more to this relationship between cultural memory and anticipation, something revealed in different ways in each of the cases above. There is a dialogic relationship between these cultural forces that is apparent here in these debates about the future of French bodies, of Paris, of the nation's borders, its idea of civilization, and its forms of linguistic expression and communication. Anticipation also has an important role to play in determining and shaping what will become the stuff of cultural memory at a given historical moment. There is, therefore, in the discourses and debates regarding the future that I explore here something to be learned about the way that nostalgia emerges in a culture. If nostalgia can be characterized as a "hypochondria" that looks backward and invents a past, the evidence I have considered here also suggests that it has origins in the ways that individuals and societies plan for and expect the future. Nostalgia is generated in advance of loss as well as in its wake. None of the objects considered in these five chapters had, as yet, in the interwar years, fully disappeared. Images of a future in which the body might lose its organic quality; in which Paris might cease to be a historic, "French" city; in which the notion of territory might become completely obsolete; in which civilization itself might (d)evolve into a future primitivism; in which the French language might lose its cultural and political raison d'être at home and abroad—these images could be used strategically in the present. For figures like the architect Le Corbusier, "the future" could serve as a means to advocate different forms of "modernization," from the transformation of cities to the overhaul of domestic spaces and ways of life. For commentators like Georges Duhamel, "the future" could be used rhetorically to signal a break with values and habits treasured as part of a national heritage, or *patrimoine*. In both of these ways of invoking "the future," "Frenchness" would come to seem a kind of anachronism, a national cultural identity seemingly fixed, out of time with the present, and aligned with a past slowly slipping away. In historical debates about the "modernity" of France, this characterization has become a form of essentialism about national cultural possibilities, feeding analyses that seek to identify and explain the origins of various French "traditionalisms" so-called. But the notion that "Frenchness" is a cultural opposite of "modernity" has a history, and "the future" is a fundamental part of that past.

Notes

Introduction: "The Future": A Useful Category of Historical Analysis

1. My title and framework here are inspired by Joan Wallach Scott's classic essay, "Gender: A Useful Category of Historical Analysis," *American Historical Review* 91.5 (December 1986): 1053–75. The structure of Scott's critical definition of gender as both "a constitutive element of social relationships based on perceived differences between the sexes, and...a primary way of signifying relationships of power" (1067) has informed my own reading of "the future" as both a temporal field imagined and anticipated *and* a "way of signifying" or articulating a variety of cultural and political phenomena in interwar France. All translations are my own unless otherwise indicated.

2. Eugène Minkowski, *Lived Time: Phenomenological and Psychopathological Studies,* trans. Nancy Metzel (Evanston, IL: Northwestern University Press, 1970), 6. Originally published as *Le Temps vécu: études phénoménologiques et psychopathologiques* (Paris: Collection de l'évolution psychiatrique, 1933). Born in Saint Petersburg in 1885, Minkowski studied medicine in Warsaw and Munich and later pursued philosophy and eventually psychiatry. In 1915, he joined the French army and moved to Paris after 1918. He was the editor of the psychiatric journal *L'Evolution psychiatrique.* See Yves Pélicier's "Vivre le temps: Eugène Minkowski," in the French edition, Eugène Minkowski, *Le Temps vécu: études phénoménologiques et psychopathologiques* (Paris: Presses Universitaires de France, 1968), v–xi.

3. Eugène Minkowski, *Lived Time,* 6–7.

4. See Henri Bergson, *Introduction à la métaphysique: Essai sur les données immédiates de la conscience* (Paris: F. Alcan, 1889). For a more in-depth discussion of memory in Bergson's work, see *Matière et mémoire* (Paris: F. Alcan, 1896).

5. Minkowski, *Lived Time,* 6.

6. Ibid., 79–91, 180–93. In addition to activity and expectation, Minkowski's analysis of the lived future explored desire and hope, prayer and the ethical act. In *The Culture of Time and Space, 1880–1918* (Cambridge: Harvard University Press, 1983), historian Stephen Kern discusses Minkowski's work, emphasizing the relationship between the psychiatrist's treatment of temporality and his experience of the war (89–90 and 280–82).

7. For an overview of the varied deployment of "memory" and debates about its workings in the humanities and social sciences, see Susannah Radstone's edited collection, *Memory and Methodology* (New York: Berg, 2000). See also Wulf Kansteiner, "Memory: A Methodological Critique of Collective Memory Studies," *History and Theory* 41.2 (May 2002): 179–97. Scholars from a number of fields refer frequently to the study by Frances Yates, *The Art of Memory* (Chicago: University of Chicago Press, 1966). Yates's discussion of the distinctions between Renaissance, medieval, and ancient mnemonic systems has been foundational to the development of a field of "memory studies" within and beyond history.

8. One of the classic studies in this area is Paul Fussell's *The Great War and Modern Memory* (New York: Oxford University Press, 1975). This work continues to influence scholarly studies of literature and "modern memory," including Patrick Quinn and Steven Trout, eds., *The Literature of the Great War Reconsidered: Beyond Modern Memory* (New York: Palgrave, 2001); See also Jay Winter, *Sites of Memory, Sites of Mourning: The Great War in European Cultural History* (Cambridge: Cambridge University Press, 1995), and Jay Winter and Emmanuel Sivan, eds., *War and Remembrance in the Twentieth Century* (Cambridge: Cambridge University Press, 1999). Works focusing on the French context include Omer Bartov, "Martyrs' Vengeance: Memory, Trauma and Fear of War in France, 1918–1940," *Historical Reflections/ Réflexions historiques* 22.1 (1996): 47–76; Daniel Sherman, *The Construction of Memory in Interwar France* (Chicago: University of Chicago Press, 1999); Allen Douglas, *War, Memory, and the Politics of Humor: The Canard Enchaîné and World War I* (Berkeley: University of California Press, 2002); Debra Kelly, ed., *Remembering and Representing the Experience of War in Twentieth-Century France: Committing to Memory* (Lewiston: E. Mellen Press, 2000); and Annette Becker, "Memory Gaps: Maurice Halbwachs, Memory, and the Great War," *Journal of European Studies* 35.1 (2005): 102–13.

9. See Pierre Nora, ed., *Les Lieux de mémoire* (Paris: Gallimard, 1984–1992); Nora's introduction to the collection appeared in English translation as, "Between Memory and History," trans. Marc Raudebush, *Representations, Special Issue: Memory and Counter-Memory* 26 (spring 1989): 7–25. A significant portion of the original project has been translated into English as *Realms of Memory: Rethinking the French Past,* 3 vols., ed. Lawrence D. Kritzman, trans. Arthur Goldhammer (New York: Columbia University Press, 1996–1998).

10. Reflections on the approach and impact of the *Lieux de mémoire* project abound. Sherman, for example, notes that "Nora's overall schema . . . is too broad and, in a literal sense, too categorical to illuminate the dynamics of interwar commemoration in any detail." See *The Construction of Memory,* 3. For a useful critical outline, see Nancy Wood, "Memory's Remains: *Les Lieux de mémoire,*" in *Vectors of Memory: Legacies of Trauma in Postwar Europe* (New York: Berg, 1999), 15–38. A helpful review essay that historicizes Nora's collection while pointing to its inclusions and exclusions, particularly with respect to the colonial past, is Hue-Tam Ho Tai's "Remembered Realms: Pierre Nora and French National Memory," *American Historical Review* 106.3 (June 2001): 906–22.

11. See Richard Terdiman, *Present Past: Modernity and the Memory Crisis* (Ithaca, NY: Cornell University Press, 1993), 3; and Matt Matsuda, *The Memory of the Modern* (Oxford: Oxford University Press, 1996). These scholars have considered the intersections between "memory" and "modernity" from the nineteenth century to the outbreak of the First World War. A study of the politics of war monuments and memorials after 1918, Sherman's *The Construction of Memory* examines the material and visual culture of remembrance and commemoration. In *The Vichy Syndrome: History and Memory in France since 1944,* trans. Arthur Goldhammer (Cambridge, MA: Harvard University Press, 1991), Henry Rousso has emphasized the postwar memory and repression of French collaboration and resistance during World War II. The work of Benjamin Stora and others has contributed to the ongoing discussion of the Algerian war and the legacies of decolonization, a history that resonates with contemporary issues of culture, citizenship, racial and religious difference in France. See Stora's, *La Gangrène et l'oubli: la mémoire de la guerre d'Algérie* (Paris: La Découverte, 1991);

Anne Donadey, "Une certaine idée de la France: The Algeria Syndrome and Struggles over French Identity," in *Identity Papers: Contested Nationhood in Twentieth-Century France*, ed. Steven Ungar and Tom Conley (Minneapolis: University of Minnesota Press, 1996), 215–32; Richard Derderian, "Algeria as a lieu de mémoire: Ethnic Minority Memory and National Identity in Contemporary France," *Radical History Review* 83 (spring 2002): 28–43; Paul Silverstein, *Algeria in France: Transpolitics, Race, and Nation* (Bloomington: Indiana University Press, 2004); Alec G. Hargreaves, ed., *Memory, Empire, and Postcolonialism: Legacies of French Colonialism* (New York: Lexington Books, 2005); and Todd Shepard, *The Invention of Decolonization: The Algerian War and the Remaking of France* (Ithaca, NY: Cornell University Press, 2006).

12. For more on this ideology, see Herman Lebovics, *True France: The Wars Over Cultural Identity, 1900–1945* (Ithaca, NY: Cornell University Press, 1992).

13. Svetlana Boym, *The Future of Nostalgia* (New York: Basic Books, 2002).

14. Boym develops two categories for examining nostalgia: the restorative and the reflective. While restorative nostalgia seeks to recreate and revive a "lost" past, reflective nostalgia lingers in the experience of loss itself, the pain of exile, and the impossibility of return.

15. On the notion of "collective memory," Nora and others take as a theoretical point of departure the work of the French sociologist Maurice Halbwachs. While Bergson's work emphasized the subjective experience of time and memory, Halbwachs argued that memory is always articulated in and through social groups and processes, that "while the collective memory endures and draws strength from its base in a coherent body of people, it is individuals as group members who remember." See Maurice Halbwachs, *The Collective Memory*, trans. Francis J. Ditter and Vida Yazdi Ditter (New York: Harper Collins, 1950; reprinted in 1980), 48. For more on Halbwachs, see Lewis Coser's introduction to Maurice Halbwachs, *On Collective Memory*, ed. and trans. Lewis Coser (Chicago: University of Chicago Press, 1992), 1–34.

16. I am indebted to Jennifer Jones for suggesting I organize the book along these lines.

17. The interwar is, historiographically speaking, exceptionally "overdetermined" in this regard, a period defined in terms of the memory of the First World War and anticipation of the Second. Historical studies and explanations rely inevitably on these event bookends to understand the period as years "in between." For example, the French historian Eugen Weber has designated "the 1920s [as] *l'après guerre*, lively and optimistic [while] the 1930s are distinctly *l'avant guerre*, increasingly morose and ill at ease." See Weber's *The Hollow Years: France in the 1930s* (New York: Norton, 1994), 8. Michael Miller has described the period in terms of a "feeling of living between a war that had passed and a war that was coming," a mood expressed in the futuristic and spy literature that appeared between the world wars. See *Shanghai on the Métro: Spies, Intrigue, and the French Between the Wars* (Berkeley: University of California Press, 1995), 13.

18. In his study, *Futures Past: On the Semantics of Historical Time* (New York: Columbia University Press, 2004), Koselleck examines time as a historical and historiographical phenomenon. Like Nora, Koselleck has also emphasized the historical transformation of conceptions of past and future. Whereas Nora draws particular attention to the late 1930s in France as the moment when, with the fall of the Third Republic, memory lost its collective and communal character, Koselleck discusses the modern period in general as one in which conceptions of the future increasingly emphasized its uncertainty and unpredictability. He argues for a divide in the history of perceptions of past and future, a break between a Christian eschatological sense of the future determined by—and continuous with—past experience and an open-ended, secular future of progress that superseded it in the West after the seventeenth century.

19. In "Visions of the Postwar: The Politics of Memory and Expectation in 1940s France," *History and Memory* 10.2 (1998): 68–101, Jon Cowans draws on Koselleck, observing that, in their emphasis on memory, historians have tended to neglect expectation and visions of the future as cultural and political forces. While I agree with Cowans on this point, I would add

that the tension between past and future had an important life in France before the watershed moment of 1940 he chooses as his starting point. The "inter" of the interwar (a perspective on the period with contemporary as well as historical and historiographical meaning) makes this moment a crucial one for the examination of the intricate relationship between memory and anticipation.

20. I am influenced here by Bruno Latour's *We Have Never Been Modern*, trans. Catherine Porter (Cambridge, MA: Harvard University Press, 1993). A number of historical studies of the twentieth century have interrogated the "modern" and the "traditional" in the French context. Informed by the *Lieux de mémoire* project, Romy Golan's *Modernity and Nostalgia: Art and Politics in France between the Wars* (New Haven, CT: Yale University Press, 1995) examines the visual and artistic production of the interwar years as evidence of "a period of increasing political, economic, and cultural entrenchment," x. Interrogating the terms *modernity* and *tradition*, Shanny Peer's *France on Display: Peasants, Provincials, and Folklore in the 1937 World's Fair* (Albany, NY: SUNY Press, 1998) considers French exhibits that showcased rural and regional life at the same time that they embraced technological innovation. For a useful overview of works that deal with the post-1945 period, see the review article by Herrick Chapman, "Modernity and Identity in Postwar France," *French Historical Studies* 22.2 (spring 1999): 291–314. Pointing to the ways that numerous scholars (particularly those working in North America) have reinscribed even when they seek to challenge "narratives of modernization" in their cultural historical analyses, Jackie Clarke has objected strongly to characterizations of a peculiarly French "struggle between tradition and modernity" in the twentieth century that privileges American economic and cultural methods and forms as the measures of advancement and "progress." See, for example, her article "France, America, and the Metanarrative of Modernization," *Contemporary French and Francophone Studies* 8.4 (2004): 365–77.

1. Machines for Being

1. *Le Miroir du Monde XXXe Siècle,* special Christmas issue, December 9, 1933. The illustrated magazine was published weekly from March 1930 through December 1937. It then fused with *Le Monde illustré,* eventually becoming known only by the latter title in 1945. The magazine subsequently merged with other publications several times, with name changes at every turn from *France-Illustration* in 1948 to *Nouveau Femina* in 1956.

2. *VU,* for example, published a special issue devoted to "the next war": "La Prochaine guerre," no. 152, February 11, 1931. In keeping with this theme, two years later, the magazine published "La Fin d'une civilisation," no. 259, March 1, 1933. In this issue, a number of articles addressed the implications of rationalization and mechanization. This included a piece by E. Weiss entitled "La machine rend l'homme inutile," 283–85, and a contribution from household expert Paulette Bernège entitled "Le Machinisme au service de la ménagère," 296–97.

3. "Féeries de l'avenir," *Lecture pour tous,* December 1932. The special issue on the future included a series of images of "Paris in the 21st Century."

4. See for example, E. Weiss, "Verrons-nous quelque jour la motocyclette aérienne," *Sciences et voyages,* no. 85, March 14, 1921, 14; "La TSF supprimera-t-elle l'affiche électorale?" *Sciences et voyages,* no. 261, August 28, 1924, 13; "La mode féminine connaîtra-t-elle le chapeau TSF?" *Sciences et voyages,* no. 265, September 25, 1924, 4 (author unknown); and Roger Simonet, "La terre, disparaîtra-t-elle en 1939?" *Sciences et voyages,* no. 749, January 4, 1934, ii–iii.

5. *Le Miroir du Monde XXXe Siècle,* December 9, 1933, 1.

6. "Cur XLVII, prince des dégusteurs et suavités interplanétaires" (pseudonym, actual author unknown), "Un millénaire de gastronomie," *Le Miroir du monde XXXe Siècle,* December 9, 1933, 30–32. "Curnonsky" was the pseudonym of Maurice Edmond Sailland. See Curnonsky and Marcel Rouff, *La France gastronomique. Guides des merveilles culinaires et*

des bonnes auberges de France (Paris: F. Rouff, 1921). This actual "Cur" also co-founded the Académie des gastronomes with Rouff in 1930. Historian Pascal Ory discusses Curnonsky's nostalgic perspective on French traditional and regional cuisine in his essay, "Gastronomy," in *Realms of Memory: The Construction of the French Past,* vol. 2, *Traditions,* ed. Pierre Nora, trans. Arthur Goldhammer (New York: Columbia University Press, 1997), 443–67. For more on Sailland/Curnonsky, see Simon Arbellot, *Curnonsky: Prince des gastronomes* (Paris: Productions de Paris, 1965). See also, the discussion of Curnonsky's role in defining "French" cuisine in the interwar years in Stephen Harp, *Marketing Michelin: Advertising and Cultural Identity in Twentieth-Century France* (Baltimore: Johns Hopkins University Press, 2001), 225–68.

7. "Jacqueline IV" (pseudonym, actual author unknown), "Chez le grand couturier: Les dernières super-élégances," in "Féeries de l'avenir," *Lecture pour tous,* December 1932, 29–36.

8. "Cur XLVII," "Un millénaire de gastronomie," 31.

9. Ibid.

10. See Charles Maier, "Between Taylorism and Technocracy: European Ideologies and the Vision of Industrial Productivity in the 1920s," *Journal of Contemporary History* 5.2 (1970): 27–61. On technocracy and the advocates of "modernization" in France, see Richard Kuisel, *Capitalism and State in Modern France: Renovation and Economic Management in the Twentieth Century* (Cambridge: Harvard University Press, 1981). In "La Vie Future: Some French Responses to Technological Society," *Journal of European Studies* 6.23 (1976): 172–89, Paul Gagnon explores these changes, focusing on French responses to technology and Americanization in the 1930s. On the earlier impact of Taylorism in France see George Humphreys, *Taylorism in France 1904–1920* (New York: Garland, 1986); Patrick Fridenson, "Un tournant taylorien de la société française," *Annales: Economies, Sociétés, Civilisations* 42.5 (1987): 1031–60; and Matthias Kipping, "Consultancies, Institutions, and the Diffusion of Taylorism in Britain, Germany and France, 1920s to 1950s," *Business History* 39.4 (1997): 67–83. Marjorie Beale's study of advertising in the first half of the twentieth century, *The Modernist Enterprise: French Elites and the Threat of Modernity 1900–1940* (Stanford: Stanford University Press, 1999), examines the anxieties French elites expressed regarding mass democracy, Taylorism, and Fordism after World War I.

11. See Anson Rabinbach, *The Human Motor: Energy, Fatigue, and the Origins of Modernity* (New York: Basic Books, 1990).

12. Leonard Smith, Stéphane Audoin-Rouzeau, and Annette Becker, *France and the Great War, 1914–1918* (Cambridge: Cambridge University Press, 2003), 96.

13. Jay Winter, "Victimes de la guerre: morts, blessés, et invalides," *Encyclopédie de la grande guerre 1914–1918: Histoire et culture,* ed. Stéphane Audoin-Rouzeau and Jean-Jacques Becker (Paris: Bayard, 2004): 1075–86. On the issue of wartime consent, suffering, and the impact of these losses in France, see the seminal study by Jean-Jacques Becker, *The Great War and the French People,* trans. Arnold Pomerans (New York: Berg, 1985).

14. On the challenges of demobilization in the immediate aftermath of the war, see Bruno Cabanes, *La Victoire endeuillée: La sortie de guerre des soldats français (1918–1920)* (Paris: Editions du Seuil, 2004). On the experiences of veterans, the history of their organizations, and forms of political engagement through the interwar years, see the classic study by Antoine Prost, *In the Wake of War: "Les anciens combattants" and French Society,* trans. Helen McPhail (New York: Berg, 1992).

15. Smith et al., *France and the Great War,* 96.

16. See Painlevé's introductory remarks in Amar's, *La prothèse et le travail des mutilés* (Paris: H. Dunod and E. Pinat, 1916), 2. Painlevé would go on to serve as minister of war in 1917, and again in 1925 and 1926. Published during the war, Amar's work set the terms for rehabilitation and reeducation in the years that followed. Before the First World War, he published *Le Rendement de la machine humaine* (Paris: J.-B. Baillère et fils, 1909), a version

of a thesis he submitted to the Faculté des sciences in Paris. Amar's later publications included *Le Moteur humain et les bases scientifiques du travail professionel* (Paris: H. Dunod and E. Pinat, 1914); *Le Devoir agricole et les blessés de guerre* (Paris: H. Dunod and E. Pinat, 1917); *The Physiology of Industrial Organisation and the Re-employment of the Disabled,* trans. Bernard Miall (London: The Library Press, 1918). This title was originally published as *Organisation physiologique du travail* (Paris: H. Dunod and E. Pinat, 1917); *L'Orientation professionelle* (Paris: H. Dunod, 1920); *Le Travail humain* (Paris: Impr. Plon-Nourrit et Cie., 1923); and a study of depopulation entitled *La Dénatalité devant la science* (Paris: Musée social, 1931).

17. Rabinbach, *The Human Motor,* 8. Rabinbach outlines the progress of Amar's career, placing his professional evolution within the context of a larger European interest in the science of work. See also William Schnieder, "The Scientific Study of Labor in Interwar France," *French Historical Studies* 17.2 (fall 1991): 410–47. While he mentions Amar, Schneider focuses on Edouard Toulouse, Jean-Marie Lahy, Henri Laugier, and Henri Piéron, the physiologists and psychologists who engaged with the problem of labor in the interwar years.

18. For more on these developments, see Rabinbach, *The Human Motor,* 238–70.

19. Ibid., 185–88.

20. Amar, *The Physiology of Industrial Organisation,* 228–29.

21. Ibid., 250.

22. On the issue of pensions and assistance, see Rabinbach, *The Human Motor,* 266.

23. See Mary Louise Roberts, *Civilization without Sexes: Reconstructing Gender in Postwar France, 1917–1927* (Chicago: Chicago University Press, 1994).

24. Amar, *The Physiology of Industrial Organisation,* 250–52. The American physician Silas Weir Mitchell had identified the phantom-limb phenomenon in 1867. In his study, Amar referred to a French translation of Mitchell's post–Civil War work entitled *Lésions des nerfs,* published in 1867. A proponent of the "rest cure" that secluded the patient, removing all stimuli thought to bring on illness, Mitchell had been particularly interested in neurasthenia, a category of nervous disorder that included a variety of physical and psychological symptoms. See T. J. Jackson Lears, *No Place of Grace: Antimodernism and the Transformation of American Culture 1880–1920* (New York: Pantheon Books, 1981), 50–53.

25. See Amar, *The Physiology of Industrial Organisation,* 243–46.

26. Amar, *La prothèse et le travail des mutilés,* 10–12. On the dehumanization of labor in modern industry, see Bruce Mazlish, *The Fourth Discontinuity: The Co-Evolution of Humans and Machines* (New Haven: Yale University Press, 1993), 65–68. My reading is also informed by the analysis of the impact of mechanization and scientific management on the body in Bill Brown, "Science Fiction, the World's Fair, and the Prosthetics of Empire, 1910–1915," *Cultures of United States Imperialism,* ed. Amy Kaplan and Donald E. Pease (Durham, NC: Duke University Press, 1993), 129–163.

27. Amar, *La prothèse et le travail des mutilés,* 10–11.

28. Ibid., 12.

29. Ibid., 11.

30. See Amar, *The Physiology of Industrial Organisation,* 302–5. I am indebted to Jonathan Kahana for suggesting that I think about Amar's use of images along these lines.

31. In *Bodies and Machines* (New York: Routledge, 1992), Mark Seltzer notes that Henry Ford's fantasy of the automated factory included the use of the disabled body as an ideal against which technological progress could be measured. According to Seltzer, "The production of the Model T required 7882 distinct work operations, but Ford noted, only 12% of these tasks—only 949 operations—required 'strong, able-bodied and practically physically perfect men.' Of the remainder—and this is clearly what he sees as the major achievement of his method of production—'we found that 670 could be filled by legless men, 2,367 by one-legged men, two by armless men, 715 by one-armed men and ten by blind men," 157.

32. Roberts addresses these issues in greater detail in her section entitled "La Femme Moderne," in *Civilization Without Sexes*, 17–88. See also Sian Reynolds, *France between the Wars: Gender and Politics* (New York: Routledge, 1996).

33. A. Chistofleau, "Que sera la vie domestique future?" excerpt from *Les Dernières nouveautés de la science et de l'industrie* (Paris: Hachette, 1925), reprinted in *Culture Technique* 3 (September 15, 1980): 212–215.

34. Ibid., 212–13.

35. See Christine Frederick, *The New Housekeeping: Efficiency Studies in Home Management* (New York: Doubleday, Page & Company, 1913). Frederick had published an article entitled "The New Housekeeping: How it Helps the Woman Who Does Her Own Work," in *Ladies' Home Journal* 13, September 1912, 70–71. She went on to publish several articles and books, including *Household Engineering: Scientific Management in the Home* (Chicago: American School of Home Economics, 1919). *The New Housekeeping* appeared in France as *La Tenue scientifique de la maison,* trans. Henri Le Chatelier (Paris: H. Dunod & E. Pinat, 1918). Le Chatelier, who wrote a preface to the volume, was a chemist at the Sorbonne and a major French proponent of Taylorism during the interwar years. It is worth noting that Le Chatelier also contributed a preface to Jules Amar's *Organisation physiologique du travail.* On technology and the movement for domestic rationalization between the wars, see Robert Frost, "Machine Liberation: Inventing Housewives and Home Appliances in Interwar France," *French Historical Studies* 18.1 (spring 1993): 109–30. See also Ellen Furlough's "Selling the American Way in Interwar France: Prix Uniques and the Salon des Arts Ménagers," *Journal of Social History* 26.3 (spring 1993): 491–519. Another important study is Jackie Clarke's "Homecomings: Paulette Bernège, Scientific Management, and the Return to the Land in Vichy," in *Vichy, Resistance, Liberation: New Perspectives on Wartime France,* ed. Hanna Diamond and Simon Kitson (New York: Berg Publishers, 2005), 171–82. Drawing attention to a "tradition-modernity binary" in the scholarship on wartime and interwar France, Clarke sees Bernège's work as an example of the "ambivalence [at] the heart of the rationalization project" rather than "a confrontation between reactionary and modernizing forces" in France during the period, 179.

36. For an overview of Bernège's ideas, see Martine Martin, "La rationalization du travail ménager en France dans l'entre-deux-guerres," *Culture Technique* 3 (September 15, 1980): 157–65. Bernège also became involved with the Salon des art ménagers inaugurated by the Office des recherches et inventions in the 1920s, editing the magazine *L'Art ménager* noted above.

37. On the "new woman" in interwar France, see Roberts, *Civilization Without Sexes,* and Whitney Chadwick and Tirza True Latimer, *The Modern Woman Revisited: Paris Between the Wars* (New Brunswick, NJ: Rutgers University Press, 2003). More recently, Roberts has examined this figure at the end of the nineteenth century in *Disruptive Acts: The New Woman in Fin-de-siècle France* (Chicago: University of Chicago Press, 2002). On the German case during this period, see Renate Bridenthal and Claudia Koonz, "Beyond *Kinder, Küche, Kirche:* Weimar Women in Politics and Work," in *When Biology Became Destiny: Women in Weimar and Nazi Germany,* ed. Renate Bridenthal, Attina Grossman, and Marion Kaplan (New York: Monthly Press Review, 1984).

38. Paulette Bernège, "Aux femmes de bonne volonté," *Mon chez moi,* no. 21, May 15, 1925, 24.

39. Paulette Bernège, "Vers une cuisine automatique" *Mon chez moi,* no. 4, October 1, 1923, 25–27.

40. See *Mon chez moi,* no. 36, August–September, 1926.

41. Paulette Bernège, "Le Machinisme au service de la ménagère," *VU,* no. 259, March 1, 1933, 296–297.

42. Paulette Bernège, "Le bureau de la ménagère," *Mon chez moi,* no. 22, June 15, 1925, 71.

43. Maurice Ponthière, "En lisant Mrs. Christine Frederick," *Mon chez moi*, no. 2, August 1, 1923, 9.

44. Paulette Bernège, "La Léssive moderne," *Mon chez moi*, no. 10, May 1, 1924, 85.

45. Paulette Bernège, "Vers une cuisine automatique," 38.

46. Paulette Bernège, "La Léssive moderne," 85.

47. Paulette Bernège, "Vers une cuisine automatique," *Mon chez moi*, 25.

48. Paulette Bernège, *Etats géneraux du féminisme*, Proceedings of a conference organized by Conseil national des femmes françaises (Paris, February 14–16, 1929), 32. Cited in Martin, "La rationalization du travail ménager en France," 159.

49. Paulette Bernège, *De la méthode ménagère*, 2nd ed. (Paris: Dunod, 1934), 72. The book was originally published by Dunod in 1928.

50. Bernège borrowed this logic of the continuing sexual division of labor despite the application of mechanization and rationalization to the home from Frederick. Frederick had already articulated a theory of the difference between rationalization of the home and the factory. See Maurice Ponthière, "En lisant Mrs. Christine Frederick," *Mon chez moi*, no. 2, August 1, 1923, 9.

51. Paulette Bernège, "Quand une femme construit sa cuisine," *L'Art ménager*, August 1933, reprinted in *Culture Technique* 3 (September 15, 1980): 173–75.

52. Jean Labadie, "A la recherche du 'home scientifique,'" in *Science et la vie* 28.102 (December 1926): 546–56.

53. Charlotte Perriand, "Wood or Metal?" *The Studio* 97 (March 1929): 278–79.

54. Ibid.

55. Charlotte Perriand, *A Life of Creation* (New York: Monacelli Press, 2003), 25. Originally published as *Une vie de création* (Paris: Editions Odile Jacob, 1998).

56. Le Corbusier referred to this notion of the "House-Machine" in articles that would later be assembled under the title *Vers une architecture* (Paris: G. Cres, 1923). He reiterated this idea of the "mass-production" home as a "machine for living" in *L'Art décoratif d'aujourd'hui* (Paris: G. Cres, 1925). Both of these titles have been reprinted in English translation in their entirety as *Towards a New Architecture* (translated by John Rodker) and *The Decorative Art of Today* (translated by James Dunnett) in the collection Le Corbusier, *Essential Le Corbusier: L'Esprit Nouveau articles* (Oxford: Reed Educational and Professional Publishing, 1998).

57. Le Corbusier, *Precisions on the Present State of Architecture and City Planning: With an American Prologue, a Brazillian Corollary Followed by the Temperature of Paris and the Atmosphere of Moscow* (Cambridge: MIT Press, 1991), 86. This collection of lectures was originally published as *Précision sur un état présent de l'architecture et de l'urbanisme* (Paris: Crès et Cie, 1930). During these lectures, Le Corbusier acknowledged Perriand's contribution to the execution of his theories. Referring to Perriand as his "design associate for the interior equipment of dwellings," Le Corbusier went on to note, "While I am speaking to you here in Buenos Aires, we are having a big stand at the Salon d'Automne in Paris showing in an unanswerable manner the principle of the 'equipment of the modern dwelling,'" 113.

58. Le Corbusier, *The Decorative Art of Today*, 110.

59. I explore Le Corbusier's project of urbanism through designs for the "Radiant City" and plans for Paris in chapter 2, "The City of the Future."

60. Le Corbusier, *Precisions*, 105.

61. Ibid., 89–90.

62. Ibid., 109.

63. Ibid., 111.

64. Ibid., 90.

65. Ibid., 108–9.

66. Le Corbusier, *The Decorative Art of Today*, 72.

67. Ibid., 76.

68. Le Corbusier, *Precisions*, 108.

69. Le Corbusier, *The Decorative Art of Today,* 72.

70. Le Corbusier, *Precisions,* 108.

71. Ibid., 111.

72. Le Corbusier, *The Decorative Art of Today,* 70.

73. Ibid., 72–73.

74. For a design genealogy of the chair, see Volker Fischer's *The LC4 Chaise Longue by Le Corbusier* (Frankfurt: Verlag, 1997). The chair, as well as Perriand's manifesto, is discussed in George Marcus, *Le Corbusier: Inside the Machine for Living, Furniture and Interiors* (New York: Monacelli Press, 2000).

75. Perriand, "Wood or Metal?" 278.

76. See Le Corbusier and Pierre Jeanneret, *Oeuvre complète 1929–1934* (Zurich: Editions H. Girsberger, 1941), 42–43.

77. Perriand, *A Life of Creation,* 29.

78. Le Corbusier, *Precisions,* 116–18.

79. Ibid., 118.

80. Le Corbusier, *The Decorative Art of Today,* 74.

81. Le Corbusier, *Precisions,* 118.

82. Le Corbusier, *The Decorative Art of Today,* 103.

83. Alice T. Friedman, "Being Modern Together: Le Corbusier's Villa Stein-de Monzie," in *Women and the Making of the Modern House: A Social and Architectural History* (New York: Harry N. Abrams, 1998), 92–125. Examining the design of the Villa Stein, Friedman's essay looks closely at how "the relationships among the people who were part of that household challenged the clients and their architect to conceive of domestic space in a new way," arguing that "the house that resulted not only was an unprecedented work of modern architecture but also...represented a creative breakthrough for the architect,"96. One of the conflicts that arose between Le Corbusier and the inhabitants was over the question of furnishings. Apparently, Le Corbusier "never quite got used to the fact that the house was filled with heavy, dark furniture," 119.

84. Le Corbusier, *Precisions,* 101.

85. Perriand, "Wood or Metal?" 278.

86. The advertisement appeared numerous times in *Illustration* in the 1920s. While Marcus points to the design link between the LC *chaise* and the "Surrepos," he does not explore further Le Corbusier's use of the language of prosthesis to discuss furniture in general. The idea that the Surrepos was a model for the LC *chaise* is also discussed in Charlotte Benton, "Le Corbusier: Furniture and the Interior," *Journal of Design History* 3.2/3 (1990): 103–24, 113. See also Magaret Campbell's "What Tuberculosis Did for Modernism: The Influence of a Curative Environment on Modernist Design and Architecture," *Medical History* 49.4 (October 2005): 463–88.

87. Professeur Bernard Paulet, "Toute la vie dans un fauteuil," *Le Miroir du monde,* December 9, 1933, 52–54.

88. Alain Saint-Ogan, *Zig et Puce au XXIe siècle* (Paris: Editions Glénat, 1997). This edition is a reprint of a collection originally published by Hachette in 1935. The cartoons first appeared in series in the weekly *Dimanche illustré* and Hachette published them chronologically.

89. "Quelle serait la découverte qui ferait le plus bien aux hommes?" was the title of the magazine's lead story during a series of issues in 1926. Responses were published in the magazine throughout the year.

90. Charles Richet cited in "Quelle serait la découverte qui ferait le plus bien aux hommes?" *Sciences et voyages,* no. 354, May 10, 1926, 4.

91. Barrier cited in ibid.

92. Renault cited in "Quelle serait la découverte qui ferait le plus bien aux hommes?" *Sciences et voyages,* no. 355, May 17, 1926, 12.

93. Rateau cited in "Quelle serait la découverte qui ferait le plus bien aux hommes?" *Sciences et voyages,* no. 356, May 24, 1926, 6.

94. Boulenger cited in "Quelle serait la découverte qui ferait le plus bien aux hommes?" *Sciences et voyages,* no. 364, August 19, 1926, 1.

95. Hanriot cited in ibid.

96. Maurice Bourdet, "La stérilisation des sentiments," *Le Miroir du Monde XXXe Siècle,* December 9, 1933, 49–51. Bourdet's submission came in the form of a "future" report on a speech delivered by "Professeur Nietzsche-Bergson Rognonas" in 2933.

97. Ibid., 51.

2. The City of the Future

1. The popular magazine *Illustration* cited the *Faux* Paris project, October 2, 1920, 245–46. The project appeared again several years later in an article describing Jacopozzi's lighting of the Eiffel tower, *Illustration,* December 10, 1927, xxx–xxxi. This lighting display is also mentioned briefly in Joseph Harriss's historical overview, *The Eiffel Tower: Symbol of an Age* (London: Paul Elek, 1976), 190. For a military discussion of the *Faux* Paris project, see Lieutenant Colonel Arsène Vauthier, *Le Danger aérien et l'avenir du pays* (Paris: Editions Berger-Levrault, 1930), 141–43.

2. A fascinating analysis of the bombardment of civilians in Paris during the war is Susan Grayzel's "'The Souls of Soldiers'": Civilians under Fire in First World War France," *The Journal of Modern History* 78.3 (September 2006): 588–622.

3. See Jay Winter and Jean-Louis Robert, eds., *Capital Cities at War: Paris, London, Berlin, 1914–1919* (Cambridge: Cambridge University Press, 1997), 6.

4. Winter notes that while the location of the city made for important differences with respect to London and Berlin, there are nevertheless "many parallels [that] remain within wartime metropolitan history," *Capital Cities at War,* 9.

5. A brief discussion of these attacks and the war coverage in the French press can be found in Benjamin Martin's *France and the Après Guerre, 1918–1924* (Baton Rouge: Louisiana State University Press, 1999), 2–9. For maps of the air raids on the city and the German bombardment of Paris in 1918, see Martin Gilbert, *Routledge Atlas of the First World War* (New York: Routledge, 2002), 66–67. Drawing on a 1930 study by Jules Poirier, Grayzel estimates 275 deaths "from air raids alone" and "close to 1500" casualties from bombardments of all kinds, "'The Souls of Soldiers'," 595–96.

6. On the cultural movements and politics of the fin-de-siècle, see Vanessa Schwartz, *Spectacular Realities: Early Mass Culture in Fin-de-siècle Paris* (Berkeley: University of California Press, 1998) and Deborah Silverman, *Art Nouveau in Fin-de-Siècle France: Politics, Psychology and Style* (Berkeley: University of California Press, 1989).

7. A useful overview of the city's history in the nineteenth and twentieth centuries is Bernard Marchand's *Paris, histoire d'une ville* (Paris: Editions du Seuil, 1993). See also Norma Evenson, *Paris: A Century of Change, 1878–1978* (New Haven, CT: Yale University Press, 1979) and, more recently, Patrice Higonnet's *Paris: Capital of the World* (Cambridge: Harvard University Press, 2002). On Paris as a site of unrest, see Priscilla Pankhurst Ferguson, *Paris as Revolution: Writing the Nineteenth-Century City* (Berkeley: University of California Press, 1994). On the Paris Commune of 1871, see Rupert Christiansen, *Paris Babylon: The Story of the Paris Commune* (New York: Viking Press, 1995). On the development of communist activity around the city, see Tyler Stovall, *The Rise of the Paris Red Belt* (Berkeley: University of California Press, 1990). David Harvey's *Paris: Capital of Modernity* (New York: Routledge, 2003) explores issues of class, revolution, and reaction in and around the city from 1848 to 1871.

8. For an overview of the history of the manuscript, see Piero Gondola Della Riva's preface to Jules Verne, *Paris au XXe siècle* (Paris: Hachette, 1994), 11–21.

9. Jules Verne, *Paris in the Twentieth Century,* trans. Richard Howard (New York: Random House, 1996), 24. Fans of Verne's science fiction have emphasized the uncanny nature of these predictions of twentieth-century life and technology. See, for example, David Platten, "A Hitchhiker's Guide to Paris: *Paris au XXe siècle,*" in *Jules Verne: Narratives of Modernity,* ed. Edmund Smyth (Liverpool: Liverpool University Press, 2000), 78–93.

10. Albert Robida, *Le Vingtième siècle* (Paris: G, Decaux, 1883); *Le Vingtième siècle: La vie éléctronique* (Paris: Librairie illustrée,1892); and *La Guerre au vingtième siècle* (Paris: G. Decaux, 1897).

11. These images are reproduced in the collection Isaac Asimov, ed., *Futuredays: A Nineteenth-Century Vision of the Year 2000* (New York: Henry Holt and Company, 1986). The collection includes a brief text by Asimov, reproductions of Côté's illustrations, as well as a short account by Christopher Hyde, a writer who acquired a set of the original cards in Paris in the 1970s.

12. Tony Garnier, *La Cité industrielle, étude pour la construction des villes* (Lyon: Baise et Goutagny, 1917). For a discussion that places Garnier within the broader contexts of metropolitan and colonial French architectural and urban modernities, see the chapter entitled "Techno-cosmopolitanism" in Paul Rabinow, *French Modern: Norms and Forms of the Social Environment* (Chicago: University of Chicago Press, 1989), 277–319.

13. The influenza epidemic that followed the First World War took millions of lives beyond those already lost on the battlefield. On the epidemic in France, see Patrick Zylberman, "A Holocaust in a Holocaust: The Great War and the 1918 'Spanish' Flu Epidemic," in *The Spanish Flu Epidemic of 1918: New Perspectives,* ed. Howard Philips and David Kilingray (New York: Routledge, 2001), 191–201.

14. Octave Joncquel, *Les Titans du ciel* (Amiens: Librairie Edgar Malfère, 1921), 11. Joncquel wrote a sequel to this novel, *L'Epopée martienne: L'Agonie de la Terre* (Amiens: Librairie Edgar Malfère, 1922).

15. André Maurois, *Deux fragments d'une histoire universelle, 1992* (Paris: Editions des Portiques, 1928); Léon Daudet, *Le Napus, fléau de l'an 2227* (Paris: Flammarion, 1927); and Jacques Spitz, *La Guerre des mouches* (Paris: Nouvelles Editions Marabout, 1978). The book was originally published by 1938 in Paris by Gallimard. French writers like Maurois and Daudet published works of science fiction in addition to their other literary and political activities in the period. The French feminist Madeleine Pelletier's *Une vie nouvelle* (Paris: Editions Figuière, 1932) was also set in the capital of the future. A useful overview of the genre in France is Jean-Marc Gouanvic's *La Science-fiction française au XXe siècle, 1900–1968: un essai socio-poétique d'un genre d'émérgence* (Amsterdam: Editions Rodopi, 1984).

16. See Annie Deperchin, "Des déstructions aux reconstructions," in *Encyclopédie de la Grande Guerre, 1914–1918: Histoire et culture,* ed. Stéphane Audoin-Rouzeau and Jean-Jacques Becker (Paris: Bayard, 2004), 1125–39. For a more detailed overview of the damage and the strategies of the French government after the conflict, see Hugh Clout, *After the Ruins: Restoring the Countryside of Northern France* (Exeter: University of Exeter Press, 1996).

17. In his study, *Paris: An Architectural History* (New Haven, CT: Yale University Press, 1993), historian Anthony Sutcliffe has noted that, in addition to problems of social hygiene and sanitation, the urgent need to rebuild devastated areas created a new and pressing interest in urban planning in France, 141.

18. The Chamber of Deputies officially voted in favor of the law on February 26, 1919. Joseph Cornudet reported to the chamber on May 28, 1915. The deputies reiterated their support for the proposal in their meetings on July 27 and 28, 1917. For the reading and voting of the law, see *Journal official de la République Française* (hereinafter *JO*), *Chambre des députés: Débats,* February 26, 1919, 861–63. The law was voted, but then published late due to an oversight. The official text of the law appeared as "*Loi conçernant les plans d'éxtension et d'aménagement des villes,*" in *JO, Bulletin des lois,* March 15, 1919, 1er séction, partie principale, 558–63.

19. *JO, Chambre des députés, Débats parlémentaires,* May 28, 1915, 786.

20. Ibid., 787.

21. Ibid.

22. See Léon Rosenthal, *Villes et villages français après la guerre. Aménagement, réstauration, embellissement, éxtension* (Paris: Payot, 1919).

23. Rosenthal cites Bourgeois's report to the Chamber, *Villes et villages français après la guerre,* 241–42. While the accuracy of these statistics may be disputed, the perceived and reported scale of destruction is significant in its own right.

24. *JO, Chambre des députés, Débats parlémentaires,* May 28, 1915, 789.

25. Ibid., June 1, 1915, 805–6.

26. Ibid., May 28, 1915, 784.

27. J.-Marcel Auburtin and Henri Blanchard, *La Cité de demain dans les régions dévastées* (Paris: Armand Colin, 1917), 89.

28. Ibid., 96.

29. See Daniel Sherman, *The Construction of Memory in Interwar France* (Chicago: University of Chicago Press, 1999).

30. Rosenthal, *Villes et villages français après la guerre,* 240–42. Rosenthal's rhetoric was in keeping with French propaganda and popular perceptions regarding the brutality of the German army and the victimization of France. For discussion of the German invasion of 1914, including debates about accusations of atrocities, see John Horne and Alan Kramer, *German Atrocities: A History of Denial* (New Haven, CT: Yale University Press, 2001).

31. Rosenthal, *Villes et villages français après la guerre,* 242–43.

32. Rosemary Wakeman, "Nostalgic Modernism and the Invention of Paris in the Twentieth Century," *French Historical Studies* 27.1 (winter 2004): 115–44.

33. *JO, Chambre des députés, Débats parlémentaires,* May 28, 1915, 794.

34. Ibid.

35. Evenson, *Paris: A Century of Change,* 54.

36. For overviews of these developments and changes, see ibid.; Sutcliffe, *Paris: An Architectural History;* and Marchand, *Paris, histoire d'une ville.* For statistics on population and growth in Paris, see Daniel Noin and Paul White, *Paris* (New York: Wiley, 1997), 17–33.

37. Maurice Talmeyr, "Les Bouleversements de Paris: La capitale de demain," *Revue des deux mondes,* July 15, 1923, 436–452.

38. Ibid., 442–43. For a detailed study of images of Paris in the interwar years, including representations of the capital as a "menace" and a "monster," see Evelyne Cohen, *Paris dans l'imaginaire national de l'entre-deux-guerres* (Paris: Publications de la Sorbonne, 1999).

39. *JO, Chambre des députés, Débats parlémentaires,* May 28, 1915, 784.

40. Sutcliffe, *Paris: An Architectural History,* 83. Baron Georges Haussmann was the prefect of the Seine under Louis Napoleon. Apart from Sutcliffe's treatment, Haussmannization is discussed in a number of histories of the capital. See for example Françoise Choay, *The Modern City: Planning in the Nineteenth Century* (New York: Braziller, 1969); Jeanne Gaillard, *Paris, la ville, 1852–1870: l'urbanisme parisien à l'heure d'Haussmann* (Paris: Champion, 1977); and Rabinow, *French Modern.*

41. Many of the guidelines that were and are still considered "sacred" to the Parisian architectural landscape were established during this period. While these norms have since been adjusted, the mark of Haussmannization is still quite visible in Paris today. From the facades of so many Parisian buildings, to the boulevards that divide the city and link its key monuments, the transformation that occurred in the nineteenth century still defines much of the city's contemporary aesthetic and layout. See Sutcliffe, *Paris: An Architectural History,* 104. See also Sharon Marcus, "Haussmannization as Anti-Modernity: The Apartment House in Parisian Urban Discourse, 1850–1880," *Journal of Urban History* 27.6 (September 2001): 723–45; and David Jordan, "Haussmann and *Haussmannization:* The Legacy for Paris," *French Historical Studies* 27.1 (winter 2004): 87–113. Jordan comments on the "homogenous cityscape" that

emerged during and after Haussmann's regulations were established. He also points to the predominance of "preservationists" in first part of the twentieth century, noting, "From 1914 until well after World War II, transformations of Paris, at least in the old core of the city, were minimal," 97.

42. See Robin Walz, *Pulp Surrealism: Insolent Popular Culture in Early 20th-century Paris* (Berkeley: University of California Press, 2000), 14. See also Margaret Cohen's, *Profane Illumination: Walter Benjamin and the Paris of Surrealist Revolution* (Berkeley: University of California Press, 1993). On the issue of state control and Haussmannization, see Harvey, *Paris: Capital of Modernity*, 146–50.

43. For more on this point, see Sutcliffe, *Paris: An Architectural History*, 170–74.

44. *JO, Chambre des députés, Débats parlémentaires*, May 28, 1915, 794.

45. See Gérard Monnier, Claude Loupiac, and Christine Menguin's *L'Architecture moderne en France*, vol. 1, *1889–1940* (Paris: Picard, 1997), 143.

46. The term refers to the area outside the fortified wall, while *intra-muros* refers to the 20 *arrondissements* that still make up Paris "proper." On the fortifications up to the end of the First World War, see Maric Charvet, *Les Fortifications de Paris: De l'hygiénisme à l'urbanisme, 1880–1919* (Rennes: Presses universitaires de Rennes, 2005). See also Jean-François Cohen, *Des fortifs au périf: Paris, les seuils de la ville* (Paris: Picard, 1991).

47. *JO, Chambre des députés, Débats parlémentaires*, March 14, 1919, 1193.

48. Ibid., March 13, 1919, 1183.

49. Ibid.

50. Ibid., 1184.

51. Ibid., March 14, 1919, 1192.

52. Ibid., March 13, 1919, 1159.

53. Ibid., March 14, 1919, 1192. Harvey's study deals with this history. His chapter on the building of the Sacré Coeur basilica and the legacies of the Commune of 1871 is particularly useful for our understanding of how the history of this particular revolution was written and rewritten into the structures and landscape of the city, *Paris: Capital of Modernity*, 311–40.

54. *JO, Chambre des députés, Débats parlémentaires*, March 13, 1919, 1159.

55. Ibid., 1185. Rozier's comments, as well as the whole issue of the city's fortifications are discussed in further detail in Cohen's *Des fortifs au périf* and Charvet's *Les Fortifications de Paris*.

56. For a more detailed account of the CIUP's construction and history, see Bernard Lemoine, *La Cité internationale universitaire de Paris* (Paris: Editions Hervas, 1990), 28.

57. "Discours de M. André Honnorat," text of speech given November 14, 1936, and reprinted in *La Maison internationale de la Cité Universitaire de Paris* (Paris: Imprimerie P. et A. Davy, 1936), 29.

58. Henry Spont, *La Cité Universitaire* (Paris: Jules Simon, 1923), 15.

59. Ibid., 3.

60. Henri-Paul Nénot, quoted in Pierre Lyautey et al., "Doit-on excommunier les gratte-ciel: Paris 1940?" *VU*, no. 119, June 25, 1930, 618.

61. Henri Bourrelier, *La Vie du quartier Latin des origines à la Cité universitaire* (Paris: Michel Bourrelier, 1936), 228.

62. "Discours de M. Jean Zay," text of speech given November 14, 1936, and reprinted in *La Maison internationale de la Cité Universitaire de Paris* (Paris: Imprimerie P. et A. Davy, 1936).

63. "Discours de M. André Honnorat," 3.

64. Lemoine, *La Cité internationale universitaire de Paris*, 28.

65. Cornudet, *JO, Chambre des députés, Débats parlémentaires*, March 14, 1919, 1185.

66. Talmeyr, "Les Bouleversements de Paris," 442.

67. Vauthier, *Le Danger aérien et l'avenir du pays*, 231–291.

68. Edmond Blanc, "Inquiètudes aériennes: La défense du ciel de Paris," *Sciences et voyages,* March 14, 1935, 273.

69. Unknown author, interview with Auguste Perret entitled "Ce que j'ai appris à propos des villes de demain. C'est qu'il faudrait les construire dans des pays neufs," *Intransigeant,* November 25, 1920, 4.

70. Le Corbusier, *Toward an Architecture,* trans. John Goodman (London: Frances Lincoln, 2008), 116. The book was originally published as *Vers une architecture* (Paris: Editions Crès et Cie., 1923).

71. It was during this period that he abandoned his real name, Charles Edouard Jeanneret, and adopted the pseudonym Le Corbusier. For more on the architect's life and career, see Françoise Choay, *Le Corbusier* (New York: Braziller Books, 1960). On the period from 1907 to 1922, see Stanislas Moos, *Le Corbusier before Le Corbusier* (New Haven, CT: Yale University Press, 2002).

72. Le Corbusier, *The City of Tomorrow and Its Planning,* trans. John Rodker, in *Essential Le Corbusier: L'Esprit Nouveau Articles* (Oxford: Reed Educational and Professional Publishing, 1998), 25. Originally published as *Urbanisme* (Paris: Editions Crès et Cie., 1925).

73. Building on earlier designs like the "Plan Voisin" (1925), Le Corbusier's plans for the "Radiant City," including plans for Paris, appear in *La Ville Radieuse: Eléments d'une doctrine d'urbanisme pour l'équipment de la civilisation machiniste* (Paris: Editions Vincent Fréal et Cie., 1964). This collection was originally published in Boulogne in 1935 by Editions de l'architecture d'aujourd'hui. It is available in English translation as Le Corbusier, *The Radiant City,* trans. Pamela Knight, Eleanor Levieux, and Derek Coltman (New York: Orion Press, 1975).

74. Le Corbusier, *The City of Tomorrow,* 50.

75. On the tower's history, see Harriss, *The Eiffel Tower.* Another exploration of the mystique of the tower's identification with Paris and the nation as a whole is Roland Barthes' *The Eiffel Tower and Other Mythologies,* trans. Richard Howard (Berkeley: University of California Press, 1979).

76. Léandre Vaillat's, "L'Architecture au Salon des artistes décorateurs," *Le Temps,* May 12, 1923, 3–4.

77. Albert Léon Guérard, *L'Avenir de Paris,* 13. An expatriate, Guérard had a perspective on the differences and links between American and French culture that was informed by extensive experience in both countries. Born in France in 1880, he moved to the United States in 1907 where he taught at a number of American institutions including Stanford University. During his career, he wrote on a range of topics including urbanism, international language, literature, and democracy.

78. Le Corbusier, "Professeur de prévisions?" (1932), Fondation Le Corbusier, Paris (hereinafter FLC) B3/5/2. The essay later appeared in Le Corbusier, *La Ville radieuse.*

79. Le Corbusier, *The City of Tomorrow,* xxv.

80. See "Le Corbusier talks of the city of the future, an exclusive interview" published in *Beaux Arts,* January 7, 1938, and an interview published by London General Press between 1933 and 1937 entitled "The Radiant City of the Future: Indoor Streets and Overhead Traffic: Ribbons of Houses Across Wide Open Spaces," by Le Corbusier, FLC B1/15/341 and A2/1987; See also "La Cité future de travail" and "Paris sera-t-il la premiere grande ville moderne du monde?" *Science et industrie* no. 154, 1926, 25–37.

81. Guérard, *L'Avenir de Paris,* 17.

82. "Arthenay," "Les gratte-ciel vont-ils conquérir l'Europe?" *Sciences et voyages,* no. 767, May 10, 1934, 1. For a thorough account of French writing about the skyscraper in this period, see Isabelle Gournay's "Quand la France decouvrait le gratte-ciel," *Architecture aujourd'hui,* no. 263 (1989): 44–54. Evenson also gives a detailed account of the fate of the tower in the French capital in *Paris.* See "The Tower Triumphs," *Paris: A Century of Change,* 175–98.

83. Roger, "Cité future" *Science et la vie*, no. 138, December 1928, inside front cover. This caption accompanied an illustration of a skyscraped city, busy with traffic.

84. Pierre Lyautey et al., "Doit-on excommunier les gratte-ciel," 615–616. The nephew of Maréchal Hubert Lyautey, Pierre Lyautey was a journalist who traveled extensively around the world.

85. On Van Dongen, see Charles Wentinck, *Van Dongen* (Amsterdam: J. M. Meulenhof, 1964). Van Dongen moved to Paris in 1897, becoming a French citizen in 1929. He participated in the Fauvist and Expressionist movements in painting.

86. *VU* also asked participants about the possibility that Paris might, at some point, become the capital of a "United States of Europe," Lyautey, "Doit-on excommunier les gratte-ciel," 615. Laprade's images also appeared in another article the following year that used the same catchy title. See M.-J. Dupré, "Doit-on excommunier les gratte-ciel?...Paris 1940," *La Cité moderne*, no. 6, February 1931, 5–9. He is perhaps best known for his design of the Palais de la Porte Dorée built for the Exposition Coloniale of 1931.

87. Lyautey, "Doit-on excommunier les gratte-ciel," 616.

88. Jean Labadie, "A la recherche du home scientifique" *Science et la vie* no. 102, December 1925, 546–56.

89. Le Corbusier quoted in Lyautey, "Doit on excommunier les gratte-ciel," 616.

90. Le Corbusier, "What About an Air War?" in *The Radiant City*, 60–61. The first note in this discussion of aerial threats instructed readers to consult Vauthier's *Le Danger aérien*.

91. Louis Dausset quoted in Lyautey, "Doit-on excommunier les gratte-ciel," 616–17.

92. Van Dongen quoted in ibid.

93. André de Fels, Deputy of *Seine-et-Oise*, quoted in ibid.

94. André de Fels, quoted in ibid.

95. Louis Bonnier, "Les Transformations et l'avenir de Paris," Part II, *La Construction moderne*, supplement, no. 5, June 8, 1930, 41–50. The first part of the article appeared in *La Construction moderne*, no. 3, May 11, 1930, 25–40.

96. Bonnier, "Les Transformations et l'avenir de Paris," part II, June 8, 1930, 46.

97. See for example, "Féeries de l'avenir: Paris au 21e siècle," *Lecture pour tous*, February 1932.

98. See for example, the discussion of New York in the section entitled "Pain or Pleasure" in Le Corbusier, *The City of Tomorrow*, 60.

99. Bonnier, "Les Transformations et l'avenir de Paris," 46.

100. On this push to restore order and return to normal, see Jean-Jacques Becker and Serge Bernstein's *Nouvelle histoire de la France contemporaine: Victoire et frustrations, 1914–1929*, vol. 12 (Paris: Editions du Seuil, 1990). Another version of this perspective can be found in Marc Auffret's *La France de l'entre-deux-guerres* (Paris: Culture, Arts, Loisirs, 1972). The desire to reestablish order was also tied to economic instability in the years following the war. For an overview of these issues in interwar France, see Alfred Sauvy's classic study, *Histoire économique de la France entre les deux guerres*, 4 vols. (Paris: Fayard, 1965–1970). The financial instability of the 1920s is also outlined in Philippe Bernard and Henri Dubief, *The Decline of the Third Republic, 1914–1938* (Cambridge: Cambridge University Press, 1985).

101. Jean Renoir, *Sur un air de Charleston* (1927). Pierre Lestringues wrote the film. A copy of the script entitled *Charleston* dated July 26, 1926, is located in the archives of the Bibliothèque du Film in Paris, CJ/0282/B36.

102. André Reuze, *La Vénus d'Asnières* (Paris: Fayard, 1924). While I have found no evidence that either Lestringues or Renoir was familiar with Reuze's novel, the two narratives do seem curiously similar.

103. In both instances, the results are difficult to interpret. It is unclear whether the authors intended these parodies as critique or were simply reinscribing motifs of the racism and sexual conservatism of the period.

3. The Next War

1. Lucien Febvre, "*Frontière*: The Word and the Concept," in *A New Kind of History from the Writings of Lucien Febvre,* ed. Peter Burke, trans. K. Folca (London: Routledge and Kegan Paul, 1973), 208–18. Originally published as "Frontière: le mot et la notion," *Revue de synthèse historique* 45 (1928): 31–44. In 1929, Febvre cofounded (with historian Marc Bloch) the journal *Annales d'histoire économique et sociale,* now known as *Annales. Histoire, Sciences Sociales.*

2. Febvre, *"Frontière,"* 208.

3. Ibid., 210.

4. Ibid., 216.

5. See Peter Sahlins, "Natural Frontiers Revisited: France's Boundaries since the Seventeenth Century," *American Historical Review* 95 (1990): 1423–51; Nathaniel B. Smith, "The Idea of the French Hexagon," *French Historical Studies* 6.2 (1969): 139–55; and Eugen Weber, "L'Hexagone," in *Les Lieux de mémoire,* vol. 2, book 2, ed. Pierre Nora (Paris: Gallimard, 1987), 96–116.

6. Febvre, *"Frontière,"* 214–216.

7. For a fascinating discussion of French anxieties about the "next war" in the wake of World War I, see Omer Bartov, "Martyrs' Vengeance: Memory, Trauma, and the Fear of War in France, 1918–1940," in "The French Defeat of 1940: Reassessments," a special issue of *Historical Reflections/Réflexions Historiques* 22.1 (winter 1996): 47–76.

8. While the French had been pioneers of tank technology at the end of the First World War, the continued use of models left over from the war and the commitment to their use in service of infantry contributed significantly to the defeat of 1940. For more detailed discussion of the role of tanks in French military doctrine, see Robert Doughty, *The Seeds of Disaster: The Development of French Army Doctrine, 1919–1939* (Hamden, CT: Archon Books, 1985). Doughty's seventh chapter, "The Development of the Tank" is especially useful on this issue, 136–60.

9. On this dominance of French defensive doctrine, see Robert Doughty, *The Seeds of Disaster;* Elizabeth Kier, *Imagining War: French and British Military Doctrine Between the Wars* (Princeton, NJ: Princeton University Press, 1999); and J. E. Kaufmann and H. W. Kaufmann, *Fortress France: The Maginot Line and French Defenses in World War II* (Westport, CT: Praeger Security International, 2006). While there is some debate among these authors on the legacies of World War I, the overview I have presented here reflects some of the common ground they share with respect to these developments.

10. By 1940, the line consisted of at least 55 *gros,* or artillery *ouvrages* (with 22 in the northeast), 68 small forts (with 35 in the northeast), 348 casemates and blockhouses, 78 shelters and 14 watch stations. Comprised of steel and concrete, the fortifications were meant to form a continuous line of fire between posts, while protecting these stations from one another's assault. For details on the line's military conception and design, including illustrations, see Kaufmann and Kaufmann, *Fortress France.*

11. See Roger Bruge, *Faites sauter la ligne Maginot* (Paris: Fayard, 1973); Doughty, *Seeds of Disaster;* Judith Hughes, *To the Maginot Line: The Politics of French Military Preparation in the 1920s* (Cambridge, MA: Harvard University Press, 1971); Kier, *Imagining War;* and Barry Posen, *Sources of Military Doctrine: France Britain and Germany Between the World Wars* (Ithaca, NY: Cornell University Press, 1986).

12. Nora, *Les Lieux de mémoire,* vol. 2, book 2, 9.

13. See Bernard Guenée, "Des limites féodales aux frontières politiques," in *Les Lieux de mémoire,* vol. 2, book 2, 11–34; Daniel Nordman, "Des limites d'Etat aux frontières nationales," in *Les Lieux de mémoire,* vol. 2, book 2, 35–62; Jean-Marie Mayeur, "Alsace: Une mémoire-frontière," in *Les Lieux de mémoire,* vol. 2, book 2, 63–95; Eugen Weber, "L'Hexagone"; and Emmanuel Le Roy Ladurie, "Nord-Sud," in *Les Lieux de mémoire,* vol. 2, book 2, 117–140.

14. See Annie Deperchin, "Des destructions aux reconstructions," in *Encyclopédie de la Grande Guerre, 1914–1918: Histoire et culture,* ed. Stéphane Audoin-Rouzeau and Jean-Jacques Becker (Paris: Bayard, 2004), 1125–39. For a more detailed overview of the damage and the strategies of the French government after the conflict, see Hugh Clout, *After the Ruins: Restoring the Countryside of Northern France* (Exeter: University of Exeter Press, 1996).

15. There is a vast literature that explores the relationship between the military and civilian fronts during the war. See, for example, Patrick Fridenson, ed., *The French Home Front, 1914–1918* (Providence, RI: Berg, 1992); Jean-Jacques Becker, *The Great War and the French People;* Leonard V. Smith, Stéphane Audoin-Rouzeau, and Annette Becker, *France and the Great War, 1914–1918* (Cambridge: Cambridge University Press, 2003). On labor, see Laura Lee Downs, *Manufacturing Inequality: Gender Division in the French and British Metalworking Industries, 1914–1939* (Ithaca, NY: Cornell University Press, 1995); and John Horne, *Labour at War: France and Britain, 1914–1918* (Oxford: Oxford University Press, 1991). For a recent interrogation of the categories "civilian" and "soldier," see Susan Grayzel, "'The Souls of Soldiers'": Civilians under Fire in First World War France," *Journal of Modern History* 78 (September 2006): 588–622.

16. Sara E. Melzer and Kathryn Norberg, *From the Royal to the Republican Body: Incorporating Seventeenth- and Eighteenth-Century France* (Berkeley: University of California Press, 1998), 1. In his examination of working-class culture and resistance in nineteenth-century France, William Sewell argues that the "corporatist idiom" of the ancien régime remained an important part of the cultural and political vocabulary and imaginary of the French working class into the nineteenth century. See his *Work and Revolution in France: The Language of Labor from the Old Regime to 1848* (Cambridge: Cambridge University Press, 1980).

17. See Ernst Kantorowicz, *The King's Two Bodies: A Study of Medieval Political Theology* (Princeton, NJ: Princeton University Press, 1957); and Antoine de Baecque, *Le Corps de l'histoire: Métaphores et politique, 1770–1800* (Paris: Calmann-Lévy, 1994).

18. See Dorinda Outram, *The Body and the French Revolution: Sex, Class, and Political Culture* (New Haven, CT: Yale University Press, 1989).

19. See Robert Nye, *Crime, Madness, and Politics in Modern France: The Medical Concept of National Decline* (Princeton, NJ: Princeton University Press, 1984).

20. Weber, "L'Hexagone," 110.

21. Jean-Marie Mayeur, "A Frontier Memory: Alsace," trans. Richard Holbrook, in *Rethinking France: Les Lieux de mémoire,* vol. 2, *Space,* under the direction of Pierre Nora; translation directed by David P. Jordan (Chicago: University of Chicago Press, 2006), 409–42, 432.

22. Ibid., 432.

23. See François Roth, *La Guerre de 70* (Paris: Fayard, 1990); and Laird Boswell, "From Liberation to Purge Trials in the 'Mythic Provinces': Recasting French Identities in Alsace and Lorraine, 1918–1920," *French Historical Studies* 23.2 (winter 2000): 129–62.

24. See Bertrand Joly, "Le souvenir de 1870 et la place de la Revanche," in *Encyclopédie de la Grande Guerre 1914–1918,* ed. Stéphane Audoin-Rouzeau and Jean-Jacques Becker, 109–24.

25. Bruge's *Faites sauter la ligne Maginot* provides a useful history of these fortifications. See also Michel Truttmann and Alain Hohnadel, *La Ligne Maginot* (Paris: Editions Tallandier, 1989).

26. See John Horne, "Corps, lieux et nation: la France et l'invasion de 1914," *Annales: Histoire, Science Sociales* 55.1 (2000): 73–109. Horne's essay is one of several in a special segment of this volume of *Annales* entitled "Le Corps dans la première guerre mondiale," including contributions by Stéphane Audoin-Rouzeau, Annette Becker, Leonard Smith, and Michèle Chossat.

27. Philippe Pétain, "Projet de note sur l'organisation défensive du térritoire," CSG, February 13, 1922, Service historique de l'Armée de Terre, Vincennes (hereinafter SHAT) 1N/25/4/1, 1.

28. Ibid., 2.

29. Ibid., 5.

30. General Débeney, "Projet d'instruction sur l'organisation défensive des frontiers," March 1,1922, SHAT 1N/25/4/1, sous-dossier 2, 6.

31. "Procès verbal de la séance du Conseil supérieure de la guerre," May 17, 1920, SHAT 1N/23/4/1a, 6.

32. "Procès verbal de la séance du Conseil supérieure de la guerre," May 22, 1922, SHAT 1N/25/4, 9.

33. General Buat, "Organisation défensive du territoire et défense nationale," Report submitted to General Guillaumat, chairman of the Commission de defense du territoire, 1924, SHAT 1N/27/7/12, 6–7.

34. Ibid., 3.

35. "Deuxième séance de la Commission chargée de l'étude de l'organisation défensive du territoire," July 3, 1922, SHAT 1N/50/2, 9.

36. "Procès verbal de la séance du CSG," May 17, 1920, SHAT 1N/23/4/1a, 2–3.

37. Ibid., 4–5.

38. While the French had sought a permanent Allied occupation of the Rhineland in 1919, they had been forced to settle for a fifteen-year occupation. The withdrawal of Allied troops from the region was to take place in three stages. See Doughty, *Seeds of Disaster,* 33 and Nicole Jordan, "The Military, the Rhineland, and the Eastern Alliances," in *The Popular Front and Central Europe: The Dilemmas of French Impotence, 1918–1940* (Cambridge: Cambridge University Press, 1992), 48–92. Hughes in *To the Maginot Line* also notes the role the occupation played in the development of the Maginot Line throughout her analysis.

39. Philippe Pétain, "Note au sujet de l'organisation défensive du territoire," May 17, 1923, SHAT 1N/51/1/2, 1.

40. Ibid., 3.

41. Ibid., 4.

42. "Commission chargée des etudes d'organisation de la defense du territoire, Ordre du jour," June 19, 1922, SHAT 1N/50/2, 2.

43. Antoine Prost, *Republican Identities in War and Peace: Representations of France in the Nineteenth and Twentieth Centuries,* trans. Jay Winter with Helen McPhail (New York: Oxford University Press, 2002), 97. Prost notes the coincidence of the building of the Maginot Line with the decommisioning of local fortifications in France seeing these projects as emblematic of postwar representations of trench warfare and combat. For an overview of the status of the fortifications in Strasbourg, see the "Rapport de Général Théodore Brécard," a member of the CSG and Military Governor of Strasbourg, October 13, 1930, SHAT 1N/31/10/4.

44. "Procès verbal de la Première séance de la Commission chargée de l'étude de l'organisation défensive du térritoire," June 19, 1922, 3.

45. Ibid., 6.

46. Ibid.

47. General Buat, "Organisation défensive du territoire et défense nationale," Report submitted to General Guillaumat, chairman of the Commission de defense du territoire, 1924, SHAT 1N/27/7/12, 14.

48. Ibid., 8.

49. "Procès verbal de Première séance de la Commission chargée de l'étude de l'organisation défensive du territoire," June 19, 1922, 6.

50. Ibid., 4.

51. "Procès verbal de la séance du Conseil supérieure de la guerre," May 22, 1922, SHAT 1N/27/D2.

52. "Procès verbal de la Première séance de la Commission chargée de l'étude de l'organisation défensive du térritoire," June 19, 1922, SHAT 1N/5/D2, 2.

53. Ibid., 6.

54. "Procès verbal de la séance du CSG," May 17, 1920, 3.

55. "Note au sujet des études sur l'organisation défensive du territoire," March 3, 1922, SHAT 1N/25/D4, sous-dossier 1, 1.

56. General Guillaumat, "Lettre à Maréchal Pétain," March 29, 1922, SHAT C-1N/50/ D1.

57. Ibid.

58. A useful overview of this and other concerns behind the construction of the Maginot Line is Enno Kraehe, "The Motives behind the Maginot Line," *Military Affairs* 8.2 (summer 1944): 109–22. See in particular the debates that took place in the Chamber of Deputies published in *Journal officiel de la République Française* (hereinafter *JO*), *Débats parlémentaires, Chambre des deputés*, March 3, 1927; November 28,1928; and December 9, 10, and 28, 1929.

59. *JO, Débats parlémentaires, Chambre des deputés*, December 10, 1929, 4235.

60. Ibid.

61. Colonel X, *La Ligne Maginot: Bouclier de la France* (Paris: Excelsior, 1939), 117–19.

62. "Faits et chiffres conçernant la ligne Maginot," Commandement en Chef des Forces Térrestres à M. le Ministre de Information (Bureau Militaire) re: l'éffort français sur terre depuis le début de la guerre, 1940, SHAT 27N/67/1.

63. Ibid., 3–4.

64. *JO, Chambre, Débats parlémentaires*, December 10, 1929, 4208.

65. Ibid., 4206.

66. Ibid., 4208.

67. Ibid., 4219.

68. Ibid., December 28, 1929, 4766.

69. Ibid., 4769.

70. Ibid.

71. Charles de Gaulle, *The Army of the Future* (London: Hutchinson, 1940). Originally published as Charles de Gaulle, *Vers l'armée de métier* (Paris: Plon, 1934).

72. De Gaulle, *The Army of the Future*, 11–12.

73. Ibid., 19.

74. Ibid., 31.

75. Ibid., 111.

76. Ibid., 33–34.

77. Ibid., 69.

78. Lieutenant Colonel Arsène Vauthier, *Le Danger aérien et l'avenir du pays* (Paris: Berger-Levrault, 1930), ix.

79. Ibid., x.

80. See Lyautey's preface to Vauthier, *Le Danger aérien et l'avenir du pays*, vii.

81. Vauthier, *Le Danger aérien*, 53.

82. Ibid., 72.

83. Ibid., 15–16.

84. Ibid., 18.

85. Ibid., ix–x.

86. Colonel A. Grasset, "Où en est la sécurité nationale?" in *L'Europe en armes*, a special issue of *La Petite Illustration*, December 19, 1936, 7.

87. Paul Bénazet, *Défense nationale: Notre sécurité* (Paris: Grasset, 1938), 64.

88. Ibid., 104, 111.

89. "La Prochaine guerre," special issue of *VU*, no. 152, February 11, 1931.

90. Robert Chenevier, "La Défense passive," a special issue of *La Petite Illustration*, July 15, 1939.

91. See Karen Offen, "Depopulation, Nationalism, and Feminism in Fin-de-siècle France," *American Historical Review* 89 (1984): 648–70; and Elinor Accampo, "The Gendered Nature

of Contraception in France: Neo-Malthusianism in France, 1900–1920," *Journal of Interdisciplinary History* 34.2 (autumn 2003): 235–62.

92. On the impact of the war on French gender ideology, see Mary Louise Roberts, *Civilization without Sexes: Reconstructing Gender in Postwar France, 1917–1927* (Chicago: University of Chicago Press, 1994). On the question of race, see Elisa Camiscioli, "Producing Citizens, Reproducing the 'French Race': Immigration, Demography, and Pronatalism in Early Twentieth-Century France," *Gender and History* 13.3 (November 2001): 593–621.

93. General Hellot, "Note sur l'organisation defensive des frontiers," January 20, 1922, SHAT 1N/50/2/#399.

94. General Guillaumat, "Rapport au Ministre sur l'organisation défensive des frontières," November 6, 1926, SHAT 1N/28/D8/2b, 3.

95. See Hughes, *To the Maginot Line*, 159; and Kraehe, "Motives behind the Maginot Line," 113.

96. General Guillaumat, "Rapport au Ministre sur les Principes de l'oganisation defensive du territoire," March 27, 1923, SHAT1N/50/4/2, 8.

97. "Procès verbal de la séance du CSG," 17 May 1920, SHAT 1N27/D1, 3.

98. Lieutenant Colonel Chauvineau, *Etude sur la fortification permanente dans la défense des frontières,* October 1923, SHAT 7N/3780/5, 18.

99. Ibid., 13–14.

100. "Procès verbal de la séance du CSG," October 12, 1927, SHAT 1N/29/4/8, 26.

101. "Note lue par le Général Filloneau devant le CSG," July 4, 1927, 9.

102. Alliance nationale contre la dépopulation, "La dénatalité, c'est l'éffondrement de la défense nationale" *Natalité: Organe bimestrial de l'Alliance nationale contre la dépopulation* no. 24, March 1939, SHAT 7N/2540. The French doctor and demographer Jacques Berthillon founded the alliance in 1896. For more on pronatalism and the alliance after the war, see Marie-Monique Huss, "Pronatalism in the Inter-war Period in France," *Journal of Contemporary History,* 25.1 (1990): 39–68; Cheryl Koos, "Gender, Anti-Individualism, and the Pronatalist Backlash against the Femme Moderne, 1933–1940," *French Historical Studies* 19.3 (spring 1996): 699–723; and Andrés Horacio Reggiani, "Procreating France: The Politics of Demography, 1919–1945," *French Historical Studies* 19.3 (spring 1996): 725–54. On the period before 1914, see Joshua Cole, *The Power of Large Numbers: Population, Politics, and Gender in Nineteenth Century France* (Ithaca, NY: Cornell University Press, 2000).

103. Alliance nationale contre la dépopulation, "La dénatalité, c'est l'éffondrement de la défense nationale," 2.

104. Advertisement for Palmolive shaving cream in *Match,* April 11, 1940, 4.

105. Advertisement for *Banania* in *Match,* January 19, 1940, 2. The military theme was not a new one for *Banania.* The company had, since 1915, used an illustration of a Senegalese *tirailleur* as the face of the brand. On the racial politics of this campaign, see Leora Auslander and Thomas C. Holt, "Sambo in Paris: Race and Racism in the Iconography of the Everyday," in *The Color of Liberty: Histories of Race in France,* ed. Susan Peabody and Tyler Stovall (Raleigh: University of North Carolina Press, 2002), 147–76.

106. Advertisement for *Banania* in *Match,* March 28, 1940, 2.

107. Advertisement for Nestlé in *Match,* April 4, 1940, 8.

108. Fernand Braudel, *The Identity of France,* vol. 1, *History and Environment,* trans. Sian Reynolds (New York: Harper and Row, 1988), 309. Originally published as *L'Identité de la France,* vol. 1, *Espace et histoire* (Paris: Flammarion, 1986).

4. The Future Is a Foreign Country

1. The title of this chapter refers to David Lowenthal's *The Past Is a Foreign Country* (Cambridge: Cambridge University Press, 1985). Lowenthal cites the architectural critic Reyner Banham who noted in 1976 that "a generation ago, visionary planners saw the

future as almost 'another country,' which one might visit like Italy, or even try to re-create in replica," 3.

2. Eugène Brieux, *Les Américains chez nous*, in *La Petite Illustration, supplément théâtre*, no. 11, February 7, 1920, 1–30. See the review of Brieux's play by Le Semanier entitled "Nos amis d'Amérique," published in *Illustration*, February 7, 1920, 110. The play was also scheduled to open in New York later that year. See Alexander Woollcott, "Second Thoughts on First Nights: '*Les Américains chez nous,*'" *New York Times Book Review*, March 7, 1920, X6. Already in his mid-fifties by the outbreak of the war, Brieux became committed to helping soldiers blinded during the conflict. See Mrs. George S. Kessler's letter to the editor dated August 11, 1916, "Brieux on the Blind: War's Victims Who Must Be Treated Like Drowning Persons," *New York Times*, August 13, 1916, E2. For an intriguing discussion of Brieux's theatrical treatment of the themes of motherhood, reproduction, and depopulation, see Jean Elisabeth Pedersen, *Legislating the French Family: Feminism, Theater, and Republican Politics, 1870–1920* (New Brunswick, NJ: Rutgers University Press, 2003), 162–91.

3. Brieux, *Les Américains chez nous*, 26–27.

4. Ibid., 23.

5. Ibid., 16.

6. Ibid., 28.

7. See Jean-Baptiste Duroselle, *La France et les Etats-Unis des origines à nos jours* (Paris: Seuil, 1976); Tony Judt, *Past Imperfect: French Intellectuals, 1944–1956* (Berkeley: University of California Press, 1992); Richard Kuisel, *Seducing the French: The Dilemma of Americanization* (Berkeley: University of California Press, 1993); Jean-Philippe Mathy, *Extrême Occident: French Intellectuals and America* (Chicago: University of Chicago, 1993); Philippe Roger, *The American Enemy: The History of French Anti-Americanism*, trans. Sharon Bowman (Chicago: University of Chicago Press, 2006). Two other useful overviews can be found in Michel Winock, *Nationalism, Anti-Semitism, and Fascism in France*, trans. Jane Marie Todd (Stanford, CA: Stanford University Press, 1998); and Pierre Milza, "Anti-américanisme," in *Dictionnaire historique de la vie politique française au XXe siècle*, ed. Jean-François Sirinelli (Paris: Presses universitaires de France, 1995), 29–33.

8. On this "cultural distance" and the pitfalls of "culturalism," see Eric Fassin, "Fearful Symmetry: Culturalism and Cultural Comparison after Tocqueville," *French Historical Studies* 19.2 (fall 1995): 451–60. Fassin examines the ways that American and French studies of French and American culture respectively tend to fix both "Frenchness" and "Americanness." Fassin considers this reciprocity with respect to gender in "The Purloined Gender: American Feminism in a French Mirror," *French Historical Studies* 22.1 (winter 1999): 113–38.

9. Georges Duhamel, *America the Menace: Scenes from the Life of the Future*, trans. Charles Milner Thompson (New York: Arno Press, 1974). Reprint edition of the English translation originally published by Houghton Mifflin in 1931. The first French edition was published as *Scènes de la vie future* (Paris: Mercure de France, 1930).

10. See Bernadette Galloux-Fournier, "Un regard sur l'Amérique: voyageurs français aux Etats-Unis (1919–1939)," *Revue d'histoire moderne et contemporaine* 37 (April–June 1990): 308–23. Galloux-Fournier estimates that 127 travel narratives were written between 1919 and 1939 by French travelers to the United States and counts another 67 essays based on travelers' experiences, 311. In *The Menace in the West: The Rise of French Anti-Americanism in Modern Times* (Westport, CT: Greenwood Press, 1978), historian David Strauss estimates that "175 book-length travel volumes were published in France" from 1917–1932, 8.

11. Citing Drieu la Rochelle, Mary Louise Roberts discusses the ways the image of a "civilization without sexes" "served as a primary referent for the ruin of civilization itself in postwar France." See *Civilization without Sexes: Reconstructing Gender in Postwar France, 1917–1927* (Chicago: University of Chicago Press, 1994), 2–4.

12. Paul Gagnon, "French Views of the Second American Revolution," *French Historical Studies* 2.4 (autumn 1962), 430–49, 430. Gagnon explores a set of related issues in "La Vie

future: Some French Responses to the Technological Society," *Journal of European History* 6 (1976): 172–89.

13. See René Rémond, *Les Etats-Unis devant l'opinion française, 1815–1852*, 2 vols. (Paris: Librairie Armand Colin, 1962).

14. Mathy, *Extrême Occident*, 26.

15. For a detailed study of the four decades leading up to the First World War, see Jacques Portes, *Fascination and Misgivings: The United States in French Opinion, 1870–1914* (Cambridge: Cambridge University Press, 2000).

16. The notion of an "American peril" was most clearly expressed in Octave Noel's *Le Péril américain* (Paris: De Soye et fils, 1899). Noel's thoughts originally appeared in a series of articles published in the Catholic publication *Le Correspondant*. See Roger's discussion of Noel in his chapter devoted to this critical episode in French-American relations, "From Havana to Manila: An American World?" in *The American Enemy*, 129–56.

17. André Siegfried, "L'Europe devant la civilisation américaine," *Revue des deux mondes*, April 15, 1930, 757–73, 759.

18. Mathy, *Extrême Occident*, 29–30.

19. Judt, *Past Imperfect*, 187–89.

20. Mathy, *Extrême Occident*, 28.

21. Milza, "Anti-américanisme," 30.

22. Judt, *Past Imperfect*, 188.

23. In his review of Brieux's play, "Nos amis d'Amérique," Le Semanier commented on the playwright's efforts and also on a range of French responses to America in the years leading up to the production. On the impact of the U.S. presence in France after 1917, see Roger's chapter "The Other Maginot Line," in *The American Enemy*, 257–76. For an interesting comparative study of racial attitudes and representations, see Jennifer D. Keene, "French and American Racial Stereotypes During the First World War," in *National Stereotypes in Perspective: Americans in France, Frenchmen in America*, ed. William L. Chew (Amsterdam: Rodopi, 2001), 261–82.

24. Milza, "Anti-américanisme," 30.

25. For a fascinating discussion of the controversy over jazz, see Jeffrey Jackson, "Making Enemies: Jazz in Inter-war Paris," *French Cultural Studies* 10.29 (June 1999): 179–99.

26. On these visits, see Galloux-Fournier, 310 and 315. See also Edouard Herriot, *Impressions d'Amérique* (Lyon: Impressions de M. Audie et Cie., 1923) and André Tardieu, *Devant l'obstacle, l'Amérique et nous* (Paris: Emile, 1927). A useful overview of French "propaganda" efforts in the immediate postwar years is William Keylor, "'How They Advertised France'": The French Propaganda Campaign in the United States during the Breakup of the Franco-American Entente, 1918–1923," *Diplomatic History* 17.3 (summer 1993): 351–73.

27. Hyacinthe Dubreuil, *Standards: Le Travail américain vu par un ouvrier français* (Paris: Grasset, 1929). Translated as *Robots or Men?: A French Workman's Experience in American Industry*, trans. Frances Merrill and Mason Merrill (New York: Harper & Brothers, 1930). For a detailed discussion of Dubreuil's reflections, see Gagnon, "French Views of the Second American Revolution," 439–43.

28. For more on Siegfried, see Strauss, *The Menace in the West*, 70–71. During the First World War, Siegfried served as an interpreter for the British Army and later took a position working for the French delegation to the League of Nations. In 1934, Siegfried became a regular contributor to the newspaper *Le Figaro*. He was elected to the Académie française in 1944.

29. André Siegfried, *America Comes of Age*, trans. H. H. Hemming and Doris Hemming (New York: Harcourt Brace, 1927). Originally published as *Les Etats-Unis d'aujourd'hui* (Paris: Colin, 1927).

30. Lucien Romier, *Who Will Be Master, Europe or America?*, trans. Matthew Josephson (New York: Macaulay Co., 1928). Originally published as *Qui sera le maître, Europe ou Amérique?* (Paris: Hachette, 1927).

31. Paul Morand, *New York* (Paris: Flammarion, 1930). Morand's book first appeared in serial form in the *Revue de Paris* from November 1929 to February 1930. He was also the author of a number of novels, including *Champions du monde* (Paris: Grasset, 1930) set in the United States. He was elected to the Académie française in 1968. See Strauss, *The Menace in the West*, 80.

32. Paul Achard, *Un oeil neuf sur l'Amérique* (Paris: Les Lettres françaises, 1930).

33. See, for example, the reviews by Pierre Dominique, "Exploration de l'Amérique" *Nouvelles littéraires,* July 12, 1930, 4; André Chérive, "Les Livres," *Feuilleton du temps,* June 13, 1930; and Paul Reboux, "L'Amérique et nous," *Paris Soir,* June 23, 1930.

34. In addition to *Scènes,* Duhamel published two literary series, *Vie et aventures de Salavin* (published from 1920 to 1932) and *Chronique des Pasquier* (published from 1933 to 1945). He was elected to the Académie française in 1935. After the Second World War, his works included *Le Cri des profondeurs* (1951) and *Compagnons de l'Apocalypse* (1957).

35. For a discussion of Georges Duhamel's participation in and writings on the First World War, see Jean-Jacques Becker's "Preface" to Georges Duhamel, *Vie des martyres et autres récits des temps de guerre* (Paris: Omnibus, 2005), i–xxii.

36. Duhamel, *America the Menace,* v.

37. Ibid., ix.

38. Ibid., xv.

39. Ibid., 49.

40. Ibid., 44.

41. Pascal Ory, "De Baudelaire à Duhamel: L'Improbable rejet," in *L'Amérique dans les têtes: un siècle de fascinations et d'aversions,* ed. Denis Lacorne et al. (Paris: Hachette: 1986), 60. Duhamel's rhetoric has been taken up, rather than interrogated, by a number of authors and researchers interested in the historical relationship between France and the United States. Winock, for example, writes: "America is painful for us in that it does not lead us to dream about our past but forces us to be lucid about the scenes of our future life. Duhamel, despite the mediocrity of his pamphlet, found the right expression," (*Nationalism, Anti-Semitism,* 52).

42. Duhamel, *America the Menace,* xii–xiii.

43. Ibid., xii.

44. Ibid., 191.

45. Ibid., 45.

46. Ibid., 19.

47. Ibid., 181.

48. Ibid., 182.

49. In "De Baudelaire à Duhamel," Ory claims that *Scènes* "was already at its 150th printing by the end of August," 65. Art historian Romy Golan places the number of print-runs at 187 in *Modernity and Nostalgia: Art and Politics in France between the Wars* (New Haven, CT: Yale University Press, 1995), 82.

50. An extensive collection of clippings of French reviews from these and other publications can be found in the "Dossiers Bethléem" collection at the Bibliothèque de l'Arsenal in Paris.

51. J. Schyrgens, "Ma corbeille de Livres," *XXe siècle,* October 19, 1930.

52. André Rousseaux, untitled review of *Scènes de la vie future* in *Le Figaro,* June 20, 1930.

53. André Rousseaux, "Autour du livre de Duhamel," *Le Figaro,* June 28, 1930.

54. Robert Le Diable's, "Causeries Littéraires: Georges Duhamel" in *Action française,* June 12, 1930. Le Diable described a genre of writing on the state of civilization of which Duhamel's account was a prime example.

55. See the untitled review by "Franc-Nohain" in *L'Echo de Paris,* May 29, 1930. "Franc-Nohain" was the pen name of the writer Maurice Etienne Legrand.

56. Abel Hermant, "Billets de minuit: Les temps ne sont pas révolus," *Le Figaro,* May 29, 1930.

57. Maurice Constantin-Weyer, untitled review of *Scènes de la vie future*, *Action française*, September 25, 1930.

58. Jules Huret, *En Amérique. De New York à la Nouvelle Orléans* (Paris: Bibliothèque Charpentier, 1904) and *En Amérique: De San Francisco au Canada* (Paris: Bibliothèque Charpentier, 1905). For more on Huret, see Strauss, *The Menace in the West*, 33–47.

59. Georges Altman, "Chroniques du cinema," *Le Monde*, June 14, 1930.

60. Rousseaux, "Autour du livre de Duhamel."

61. Philippe Dastre, "Cinémaphobie," *Liberté*, May 30, 1930.

62. André Billy, "Les livres de la semaine, Duhamel contre l'Amérique," *Oeuvre*, June 3, 1930.

63. Gerard de Catalogne, *Dialogue entre deux mondes* (Paris: Librairie de la Revue Française, 1931). Other key titles published that same year included André Maurois' *L'Amérique inattendue* (Paris: Editions Mornay, 1931); Robert Aron and Arnaud Dandieu's *Le Cancer américain* (Paris: Age d'homme, 1931) and *Décadence de la nation française* (Paris; Editions Reider, 1931); and Charles Pomaret's *L'Amérique à la conquête de l'Europe* (Paris: Librairie Armand Colin, 1931).

64. For a brief overview of the impact of the world financial crisis on the French economy, see René Rémond's *Histoire de la France au XXe siècle* (Paris: Editions Seuil, 1996), 129–38. Galloux-Fournier makes the important point that the sense of "America" as a menace was not caused by the economic crisis. It was, instead, more of a response to American prosperity over the longer term. See "Un regard sur l'Amérique: voyageurs français aux Etats-Unis (1919–1939)," 322.

65. Duhamel, *America the Menace*, xii–xiii.

66. Ibid., xiii.

67. André Bellesort, "Encore l'Amérique," *Feuilleton du Journal des Débats*, June 11, 1930.

68. Duhamel, *America the Menace*, 1.

69. Ibid., 12.

70. Lucien Lehman, *Le Grand mirage—USA* (Paris: Edition Maisonneuve Frères, 1929), 5–6.

71. Achard, *Un oeil neuf sur l'Amérique*, 278.

72. Ibid., 8.

73. Ibid., 14.

74. Ibid., 7.

75. Ibid., 14.

76. Ibid., 44.

77. Maurois's other novels included *Climats* (1928), *Le Cercle de famille* (1932), and *Les Roses de séptembre* (1956). Maurois also wrote a number of historical and literary biographies such as *La Vie de Disraeli* (1927), *Lyautey* (1931), *Chauteaubriand* (1938), *A la recherché de Marcel Proust* (1949), *Olympia ou la vie de Victor Hugo* (1954), and *Prométhée ou la vie de Balzac* (1965). He was elected to the Académie française in 1938. See René Rémond *Histoire de la France au XXe siècle*, 201.

78. André Maurois, *En Amérique* (New York: American Book Co., 1936), 11.

79. Ibid., 15–16.

80. Ibid., 17.

81. Ibid., 18–19.

82. André Maurois, *Deux fragments d'une histoire universelle 1992* (Paris: Editions des Portiques, 1928).

83. R. P. Gillet, "Ce que j'ai vu aux Etats-Unis," *Revue de Paris*, March 1931, 322–43, 322.

84. Maurois, *En Amérique*, 11.

85. Morand, *New York*, 260.

86. Ibid., 262.

87. Ibid., 266–67.

88. Ibid., 277.

89. Ibid., 266 and 279.

90. Ibid., 274.

91. Ibid., 279–80.

92. Louis-Ferdinand Céline, *Journey to the End of Night*, trans. John P. Marks (New York: New Directions, 1960). The book originally appeared as *Voyage au bout de la nuit* (Paris: Gallimard, 1932). Céline's real name was Louis-Ferdinand Destouches. He was also the author of *Mort à credit* (1936) and a controversial anti-Semitic tract entitled *Bagatelles pour un massacre* (1937).

93. Céline, *Journey to the End of Night*, 197.

94. Ibid., 213.

95. Ibid., 184.

96. Ibid., 213

97. Duhamel, *America the Menace*, 70–71. Fassin's piece "The Purloined Gender: American Feminism in a French Mirror," discusses the emasculating figure of the American woman as a recurrent theme in French depictions of the United States.

98. Duhamel, *America the Menace*, 64.

99. Maurois, *En Amérique*, 22.

100. Gaston Rageot, "Une visite aux Etats-Unis," *Illustration*, November 1, 1930, 38–39. Roberts discusses Rageot's anxiety about the erosion of traditional gender roles as a pillar of civilization in *Civilization without Sexes*, 7–9.

101. De Catalogne, *Dialogue entre deux mondes*, 57.

102. For a discussion of this legislation, see Roberts, *Civilization without Sexes*, 93–119; and Pedersen, *Legislating the French Family*.

103. G. Hanet-Archambault, "Le Journal français de demain," *Mercure de France*, November 1, 1931, 554–572.

104. Ibid., 554.

105. Ibid., 557.

106. Ibid., 556.

107. Arthenay, "Comment les Américains conçoivent le monde de demain," *Sciences et voyages*, no. 734, September 21, 1933, 2–3. The magazine, published from 1919 to 1940, often printed articles about the latest technological developments in the United States. It used developments in America to inform a French public about scientific possibilities in the present, as well as in the future.

108. Ibid., 3.

109. Maurois, *En Amérique*, 107.

110. André Siegfried quoted in de Catalogne, *Dialogue entre deux mondes*, 277.

111. Abbé Moreux, *La Vie sur Mars* (Paris: Gaston Doin, 1924), 9–10. A number of scientists and observers paid particular attention to Mars in 1924. In August of that year, Mars came closer to the Earth than it had in the past, only 55,577,000 kilometers away. See J.-F. Merlet, "Ce que les grands astronomes français pensent de la planète Mars," *Sciences et voyages*, no. 270, October 30, 1924, 1–4; Charles Nordmann, "Allons-nous communiquer avec Mars?" *Revue des deux mondes*, July 15, 1924, 456–67; and "Après la visite de Mars," *Revue des deux mondes*, September 15, 1924, 456–67.

112. F. Boucaru, *La Planète Mars: Communication télépathique avec un astronome martien* (Paris: Figuière, 1926), 4. The classic which inspired many authors was H. G. Wells's, *The War of the Worlds* (London: William Henemann, 1898). One example from interwar France is Octave Joncquel's *Les Titans du ciel* (Amiens: Librairie Edgar Malfère, 1921). Joncquel also wrote a sequel to this novel, *L'Epopée martienne. L'Agonie de la Terre* (Amiens: Librairie Edgar Malfère, 1922).

113. Siegfried, "L'Europe devant la civilisation américaine," 763.

114. Ibid., 773.

115. Siegfried, *America Comes of Age*, 203.

116. Gillet, "Ce que j'ai vu aux Etats-Unis," 327.

117. Morand, *New York*, 265.

118. Maurois, *En Amérique*, 75.

119. Ibid., 56.

120. See de Catalogne's "Prologue" in *Dialogue entre deux mondes*, 1.

121. Rageot, "Une visite aux Etats-Unis," 38.

122. Pomaret, *L'Amérique a la conquête de l'Europe*, v.

123. Ibid., 3.

124. Achard, *Un oeil neuf sur l'Amérique*, 13.

125. Ibid., 279.

126. Morand, *New York*, 266.

127. Duhamel, *America the Menace*, 203.

128. Robert Brasillach quoted in de Catalogne's, *Dialogue entre deux mondes*, 90–91. Brasillach (1909–45) was a member of the Action française in the 1930s. A literary critic, known for his anti-Semitism, Brasillach wrote novels, including *Le Voleur d'étincelles* (1932). He also edited the weekly newspaper *Je suis partout* from 1937 to 1943 (with an absence from 1940 to 1941 following the French defeat). After supporting a policy of collaboration with the Germans during the Occupation from 1940 to 1944, Brasillach was sentenced and shot during the French purges of 1945. See René Rémond, *Histoire de la France au XXe siècle*, 208.

129. Paul Adam quoted in Paul Morand, *New York*, 263.

130. André de Fels, "Ford ou Lénine?" *Revue de Paris* 38, December 1931, 675–87. De Fels participated in the debates about the development and extension of Paris in the interwar years that I discuss in chapter 2.

131. See de Catalogne's "Prologue" in *Dialogue entre deux mondes*, 1.

132. Emile Baumann quoted in de Catalogne, *Dialogue entre deux mondes*, 181.

133. Duhamel argued that, of the "two experiments," the Russian was "purely political and ideological" while the American "describes itself as a 'civilization,' a mode of living. It touches everything," *America the Menace*, 210.

134. See Winock, *Nationalism, Anti-Semitism*, 35.

135. Jacques Spitz, *L'Agonie du globe* (Paris: Septimus et Bernard Eschasseriaux, 1977), 57. Gallimard originally published the novel in 1935. Spitz was the author of a number of science fiction novels in the period. These titles included *Les Evadés de l'an 4000* (Paris: Gallimard, 1936); *La Guerre des mouches* (Paris: Editions Jean Vigneau, 1938); *L'Homme élastique* (Paris: Editions Jean Vigneau, 1938); and *L'Expérience du Docteur Mops* (Paris: Editions Jean Vigneau, 1939). In *La science-fiction française au XXe siècle (1900–1968): Essai de socio-poétique d'un genre en émérgence* (Amsterdam: Editions Rodopi, 1994), Jean-Marc Gouanvic has noted "Spitz's novels had the double advantage of being relatively numerous and having been published (before 1939) by one of the most important French publishing houses [Gallimard]. This guaranteed them a large readership," 135.

136. Spitz, *L'Agonie du globe*, 102.

137. Ibid., 192.

138. Ibid., 71–73.

5. The International Language of the Future

1. Albert Léon Guérard, *A Short History of the International Language Movement* (London: Fisher Unwin, 1922). Readers may remember (from chapter 2) that Guérard, born in France in 1880, moved to the United States in 1907 and lived there until his death in 1959. He spent most of his career as a professor of French literature at Stanford University and published numerous books on France and French culture over the years.

2. Guérard, *A Short History,* 194.

3. Ibid., 196.

4. Ibid., 205.

5. Ibid., 196.

6. Ibid., 208. Throughout this chapter, readers will notice a series of key terms that were and continue to be used to refer to the languages discussed here. The historical authors I cite referred to French, for example, as both a "national" and an "international" language given its widespread historic uses. Esperanto, on the other hand, was considered a solely "international" language. Authors also used terms such as "artificial," "invented," "planned," and "auxiliary" to denote Esperanto's lack of/freedom from national origins and to signal its use as a second, rather than a first, language.

7. Ibid., 209.

8. Ibid., 196.

9. Zamenhof developed Esperanto in the 1870s and 1880s. The grammar, vocabulary, phonology, and semantics of the language are based on existing western European languages. Other artificial languages (such as "Ido" and "Volapuk") have competed with Esperanto, but none have achieved nearly the same success worldwide up to the present day. See Peter Forster, *The Esperanto Movement* (New York: Mouton, 1982); and Andrew Large, *The Artificial Language Movement* (New York: Basil Blackwell, 1985).

10. Guérard, *A Short History,* 195.

11. Ibid., 131

12. Albert Léon Guérard, *Beyond Hatred: The Democratic Ideal in France and America* (New York: Charles Scribner's Sons, 1925), 203–4.

13. Ibid., 190.

14. See Le Corbusier, *The Decorative Art of Today,* in *Essential Le Corbusier: L'Esprit Nouveau Articles* (Oxford: Reed Educational and Professional Publishing, 1998), 110.

15. For a fascinating analysis that draws on this interwar history to explore the phenomenon of nationalism in Central and Eastern Europe in the 1990s, see Rogers Brubaker's *Nationalism Reframed: Nationhood and the National Question in the New Europe* (Cambridge: Cambridge University Press, 1996).

16. See *Esperanto as an International Auxiliary Language,* Report of the General Secretariat of the League of Nations Adopted by the Third Assembly (Paris: Imprimerie de presses universitaires, 1922).

17. Forster, *The Esperanto Movement,* 171.

18. There is an enormous body of scholarship on the peace settlement and the League of Nations. For the reflections of two key French participants, see André Tardieu, *La Paix* (Paris: Payot, 1921), including a preface by French prime minister Georges Clemenceau; and Georges Clemenceau, *Grandeurs et misères d'une victoire* (Paris: Plon, 1930). Tardieu's text was translated as *The Truth about the Treaty* (Indianapolis: Bobbs Merrill, 1921). Clemenceau's reflection appeared in English translation as *Grandeur and Misery of Victory* (London: George C. Harrap, 1930). Margaret Macmillan's *Paris 1919: Six Months that Changed the World* (New York: Random House, 2002) is a detailed and compelling account of the events of 1919, including a discussion of the language issue in particular. See *Paris 1919,* 55–56. Other useful secondary sources include Marc Trachtenberg, *Reparation in World Politics: France and European Economic Diplomacy* (New York: Columbia University Press, 1980); Martin F. Boemeke et al., eds., *The Treaty of Versailles: A Reassessment After 75 Years* (New York: Cambridge University Press, 1998); and Sally Marks, *The Illusion of Peace: International Relations in Europe, 1918–1933,* 2nd ed. (Basingstoke: Palgrave Macmillan, 2003). For an excellent overview of the historiography of the league, see Susan Pedersen, "Back to the League of Nations," *American Historical Review* 112.4 (October 2007): 1091–1117.

19. The full text of the plan of procedure is available in English translation as "Plan of the Preliminary Conversations between the Allied Ministers," in United States Department of State,

Papers Relating to the Foreign Relations of the United States, 1919: The Paris Peace Conference (hereinafter *PPC*), vol. 1 (Washington: Government Printing Office, 1942), 386–96. In his account, Tardieu notes that Clemenceau had asked him to prepare this note. See *The Truth About the Treaty*, 88.

20. The full text of minutes recorded in English at the Council of Ten meetings, which took place from January 12 to February 14, 1919 is available in *PPC*, vol. 3. Both the British and the American delegations kept minutes in English. Unless otherwise noted, the citations that appear here are drawn from the minutes kept by Lieutenant Colonel Sir Maurice Hankey of the British delegation. Clemenceau's interpreter for the proceedings was Professor Paul Mantoux. Mantoux would later go on to publish the notes he kept for the meeting of the "Council of Four" (with representatives from Britain, the United States, France, and Italy in attendance). See Centre national de la recherche scientifique (France), *Les délibérations du Conseil des quatre (Mars 24—Juin 28, 1919): Notes de l'officier interprête Paul Mantoux*, 2 vols. (Paris: Editions du Centre de la Recherche Scientifique, 1955). Mantoux's notes later became available in English translation as Arthur S. Link, ed., *The Deliberations of the Council of Four (March 24–June 28, 1919): Notes of the Official Interpreter Paul Mantoux*, 2 vols. (Princeton, NJ: Princeton University Press, 1992).

21. See "Plan of the Preliminary Conversations," *PPC*, vol. 1, 394.

22. Ray Stannard Baker, *Woodrow Wilson and World Settlement*, vol. 1 (New York: Doubleday, 1922). Baker, President Wilson's press secretary, devoted an entire chapter to this episode in his three-volume study based on access to Wilson's papers. Entitled "The Battle of the Languages," Baker's chapter outlined the importance of this preliminary debate with respect to the world and other views of the conference's major participants.

23. A number of authors have noted the significance of the shift to official bilingualism that resulted as a watershed moment in international diplomacy. Guérard discusses the matter in *A Short History*, 23. See also Herbert Newhard Shenton, *Cosmopolitan Conversation: The Language Problems of International Conferences* (New York: Columbia University Press, 1933), 379; Harold Nicolson, *Diplomacy* (London: Oxford University Press, 1939), 231; and Keith A. Hamilton, "A Question of Status: British Diplomats and the Uses and Abuses of French," *Historical Research* 60.141 (February 1987): 125–29. Historian Benjamin Martin has noted the introduction of English as one of the initial "blows" to France during the conference in *France and the Après Guerre, 1919–1924* (Baton Rouge: Louisiana State University Press, 1999), 40.

24. *PPC*, vol. 3, 553.

25. Antoine Meillet, *Les Langues dans l'Europe nouvelle*, 2nd ed. (Paris: Payot, 1928), 248. The first edition of this study appeared in 1918. Trained at the Sorbonne, Meillet was a professor at the Collège de France and served as director of the Ecole des Hautes Etudes in Paris.

26. *PPC*, vol. 3, 553.

27. While the Japanese representatives remained silent, Baron Sonnino, the Italian Foreign Minister, resisted the introduction of official bilingualism during this debate. While he could support the use of French only, out of respect for tradition, Sonnino argued that the recognition of a second official language begged the question of the recognition of the languages of the other powers (including Italy) represented at the conference. See his remarks in ibid., 554 and 558–59.

28. Ibid., vol. 3, 553–54.

29. This argument worked to justify the consideration of English alongside French, while ruling out either Italian or Japanese as "minority" languages. It would not, in the end, be practical to recognize four official languages. In a recent history of the Alliance Française, François Chaubet mentions "the great indignation of the French" over the new bilingualism that was caused, in part, by the fact that "neither Wilson, nor Lloyd George spoke French." See his *La Politique culturelle française et la diplomatie de la langue: L'Alliance Française*

(1883–1940) (Paris: L'Harmattan, 2006), 166. In *Paris 1919*, MacMillan underlines the practical issue of languages spoken by the leaders present as a partial explanation for the introduction of English at the conference: "Since Clemenceau spoke English well and the Italian foreign minister, Sidney Sonnino, spoke it reasonably, conversations among the Big Four were often in English," 54.

30. Clemenceau, *Grandeur and Misery of Victory,* 135.

31. Ibid. MacMillan claims "Poincaré was furious when Clemenceau conceded that English would be an official language at the Peace Conference alongside French," *Paris 1919,* 34. See also J.F.V. Keiger, *Raymond Poincaré* (Cambridge: Cambridge University Press, 1997). Keiger asserts that Poincaré "had spoken firmly against such a move: 'I point out that after all that she has done, France could not tolerate having the moral benefit of the official language taken away from her,'" 251.

32. Clemenceau, *Grandeur and Misery of Victory,* 135.

33. *PPC,* vol. 3, 555.

34. Ibid., 555–56.

35. Ibid., 558.

36. Ibid., 561. As Martin notes, "Even the Prussians in 1871 had not demanded that French cede its place as the sole diplomatic language." See *France and the Après Guerre,* 40.

37. *PPC,* vol. 3, 558.

38. Ibid., 559.

39. Ibid., 557.

40. Ibid., 560.

41. Guérard, *A Short History of the International Language Movement,* 23.

42. Meillet, *Les Langues dans l'Europe nouvelle,* 254. The author had revised this second edition to include discussion of the events of the postwar period, including the 1919 peace settlement, the creation of new European states, and the progress of the international language movement (of which he was a supporter) since the end of the war.

43. Shenton, *Cosmopolitan Conversation,* 381.

44. Shenton also cites statistics regarding the number of speeches delivered in English and French during the meeting of the league. During the First Assembly in 1920, 65% of the speeches were in French, while 35% were in English. The Fifth Assembly in 1924 heard 79% of speeches in French and 21% in English. The Eighth Assembly heard 77% in French, 22% in English, and 1% in German in 1927, ibid., 381–82.

45. The American jurist and diplomat James Brown Scott wrote on the value of French as a language of diplomacy in *Le Français langue diplomatique moderne* (Paris: Pedone, 1924). Scott lamented the move to bilingualism in Paris in 1919, claiming that French had remained the official language in the case of international law. His position, however, is not supported by statistical studies of the multiple languages used in treaties since the First World War. On the widespread adoption of bilingualism, as well as statistics on the use of other languages in treaties signed between 1921 and 1930, see Manley O. Hudson, "Languages in Treaties," *The American Journal of International Law* 26.2 (April 1932): 368–72.

46. See John Milton Cooper, *Breaking the Heart of the World: Woodrow Wilson and the Fight for the League of Nations* (New York: Cambridge University Press, 2001).

47. League of Nations, "Draft Resolution Concerning Esperanto," in *Records of the First Assembly: Plenary Meetings* (Geneva, 1920), 413. The list of countries that supported the motion included Brazil, Columbia, Haiti, Chile, China, South Africa, Italy, India, Belgium, Czechoslovakia and Persia.

48. See Jean-Jacques Renoliet, *L'UNESCO oubliée: La Société des nations et la coopération intellectuelle (1919–1946)* (Paris: Publications de la Sorbonne, 1999), 11. In his detailed history of international cooperation, Renoliet notes the early collaborative efforts of the UIA and the league that led to the eventual formation of an International Commission on Intellectual Cooperation (ICIC) in 1922 and the International Cooperation Organisation (ICO)

in 1931. The UIA continues to exist to this day. For more information, see the organization's website: http://www.uia.be.

49. Benedict Anderson, *Imagined Communities: Reflections on the Origin and Spread of Nationalism* (New York: Verso Books, 1991), 6.

50. Ibid., 43.

51. League of Nations, "International Language," Committee No. 2, *Records of the First Assembly: Plenary Meetings,* Annex D (Geneva, 1920), 768.

52. League of Nations, "Report of Committee No. 2 on an International Language," in *Records of the First Assembly: Plenary Meetings,* Annex D (Geneva, 1920), 753.

53. Trained as a historian, Hanotaux had taught at the Ecole des hautes études before becoming involved in government. Elected to the National Assembly, he served as France's minister of foreign affairs at the end of the nineteenth century, later becoming a delegate to the League of Nations.

54. League of Nations, "Report of Committee No. 2 on an International Language," in *Records of the First Assembly: Plenary Meetings,* Annex D (Geneva, 1920), 753.

55. Ibid., 754.

56. Making reference to the "Provisional Rules of Procedure" under which English and French were accorded official status, these delegates suggested that Spanish, the language spoken by more of the league's member nations than any other, be recognized as well. See League of Nations, "The Use of Spanish as One of the Official Languages of the Assembly," *The Records of the First Assembly: Plenary Meetings* (Geneva, 1920), 172. See also League of Nations, "Resumption of the Debate on the Use of Spanish as one of the Official Languages of the Assembly," *Records of the First Assembly: Plenary Meetings* (Geneva, 1920), 179.

57. League of Nations, "Report on the Draft Rules of Procedure Presented by Committee No. 1" (11th Plenary Meeting, November 30, 1920), *Records of the First Assembly: Plenary Meetings,* 216.

58. League of Nations, "Report of Committee No. 2 on an International Language," 754.

59. See "Circular Letter from the Secretary General on the Teaching of Esperanto in Schools" and "Questionnaire with Regard to the Teaching of Esperanto in Schools" (both dated January 23, 1922) published in *League of Nations Official Journal* (March 1922), 293–94. The circular letter was signed by I. Nitobe (of Japan), under secretary-general for the secretary-general.

60. Forster, *The Esperanto Movement,* 173.

61. While Forster refers to this document as the "Secretary General's Report" (in *The Esperanto Movement,* 174), I will refer to "the Secretariat" as it does not appear that Drummond himself wrote the report. When the report came under scrutiny during one of the League's committee meetings in 1922, Under-Secretary Nitobe "explained that the report had been prepared under his supervision." He had also solicited the help of Dr. Edmond Privat, a delegate from Persia (and a enthusiastic supporter of Esperanto). See League of Nations, "Minutes of the Fifth Committee, Sixth Meeting, September 14, 1922," *Records of the Third Assembly: Meetings of the Committees* (Geneva, 1922), 31. Nitobe had attended the 13th World Esperanto Congress in Prague as the league's official delegate in 1921. He had also prepared an extensive report on the congress, the third section of which was published as "The Language Question and the League of Nations," *League of Nations Official Journal* (January–March 1922): 295–98.

62. *Esperanto as an International Auxiliary Language,* 5.

63. Ibid., 8.

64. Ibid., 8–9.

65. Ibid., 11.

66. Ibid., 31–32.

67. See for example Ludwik Zamenhof, *Langue internationale "Esperanto": manuel complet avec double dictionnaire* (Paris: H. Le Soudier, 1987).

68. Forster, *The Esperanto Movement*, 75.

69. *Esperanto as an International Auxiliary Language*, 8.

70. Ibid., 13.

71. See Forster, *The Esperanto Movement*, 190–199.

72. Famous participants in the movement and the journal of the same name would include Henri Barbusse, Paul Vaillant-Couturier, Romain Rolland, and Georges Duhamel. For an overview of the Clarté movement, its key members, and principal aims, see Nicole Racine, "The Clarté Movement in France, 1919–1921," *Journal of Contemporary History* 2.2, Literature and Society (April 1967): 195–208.

73. See ibid., 203. Born in France in 1873, Barbusse was 41 years old when he joined the French army in 1914. *Le Feu*, a novel that sold hundreds of thousands of copies and created controversy because of its stark portrayal of the war, won the Prix Goncourt in 1916. For a fascinating discussion of the novel's significance with respect to postwar gender anxieties, see Mary Louise Roberts, *Civilization without Sexes: Reconstructing Gender in Postwar France, 1917–1927* (Chicago: University of Chicago Press, 1994), 27–28.

74. See Henri Barbusse, "Préface," *Cours rationnel et complet d'Espéranto*, 3rd ed. (Paris: SAT-AMIKARO, 1946), 5–8. Barbusse's original preface appeared in the first edition of this textbook in 1921 and was reprinted in subsequent editions.

75. Rolland was perhaps most famous for his *Jean-Christophe* series, ten volumes that he published from 1904 to 1912. See David James Fisher, *Romain Rolland and the Politics of Intellectual Engagement* (Berkeley: University of California Press, 1988).

76. See "R. Rolland et l'Espéranto," *La Vie ouvrière*, August 6, 1919; and "L'Opinion de Romain Rolland sur l'Espéranto," *La Vie ouvrière*, April 23, 1920. These citations are for the originals of these letters that were published in French in *La Vie ouvrière*, the syndicalist paper founded in 1909. Lanti printed Esperanto translations of the letters in *Travailleur espérantiste*.

77. "R. Rolland et l'Espéranto," *La Vie ouvrière*, August 6, 1919.

78. "L'Opinion de Romain Rolland sur l'Espéranto," *La Vie ouvrière*, April 23, 1920.

79. André Baudet, "Selection and Advantages of an International Auxiliary Language." The report was published as "Annex 2" of the League of Nations 1922 report, *Esperanto as an International Auxiliary Language*, 35–42; It was also published separately by the Paris Chamber of Commerce under the French title, *Utilité et choix d'une langue auxiliaire internationale* in 1921. Its appearance made international headlines. See "Paris Business Men Would Use Esperanto," *New York Times*, February 16, 1921, 12.

80. Baudet, "Selection and Advantages of an International Auxiliary Language," 35–36.

81. Guérard would raise this issue in 1922. While he recognized the historical predominance of French, Guérard warned that the use of "French as the universal auxiliary language might give to the purely national elements in French culture a supremacy which other national cultures are not willing to acknowledge." He was skeptical that it "would...be possible to denationalize French entirely, to make it wholly universal in spirit." See *A Short History of the International Language Movement*, 31.

82. The names on the petition included the philosopher Paul Janet, mathematician (and politician) Paul Painlevé, and filmmaking pioneer Louis Lumière. The petition, along with the support of other scientific groups were all cited in the published proceedings of the "International Conference for the Use of Esperanto in the Pure and Applied Sciences" held in Paris in 1925. See "Documents et voeux," *Conférence internationale pour l'emploi de l'esperanto dans les science pures et appliqués*, Paris, May 14–17, 1925 (Paris: Imprimerie centrale espérantiste, 1925).

83. Charles Richet, "Une grande espérance: l'Espéranto," *Le Petit Parisien*, December 29, 1921, 1.

84. See James Macmillan, *Twentieth-Century France* (Oxford: Oxford University Press, 1992), 93.

85. See Renoliet, *L'UNESCO oubliée*. Renoliet's first chapter, "La Formation de l'OCI (1919–1926)" is particularly useful and notes the French rejection of Esperanto in the meetings of the league as an important example of its policies at this time.

86. Forster, *The Esperanto Movement*, 183. Forster's discussion of the ban draws on the account in Ulrich Lins and Victor Sadler, "Regardless of Frontiers: A Case Study in Linguistic Persecution," in *Man, Language and Society*, ed. Samir Ghosh (The Hague: Mouton Press, 1972), 206–15.

87. Léon Bérard, "Circulaire ministérielle du 3 juin 1922." The full text of the two-page memo, along with several critical responses, was published in *Le Monde espérantiste*, May–June 1922, 18–19. All citations refer to this version. The memo also appeared as "Dépêche ministerielle du 3 juin 1922, a M. le Recteur de l'Académie de Paris, relative à l'Espéranto," in *Bulletin de l'instruction primaire du départment de la Seine* 5 (May–June 1922), 242–44.

88. Bérard, "Circulaire ministérielle du 3 juin 1922," 18–19. In *The Moral Disarmament of France: Education, Pacifism, and Patriotism, 1914–1940* (Cambridge: Cambridge University Press, 2004), Mona Siegel states that "international solidarity" was a "fundamental principle guiding public education in the interwar years." She argues that, while teachers generally regarded it "as an extension rather than a repudiation of republican patriotic values," the French government at the time became quite anxious about its implications for the nation. Bérard's ban on Esperanto was perhaps the most salient example of their conservative fears (173–74).

89. Bérard, "Circulaire ministérielle du 3 juin 1922," 18.

90. Ibid., 19.

91. "La Sottise d'un ministre," *Le Monde espérantiste*, May–June 1922, 1.

92. "Le Ministre insiste," *Le Monde espérantiste*, January–February 1923.

93. See Bérard's response to *Ligue* president Ferdinand Buisson published in *Le Temps*, January 8, 1923, 2. The response was also reprinted in *Le Monde espérantiste*, January–February 1923, 1.

94. Siegel, *Moral Disarmament of France*, 174.

95. League of Nations, "General Discussion of the Report on Esperanto," 26–27. It is interesting to note that, while Brazil was included in the list of countries that originally filed the "Draft Resolution Concerning Esperanto" and submitted it to the league in 1920, the Brazilian delegate in this instance was most adamant in his opposition to the auxiliary language.

96. See "Esperanto as an Auxiliary International Language," Report of the Fifth Committee as submitted to the Third Assembly by the Rapporteur, Senator G. Reynald, Delegate of France in League of Nations, *Records of the Third Assembly*, Annex 15 (Geneva, 1922), 134–135.

97. League of Nations, Committee on Intellectual Cooperation, *Minutes of the Second Session*, July 26–August 2, 1923.

98. Luchaire would go on to serve as Director of the International Institute of Intellectual Cooperation based in Paris. In 1922, the Inspector-General had voiced his own resistance to Esperanto in an article entitled "Français ou Espéranto," in *Le Figaro*, July 18, 1922, 4. On Luchaire's role in international affairs during this period, see Renoliet's *L'UNESCO oubliée*.

99. These two agenda items were listed as nos. 71 and 73 (with Esperanto coming second on the schedule) for the "Ninth Meeting" of the committee held on July 31, 1923. See the "Table of Contents" of League of Nations, Committee on Intellectual Cooperation, *Minutes of the Second Session*.

100. League of Nations, Committee on Intellectual Cooperation, *Minutes of the Second Session*, 36. Gonzague de Reynold was dean of the Faculty of Philosophy at the University of Berne.

101. Ibid.

102. Ibid., 37.

103. Ibid., 38.

104. Ibid., 40–41.

105. Ibid., 41.

106. Forster, *The Esperanto Movement*, 183.

107. This categorization resulted in a lowering of tariffs on the use of the language no longer considered a "code." See Bureau International de l'Union Télégraphique, *Documents de la conférence télégraphique internationale de Paris*, vol. 1 (1925), 72–74; and vol. 2 (1925), 58, 157–60, 192, and 215.

108. Forster claims: "It is on record that Bergson had earlier expressed himself in support of Esperanto; he admitted acting under the instructions of Bérard...to 'drown' Esperanto," *The Esperanto Movement*, 177.

109. Paul Gsell, *Les matinées de la Villa Said: Propos d'Anatole France* (Paris: Bernard Grasset, 1921). Most of these exchanges had taken place before the war. Awarded the Nobel Prize in 1921, France was the author of many works of fiction and criticism, including *Le Crime de Sylvestre Bonnard* (1881), *La Rôtisserie de la reine Pédauque* (1892), *L'Affaire Crainquebille* (1901), *L'Île des Pingouins* (1908), *Les Dieux ont soif* (1912), and *La Révolte des anges* (1914). See Marie Claire Bancquart, *Anatole France* (Paris: Julliard, 1994).

110. Gsell, *Les matinées de la Villa Said*, 173.

111. Ibid., 174–75.

Afterthoughts

1. See Martin Thom's English translation of Renan's 1882 lecture, "What is a nation?" in *Nation and Narration*, ed. Homi K. Bhabha (New York: Routledge, 1990), 8–22, 19.

Index

Note: Illustrations are indicated by page numbers in italic type.